How to Become a Football Agent

Third Edition

Dr Erkut Sogut, Jamie Khan & Thomas Freismuth

First published in Great Britain in 2019, by CA Publishing House Ltd

This edition first published 2023, by CA Publishing House Ltd.

For more information, address: erkutsogut@gmail.com

Typesetting by Tom Witcomb

ISBN 978-1-7397288-5-4 (ebook)

CA Publishing House
Summit House,170 Finchley Road
London, United Kingdom
NW3 6BP

https://grow-talents.com/

Acknowledgements

With thanks, in recognition of all your support and contribution to our book:

Mesut Özil

Kieran Gibbs

Wayne Welbeck

Nassim Touihri

Max Legath

David Jackett

Carol Joy & Jacquie Agnew

Toni Ortega

Harun Arslan

Nick Robinson

Loren Roman Garcia

Luis Kircher

Rory Smith

Daniel Geey

Jessie Engelhart

Misha Sher

We Play Forward

Stéphane Ehrhart

Jörg Neubauer

Pere Guardiola

Paddy Dominguez

Matthieu Rios-Grossin

Paolo Cucalon

Dee Hong

Mesut Aslan

Nicola Giuliani

Lucas Arbelo

Ali Shariballi

Yussif Alhassan Chibsah

With special thanks also to Izabela Novoselec and Tom Witcomb

CONTENTS

Foreword

Mesut Özil

When I first met Erkut in 2011, I was at Real Madrid and he was entering his eighth year of education in Law. To begin with, despite me and my family being certain that he was the right person we were looking for, Erkut himself was hesitant at balancing his education alongside beginning to help my career. Eventually we convinced him to become firstly my lawyer and later on, my agent on the condition that he was allowed certain days of the week to dedicate to his studies. On top of this, he had actually already begun to educate agents on the importance of their roles in footballer's careers and on the law side of things.

This philosophy and approach with an emphasis on education has remained persistent and I strongly believe it is a primary reason behind Erkut's incredible and record-breaking success in the industry. He loves to educate others and share his advice, experiences and guidance with them. He is the best mentor for football agents in the world. It's as simple as that.

Throughout my own career, many people will recognise Erkut mostly for the two contract records that he broke. But this is not what he should be confined to. Erkut is an incredible mentor for me; a very good friend that I can trust with anything and that will always support me through the tough times that are inevitable at the top level of football; his commercial brain has helped me develop and grow my own personal brand; and his wisdom has led me to various different successful business ventures which I have been able to enjoy alongside him.

An agent like him is hard to come by and I am very fortunate to have had Erkut as my own. Similarly, I am sure that once you have finished this book, you will be grateful too as this is the best advice available to those who are wanting to follow in his footsteps.

Kieran Gibbs

I know for a fact that Erkut will rise, without fail, at 5am every morning, regardless of whichever country he flew in from the day before, and will be seated at his desk soon after. Everyday he takes on new challenges, from learning a sixth language to writing a novel and, most importantly for you as the reader of this, brainstorming new ideas for how to educate the next generation of agents. Then finally, he still manages to operate as a top agent, with contacts in all corners of the globe and the world of football. His acumen for networking to manufacture and maintain genuine relationships with so many people is extraordinary. He is a people person with a remarkable background and obsession with education and with bettering himself each day. This is as close as possible to the perfect combinations of attributes for a football agent to possess.

Throughout my time at Arsenal, Erkut and I created a productive and (hopefully he agrees) mutually beneficial relationship. I knew that Erkut's intentions were pure. One thing that he teaches is the trust and loyalty that an agent should show to their client and through having an authentic relationship with him, not only did I know that my best interests were cared for, but that I also naturally returned the same level of trust and loyalty back to him.

Now that I am in the latter stages of my career in Miami, I am also starting to realise that despite all his hard work throughout my career, he is a rare example of an agent who will also work tirelessly to ensure that post-career, I have enough of an education and business aptitude behind me to continue to be financially secure. I have even been persuaded to join his new agent education course as a tutor which is an exciting opportunity for me and a demonstration of the work he puts in behind the scenes. Erkut will support me on ventures outside of football and I am glad that this book includes a chapter on the careers of clients away from football. It is something that I do not take for granted and I hope those that read this and do become agents will provide the same service to their own clients. It is enormously appreciated.

For someone like Erkut to continue to release informative and unique modes of education through his masterclasses, conferences, lectures and this book, is an extremely fortunate thing for those hoping to become a part of this industry. Agency is a very hard skill to master and achieve success at, but through his remarkable dedication, high-intelligence and inherently caring nature towards his clients, Erkut has reached the very top and he willingly shares this with you here.

Introduction

Dr Erkut Sogut, Jamie Khan and Thomas Freismuth would like to welcome you to the third edition of 'How to Become a Football Agent'.

- We'll aim to answer the following questions and more:
- What is required for an agent's licence in football?
- How does an agent structure a £50 million transfer?
- What happens on deadline day?
- What does an agent do on the day of a signing?
- What strategies can an agent use in a million-euro negotiation?
- How do you sign a client?
- How do you decipher who is a good agent and who is not?
- How are commercial deals done?
- Can you represent a coach?
- What is different about being an agent in each global market?

Once again, the ever-evolving landscape of football and the agency industry brings us here. Much like the first and second edition of this book, the aim is very simple; to provide comprehensive, detailed and motivational guidance to you as the reader. Whether you are someone who aspires to pursue a career as an agent; is already involved in the football industry in some form and wants to broaden their knowledge; or is simply a lover of the beautiful game and their fascination has brought them to delve into the much-debated world of agency.

For those that are not aware of the changes that are occurring across modern football and in this era of agents, this book outlines it all. For those who do already have an idea, this guide goes deeper, enhancing your level of insight into the industry and how this influences your possible aspirations of becoming a successful agent.

Success as an agent comes in many forms. On a basic level, one may view being an agent as the man who poses in contract signing photos and is paid healthily for it. This is what the media may have led you to believe. This is far from the truth. Agents are at the very core of football and have a responsibility in almost every deal that takes place across the football world. It is an area that is commonly misunderstood and misinterpreted. This guide will also broaden your perspective of what a true and moral agent operating within the game is and hopefully inspire you to become one of these. The more educated, ethical and well-informed agents within the game the better it is for the industry and for the sport of football as a whole.

The third edition expands further than ever before to acclimatise to the modern era of football. Agency is an unpredictable profession where no two days are ever the same but this guide provides as close to an all-encompassing agent 'textbook' that will present almost every eventuality, challenge and role that an agent will face in their career. This now includes chapters that emphasise the importance of aspects such as working with female footballers; the future of football agents; the art of negotiation in the football context; social media, commercialisation and personal branding; the relevance of agents for NFT's and Cryptocurrency in football; how and when to work with trusted lawyers; and, of course, the new regulations being proposed by FIFA and how this will impact and affect the way you go about breaking into and succeeding in the industry. As well as updating and reconsidering all of the essential areas from the art of a transfer, to negotiating and networking with football clubs, to the day-to-day work of an agent; all of which continue to adapt in keeping with the evolution of football and football players.

The guide is not designed to be read just once. It is a lot of information to take in. Our best advice is to sit back, grab a highlighter or pen, and pay attention to the details. It is the kind of guide that we expect its benefits to be maximised by revisiting certain sections and chapters at various points. Remember, reading this book does not make you a successful agent; but learning from the lessons it teaches, developing the skills that it emphasises and adopting the good habits it proposes as essential, will stand you in good stead to succeed in one of the most unpredictable and challenging yet enthralling and rewarding professions in the world.

Chapter 1: The History of the Business

"It is important to know and understand the history of the profession" - Dr Erkut Sogut

Introduction

The history of football agency, and sports agency in general is fascinating. Since before the start of the 20th century, individuals have taken on roles and responsibilities that are often attributed to our modern concept of what an agent does. After the first half of the 20th century, several names began to emerge as the dominant forces across the sports industry in the talent management field. Understanding where we are in the industry today and to appreciate the evolution of the profession are important foundations for an aspiring agent.

The work of an agent has progressed and evolved alongside the changing dynamic and norms of modern sport. Many new skill sets, challenges and responsibilities have become a part of an agent's duty whilst others that may have been integral to the traditional role of an agent in the beginning are no longer a significant component of the job. The future of agency is unpredictable but there are several possible pathways which the profession might go down and different areas it might venture into, we will look into these at the end of this book.

In the Beginning

It could be argued that some men that operated within football from around the beginning of the 20th century up until 1950 were a form of football agent. These men conducted work on behalf of clubs in scouting players and had a role in mediation for their contracts and transfers. This was particularly prominent in England as well as some other European countries. During this time, football had not reached its professional era. Whilst players were paid, the wages were minimal and capped and they all worked other jobs on the side. Football was more of a hobby but the involvement of external third-parties in the movements and loyalties of the players was beginning to emerge.

Back in this era, players were viewed as commodities. This is an accusation that is often made in the modern era as well. It is an age-old worry that with clubs exchanging money (and large sums of it in the modern era) for the services of a human being, it is possible to lose sight of their rights, footballing autonomy and 'humanness'. Consequently, an anti-intermediary sentiment began to rise within football as clubs and fans believed they were an unhealthy addition and encouraged the commodification of young men playing a sport they enjoyed.

The term 'agents' wasn't used during this time and still seemed an alien concept. On the face of it, all that was happening was a handful of men willing to involve themselves in a football club would take on some kind of scouting or mediation capacity within the club. In a pre-professional era, there was no regulation in place to control, guide or restrict their activities. At this stage, it was a very primitive and basic occupation rather than a professional livelihood and commissions in the millions seemed an unrealistic development.

The earliest indication of the future that sports agency might present was through the work of the legendary Gigi Peronace. In 1957, his first ever deal broke the football transfer record as he moved John Charles from Leeds United to Juventus for £65,000, an enormous transfer fee at such a time. Peronace identified that he could utilise his status and power to entice players in the UK to opportunities in Italy. The biggest selling point was that the wages limits were still in place in the UK at the time whilst the salaries available in Italian football were unrestricted. This was epitomised when Charles collected £10,000 as a signing-on bonus at Juventus when the norm for signing-on fees in the UK was £100. Peronace had leaped at the opportunity and went on to represent clients such as Jimmy Greaves and Denis Law, continuing his pattern of finding them buying clubs in Italy where they could earn far more for their services as football players. Peronace had begun to pave the way to the future of the agency field in football.

The 1960's: The True Birth of Agency

In 1961, the maximum wage legislation in UK football was abolished and the FA adopted the same regulation as the Italian system which Peronace had used to his advantage. Playing football in the UK became more attractive as the average salaries of footballers rose by 61% by 1964. For agents, this meant there was a far greater extent of bargaining and negotiation power for them to become useful to clients. Their importance and value to players increased in direct correlation with the rise in professionalism of football and the income that they could earn from the game.

Across the pond, Mark McCormack was bringing the profession of sports agency and talent representation into the eye of the general public for the first time. Beginning in 1960, having graduated from Yale University with a degree in Law and meeting golfer Arnold Palmer on the golf circuit, McCormack rose to fame by taking on the responsibility of representing some of the world's major sports stars at the time.

As his career developed, McCormack diversified his client roster across several sports, particularly tennis and became the agent of Brazilian football legend Pelé. He founded the International Management Group (IMG) which continues to be a global powerhouse in the modern era of talent management and was part of a major merger with William Morris Endeavour (WME).

One of the biggest progressions in sports agency that was made by McComack was his extension of the agency profession into client endorsements and sponsorships. He reframed an agent's perspective of their responsibilities to their client to include prioritising boosting their marketability and popularity. He believed that in the era that sport had entered, the concept of an athlete as their own popular personal brand could "transcend borders, language, cultures and even sports itself". It was a revolutionary approach to agency and he can be credited with laying the foundations for the role of agents in modern sports and in football.

Football underwent the process of globalisation during this period of time. The sport had become a regular on television and was being viewed across the world. As a result, the popularity of football itself and the players that played it was rising exponentially. This presented further opportunities and possibilities for football agents. The metaphorical ceiling to what agents could achieve for their clients was disappearing and the scope of their responsibilities in the job description was lengthening almost endlessly.

This idea grounded itself in the 1970's. Football agents were tasked with continuing the promotion of internationalisation for the sport and the players that they represented. Their clients were now globally marketable and a new age of commercial deals and endorsements added an additional area of expertise and negotiation aptitude demanded of agents. Furthermore, part of the sport's globalisation was a relaxation in transfer restrictions and overseas deals. Agents began to ignore the traditional transfer channels within individual countries and went about forging new pathways between football clubs from across their continent and beyond.

During this decade, a couple of major figures emerged in the world of football agency. Dennis Roach was one of the best known agents at the time. He began in 1973 with none other than Johann Cruyff as his first client which helped to quickly establish himself as a desirable agent for footballers globally. Before the decade was up, Roach claimed the very first £1million deal in football as he transferred Birmingham's Trevor Francis to Nottingham Forest for the groundbreaking fee. Over his 20-year career, Roach continued to represent top talents such as Glenn Hoddle, Mark Hughes and Harry Redknapp.

Elsewhere, the now world-renowned Pini Zahavi started out on his journey in football agency in 1979. After managing clients such as Rio Ferdinand and brokering Roman Abramovich's acquisition of Chelsea Football Club, many acclaim that Zahavi is the true godfather of modern football agency and he continues to represent players of the calibre of Polish superstar, Robert Lewandowski. He has operated through the height of the transition period for agents as a broad focus across legal advice, contractual negotiations, client branding and endorsement deals became the norm of an ever-increasingly professional and lucrative sport.

Professionalisation: The 1990's and Millennial Boom

The agency field had to keep up with the evolution and modernising dynamic of football as the 21st century approached. Agents had become an integral part of football by the 1990's and after a period of many players receiving inadequate salaries after naively appointing close family relatives as representatives, they had been rightly recognised for their importance and value to players. Consequently, by the beginning of the decade, the majority of players called upon the services of an agent to assist with contract negotiations with clubs and legal advice as a minimum;

and for those that were more marketable and popular with the public, also to help seek lucrative and appropriate endorsement opportunities. The number of agents in the world of football had soared as many hopeful individuals cited it as an opportunity to make a desirable income in one of the top sports in the world. It was only a matter of time before the football industry recognised agents as professionals of the sport.

This momentous occasion came in 1994 as FIFA formally repositioned agents as professionals. With this, they implemented regulation, guidelines and criteria. This included a structured licensing system in order to obtain a licence that granted permission for individuals to operate as an agent. Many national associations implemented their own examinations that agents were required to pass, incorporating FIFA's legislation. This was in recognition of the alarmingly high rate at which new agents were entering the industry. The hope was that the exam, licensing and application fees would discourage those that were entering the industry for the wrong reasons or with an insufficient and inappropriate skillset from ever applying.

In 1996, one of the first well-known agents to pass the exam and to obtain his licence was Jorge Mendes. He has been a mainstay in the world of football agents ever since and has represented or continues to manage some of Portugal's finest footballing talent and beyond. His clients include Cristiano Ronaldo, Ruben Neves, Angel Di Maria, Joao Cancelo, Darwin Nunez and manager Jose Mourinho, to name a handful of superstars on his roster. He entered the field at a time when agency was undergoing a distinct stage of reformation but Mendes established himself as a major figure and has experienced great success since the turn of the century.

Several factors over the next few years before 2000 further added to the attraction of being a football agent and the potential lucrativeness of the profession. In 1995, the Bosman Ruling once again caused a significant alteration to the pattern of transfers in global football and the freedom that players and their agents had. With 'free agents' able to negotiate higher wages for a free transfer, the bargaining power of agents was enhanced even further and the possible commission remuneration for themselves rose in situ.

Paid television also emerged in the world of sport. Paying subscriptions to broadcasting companies in order to watch football and other sports was a new concept but one that immediately caused a jump in the financial value of the sports. Broadcasting and television rights payments were distributed amongst football clubs and player salaries benefited substantially. As always, with more money available to players, there was also more money available to their agents. Despite the implementation of licensing and examination, the number of agents in football continued to rise as the chance of representing a client who earned a large sum of money each year was too attractive to ignore.

Needless to say, popular culture also played its part in launching the agency profession into the public spotlight. The 1996 Tom Cruise film, Jerry Maguire, was Hollywood's interpretation of the world of agency. Modelled upon the life and career of NFL agent Leigh Steinberg, the film depicted agency as a glamorous, exhilarating, ultimately rewarding and lavish lifestyle. It was very successful at the box office and exposed the general public to the life of an agent, or at least what Hollywood made it out to be.

The result of this decade of change was a new wave of agents entering the business. Agents were now coming from all walks of life. Lawyers, bankers, ex-footballers, scouts, marketers, journalists, directors and almost any other profession were trying their hand in the football agency field. There was a large list of transferable skills from other industries that were readily applicable to the agency profession. However, the vast scope of agent responsibilities, capabilities and services they were demanded to provide to their clients meant that very few reached the top level and worked with the best clients. Nevertheless, across the first decade of the century and the start of the 2010's, the full force of the new wave was felt. In 2001, FIFA had 631 agents registered globally under their relatively new licensing system. By 2009 there were 5,193 across the world.

2015-2022: The Age of Deregulation

Prior to 2015, an emerging trend presented itself that coupled with the other areas of evolution in the field of football agency. There was an alarming volume of 'player representatives' that were operating without a licence. These individuals were often carrying out the same responsibilities and services for players that a licensed agent was. The difference lay in the way that they sought remuneration and commission through other forms away from the contracts and below the books through kickbacks or 'benefit in kind' payments. However, this was easy enough and meant that fans, media and football authorities observed that the growing value of agency fees being paid by clubs each year were perceived as leaking money out of the game.

This was recognised in 2009 and plans were made to change the regulation system for agents to try and encourage all agents to work above the books in accordance with FIFA's legislation. These plans came to fruition in 2015. They materialised in the form of a complete deregulation. National associations were given the option of generating their own individual regulations for agents. Apart from France and Italy who upheld their exam processes, other footballing nations withdrew such requirements. Instead the process of becoming an agent became astoundingly straightforward. An aspiring agent simply needed to pay a relatively small fee and verify that they do not have a criminal record and they were able to obtain a licence. As expected, the number of agents has inevitably risen once more and the money spent by clubs on agency fees continues to rise. The number of agents operating in the UK alone peaked well over 4,000 during this time.

Another recent development of note is large investment from American companies into agencies that has altered the landscape for football agents. For example, the merging of Stellar and Base Soccer with the Creative Artists Agency (CAA) is an enormous acquisition in the world of agency that affects the industry globally. CAA Stellar now represents over 700 clients in world football, with a total market value of €1.59billion. This indicates more of a monopoly in the market in the recent history of football agency.

There was also new terminology adopted within the world of football due to the altered positioning, regulation and hierarchy of the field. Agents became known and referred to by FIFA as 'intermediaries' to indicate their change in role and perception as mediators and 'middlemen' for transactions. Some individuals at the very top of the agency industry have also become known as 'superagents'. They boast some of the biggest names in the sport as their clients and have a significant level of power over major football clubs and control over transfers whilst collecting enormous commissions, having acted on behalf of more than one party in a single transaction.

FIFA has recently done a U-turn and as our exploration of the history of football agency reaches the present, 2023 is the year when regulation has come back into force. These regulations extend further than before in recognition of the relentlessly increasing commissions and power that agents receive in football. The regulations (chapter 2) establish new laws regarding commission caps, licensing, a new exam and a ban of multiple representation. All of this is part of becoming an agent that we will delve into throughout the book.

Summary

- Knowing and understanding the history of the profession and how it has got to the point at which it finds itself today is an important part of bettering yourself as an agent.
- Be aware how much the industry has chopped and changed and be prepared that it will continue to do so and it is your responsibility to keep up to date with these changes and adapt accordingly.

Further Reading

- The Age of Football - David Goldblatt
- Jerry Maguire - A Tom Cruise Film

Chapter 2: The New Agent Regulations

"Knowledge has a beginning but no end" - Geeta Iyengar

Why Change the Period of Deregulation?

As explained in the previous chapter, prior to 2015, there was a system in place that provided regulations and guidance for football agents globally. There were significant barriers to entry for becoming a licensed agent and to operate in the football industry. The most important obstacle was that agents were required to undertake a compulsory exam. The exam consisted of 20 multiple choice questions based upon various case studies and scenarios. 15 of these questions came from FIFA directly and the other five were created by the national football association based upon their independent laws. The exam was also available in each local language of the national football association in which the agent was acting.

The aim of such a qualification was to test the candidate's understanding of FIFA's principles and to appropriately apply the regulations in different situations. In order for the candidate to be awarded an agent's licence, they were required to achieve 80% on the exam; a total of 16 correct answers out of a possible 20. It was a difficult exam that forced aspiring agents to vigorously examine and understand all of FIFA's regulations, from player registration to transfers and status of players. The exam was not to be underestimated, reflected in just an 8-15% annual pass rate. Consequently, agent numbers were restricted. Prior to the deregulation in 2015, there were only around 500 registered and licensed agents operating in the UK, according to *The Independent* and.

The issue that arose as a result of such an intense and difficult entry process was that many individuals operated without a licence and took on the responsibilities of an agent unqualified. FIFA was concerned that this was to blame for a rising number of deals that were done below the books and epitomised the lack of transparency in the football world. Consequently, the exam was abolished in April of 2015 as part of FIFA's changes to agent regulations in an attempt to improve the industry and football as a whole.

FIFA's motivation for deregulation was in the hope that transparency would increase as all agents would become licensed. Previously, those that could not or did not want to pass the exam resorted to operating without a licence, making it difficult for FIFA to monitor. They decided it was best to leave the responsibility of deciding how to award an agency licence to the independent national football associations.

In some countries, such as France and Italy, an exam was still used, combining FIFA's and the independent football associations' regulations. However, in other countries such as the UK and Germany, the absence of an exam reduced the criteria for obtaining an agent licence to a criminal record check and an affordable annual payment. As a result, *The Independent* estimated that the number of licensed agents in the UK reached around 6000 individuals, a 1200% increase from the time when passing the FIFA exam was mandatory. This is an extraordinary rise in the number of agents under the umbrella of the FA. This was not exclusively seen in the UK; it had the same impact on the football industry worldwide.

Becoming an agent in one of the most exciting industries and sports in the world seemed an incredibly attractive opportunity to many. When the decision to deregulate football agents was made, FIFA encouraged clubs and players to implement a commission cap of 3% for agents. In reality, this was rarely adhered to. Despite FIFA's guidance commission rates were actually far higher as these statistics from before the new regulations show:

1. The average agent commission for transfers over $5million is 5.8%
2. The average agent commission for transfers between $1-$5million is 8.8%
3. The average agent commission for transfers under $1million is 16.6%
4. There were 3558 transfers that used at least one intermediary in 2019, 148 of those transfers accounted for $430million worth of commission out of the total agency fees of $653.9million for the year
5. That equates to 4.5% of transfers amounting for 65.7% of the total agency commissions

The world has seen a continuous rise in enormous transfer fees and additionally in the commissions that agents are receiving at the top end of the game. The main reason for this is the extreme growth in broadcasting revenue, commercial sponsorship and foreign investment into football clubs. In general, transfer prices and player salaries have risen, and therefore, so have agent commission fees. In 2019, USD $653.9million was paid in agency fees (FIFA TMS - these useful details can be found through platforms such as the FA Intermediary Transactions documents online). Worryingly for FIFA, there had also not been an increase in the transparency of transfers globally.

A significant proportion of these payments came out of the pockets of the clubs rather than directly from the players themselves. However, despite common misconception most of these fees were paid because of agent services on behalf of players rather than clubs although the exact breakdown of this distribution is not disclosed.

Once FIFA accepted that the 2015 deregulation of agents had not had the desired and intended effect, they sought to formulate a new approach. Hence, the idea of the regulations that were approved in December 2022 and have recently come into force on the 9th January 2023 began. After years of development and discussion (which still continues), this revamped four-pronged regulation system endeavours to rectify the mistakes made in the past and increase the standard, morality and transparency of the agency industry.

Within this chapter we will aim to provide an overview of each element of FIFA's new regulations that you will now have to comply with; hard commission caps, the new exam, multiple representation restrictions and the centralised clearing house. Each of these facets are vital for any agent to have a flawless comprehension of.

Commission Caps

One of the biggest changes to agent regulations that has come into force is that FIFA have installed commission caps, primarily to keep as much money as possible in the game. This stemmed from the feeling amongst some major figures in the football world that opposed the disproportionately high level of remuneration that agents were receiving. The hard commission restrictions implemented by FIFA for a single transaction are as follows:

Client	Service Fee Cap	
	Individual's annual remuneration less than or equal to $200,000 (or equivalent)	Individual's annual remuneration above $200,000 (or equivalent)
Individual	**5%** of the individual's remuneration	**3%** of the individual's remuneration
Engaging Entity	**5%** of the individual's remuneration	**3%** of the individual's remuneration
Engaging Entity and **Individual** (permitted dual representation)	**10%** of the individual's remuneration	**6%** of the individual's remuneration
Releasing Entity (transfer compensation)	**10%** of the transfer compensation	

Source: FIFA Football Agent Regulations

Putting the table into simple terms:

1. Individual refers to the agent acting on behalf of the player (the individual) as the client. If the player's annual remuneration is above $200,000 (or the same amount in another currency), the agent is entitled to 3% of this figure. If it is below $200,000, the agent is entitled to 5%.

2. The engaging entity simply means the 'buying club'. If the player's annual salary is above $200,000, the agent is entitled to 3% of this figure from the buying club; or 5% if it is below $200,000.

3. If prior written consent has been given by each party, and the agent represents both the player and the buying club (the only permitted form of multiple representation) the commission percentage is doubled. If the player earns less

than $200,000 annually, the agent is entitled to 10% of this, 5% from the player and 5% from the club. If the salary is over $200,000, the agent is entitled to 6% (3% from the buying club, 3% from the player).

4. Finally, if the agent represents the selling club (releasing entity) as their client, they will be entitled to 10% of the player's annual salary, regardless of whether it is above $200,000 or not.

Note: if there are multiple agents involved in one service provision, this does not entitle the agent to a commission fee any more than the relevant capped percentage in total.

The secondary aims of these reforms for FIFA are centred around the desire to maintain and protect the integrity of the sport and align agency fees with solidarity and training compensation payments that were far below the figures paid for agency fees.

An issue that remains is that the average commission of agents at the top level of football did not previously exceed 3% extortionately whilst agents operating at a lower level have been more dramatically impacted. This is demonstrated by the discrepancies shown in the 2020 UK figures below:

1. The Premier League paid £272million to agents
2. The Championship paid £40million to agents
3. League 1 paid £3million to agents
4. League 2 paid £1million to agents

This has led to speculation that the future of agent regulations may incorporate a slight variation in hard commission caps that allows for a tiered system to ensure that agents that are involved with smaller transactions and transfers are able to afford their livelihood through the industry although this remains to be seen. Remember it is part of your job as an agent to keep up with the ongoing developments around agent regulations.

An interesting clause of the new regulations is that agents acting on behalf of the selling club are entitled to a far higher commission (10%) than those acting on behalf of the player or the buying club. For agents, is it important to remember that it is vital for us to care for our clients. It may be an attractive option to act on behalf of the selling club in order to maximise our personal financial terms but this should not reduce our player clients to commodities that we simply urge to move onto another club in order to collect higher commissions. The job of the agent, regardless of which party they are acting on behalf of, is to ensure that they have their client's best interests at heart and as motivation for all the decisions and negotiations we make. Agency is a selfless business and with the introduction of commission caps, a good agent will not let such a regulation affect the quality and standard of work they provide for their clients.

The New Exam

FIFA decided, in light of the issues following the 2015 deregulation, that the best option was to reintroduce an examination process to restrict the number of individuals who could qualify as agents and to raise the overall understanding and aptitude of those operating in the industry. The FIFA Chief Legal and Compliance Officer (CLCO) has made it very clear that this exam, and the regulations as a whole, are not intended to be a project to oppose agents but to help them by improving the standards within the industry.

Agents and prospective agents should perceive the reintroduction of the exam as an opportunity to educate themselves and improve their competency, capability and knowledge as an agent rather than viewing it as a barrier to entry. Those that are knowledgeable and have a sufficient, profound understanding of what it takes to be a successful agent will pass the exam without question. We hope that this guide itself will go some way in helping to educate you towards passing it but it is important to carry out further reading. Erkut also offers a 'how to pass the agent exam' course with top sports lawyer, Daniel Geey, which offers bespoke preparation for the agent exam.

Fortunately for those who took the exam prior to 2015, they will not be required to retake the newest version of the exam and will just need to prove they have passed the exam before. Although, our advice to all agents would be to make sure that your understanding and awareness of different aspects of the industry is continually updated and aligned with the evolving game of football nonetheless. This should be to a point where if they were required to sit the modern exam, they would pass once again.

Education should be paramount and integral to our lifestyle as agents, and should be expanded and developed with a greater volume of content that is specific to the work of agents. For an agent to be successful and professional they must have a wider understanding of all regulations, case studies, cultures, systems, history, leagues, legislation and every facet and field of the industry.

We will revisit the new exam in an entirely separate chapter (chapter 5) in order to gain a full understanding of what it is likely to entail.

Agents that have obtained a licence after the 2015 deregulation are likely to have built the foundations of their careers already. However, they will be required to sit the newest exam in order to maintain their licence and status as an agent.

Another significant element that will be included is known as a 'Continuing Professional Development' (CPD) requirement. This refers to a system or infrastructure that will be implemented to enforce the on-going education of agents. Such a regulation will demand the personal responsibility of an agent to update and maintain their adequate knowledge of the industry and relevant regulations.

Multiple Representation Restrictions

Prior to the adoption of the new FIFA agent regulations, multiple representation had been the norm in the football world. The term refers to instances where the agent represented more than one party in a transfer negotiation: at least two out of the selling club, the buying club and the player themselves. These agreements would occur in order to simplify a transfer deal by directing it through a single negotiator. The agent may have had a particularly good relationship with each of the clubs and knew or represented the player involved. A multiple representation agreement would result in larger payouts to the agent, but the clubs were not forced to use this method, although they often chose to do so in order to successfully acquire a player they desired. The practice of multiple representation of up to all three parties had been possible during the time before the new regulations and offered enticing opportunities to agents who could receive remuneration from the player, the buying club and the selling club in a single transfer.

The transfer of Paul Pogba from Juventus to Manchester United in 2016 is the most publicly well-documented case of multiple, tripartite representation. In order for the agent, in this particular case the late Mino Raiola, to have legally acted as the agent of all three parties, he must have been in compliance with the multiple representation regulations of the English FA and the Italian FIGC. To be seen as adhering to these regulations, he was required to have lodged his representation agreements with the FA as well as obtaining written consent from all three parties accepting the issues of multiple representation. Prior to this, both clubs and the player must have been made explicitly aware of the inevitable conflict of interest that would arise as a result of acting on behalf of each interested party as well as disclosing the terms of representation and the fees that he was entitled to from each contract. The FA referred to this as the 'duty of disclosure of the full particulars' of each agreement to the others in order to fulfil the obligations of transparency demanded under the regulations for multiple representation.

The graphic below hopefully simplifies this example transfer and how a tripartite representation materialises:

CASE STUDY:
TRANSFER PAUL POGBA

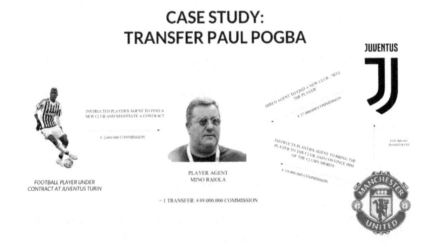

Part of the introduction of FIFA's new regulations concerns multiple representation and is aimed at combating moral and legal questions that were raised through the practice. There were ethical implications surrounding conflicts of interest as well as legal difficulties, separate from football legislation, such as tax problems. The changes made by FIFA are as follows:

1. An intermediary should only perform his/her services on behalf of one party. There is only ONE exception to this rule (2).

2. The agent can legally act on behalf of the individual player and the engaging (buying) club ONLY if the following criteria is met:

   a. Both parties are made aware of the conflict of interests that will arise as a result.

b. The details of both contracts, including the terms of service and the terms of remuneration are fully disclosed to each party.
c. Both parties have the right to seek independent legal advice on the matter.
d. The player must have a preexisting representation contract with the agent, lodged with the National Association.
3. This means that the agent is not entitled to simultaneously represent the buying club and the selling club; the selling club and the player; nor ALL THREE PARTIES.

First and foremost, the primary purpose of these new regulations is to prevent instances where the agent was able to represent all three parties. FIFA suggested these changes as a sign of intent to achieve the fundamental principles that must be met in order to improve the football industry and to increase the transparency of agents and transactions. Instead of relying upon National Associations to make their own judgements on dual representation, FIFA has attempted to synchronise and coordinate the regulations to create a more robust and consistent system. The new regulations incur sanctions and penalties if they are violated and if an agent is found to have committed a 'misconduct offence'. Penalties include punishments such as loss of remuneration for the agent from affected parties and potentially the revokement of a licence to operate. It is vital therefore that we have a clear comprehension of the limitations that the new regulations place upon the eligibility of multiple representation to avoid these sanctions affecting our livelihood.

The ethical foundations behind the new regulations are centred upon the conflicts of interest that previously arose. When an agent signs a representation agreement, they are obliged to fulfil the fiduciary, contractual duty of acting in the best interests of the party that he or she represents. For example, representing the buying and selling club is now prohibited under the new regulations as there was an obvious contradiction in trying to negotiate the lowest price for the buying club whilst pursuing the highest price possible for the selling club. By representing the buying club and the player, these conflicts might not be as prominent and have become an established and common system used by agents and clubs, especially in the United Kingdom. However, it is important to note that once an agent is responsible for more than one party, there will always be an ethical dilemma in being able to satisfactorily act in the best interests of both parties within the only legally accepted dual representation contract. Even though FIFA have ruled out the possibility of the most contradictory relationships, there is still a level of difficulty in achieving the best for the player and the buying club. This will be illustrated when you are in a scenario in which you are trying to achieve the highest salary possible for the player whilst also negotiating to minimise the expenses for the buying club that you are also representing.

The Clearing House

Many problems, issues, legal questions and ethical queries in modern football can go some way to being resolved through a centralised system. FIFA believes that, from agency fees to transfers to third party ownership, a sole location through which all of these transactions must pass through will help to eradicate dubiousness and foul play.

The key to the solution is an increase in the transparency of all global transfers and transactions that take place. In response to this, FIFA have developed and established a centralised 'Clearing House'. To ensure the success and effectiveness of this clearing house requires that all transactions within football to be passed through and documented by this single and universal system. This emphasises the necessity of transparency in mitigating the negative impact of third party ownership (you may sometimes see this abbreviated as TPO).

The presence of a clearing house to receive the exact details, financial and otherwise, of transactions between clubs, agents and players allows for FIFA to have greater capabilities to monitor where money is being lost from football clubs and the game itself. This hopes to ensure that any malpractice of agents is eradicated and prevent future ill-behaviour from taking place. A centralised clearing house positively impacts the footballing world and should go some way in solving a significant problem that FIFA faces in the criticism of agents taking money unjustifiably away from the game. This clearing house is useful for those agents that operate above the books in an ethical and legal manner as their work will be recognised as such. Prioritising policies such as using clearing houses as part of agent regulation reforms, with the view of doing everything through a centralised system, is the best approach to creating a more transparent world of football transfers and transactions.

Another topic of debate for you as an aspiring agent to consider, and to keep up to date with, is the objections to certain elements of the clearing house. Namely the requirement of publicly stating annual earnings and income. Whilst it is clearly good for global transparency in football, many are challenging the system as an invasion of privacy. In most professions it is deemed inappropriate or rude and often avoided to declare the salary of an individual in a given year and yet the clearing house completely contradicts this. Especially in volatile countries, this may endanger agents if their salary is known to others. Keep an eye on the clearing house and hopefully an ethical and suitable solution is found.

Expert's View: Dr Erkut Sogut

"It was once a privilege of mine to be invited to the FIFA agent consultations and to spend a few years as the vice-president of the Professional Football Agents Association (PROFAA) during the discussions of the new regulations. I believed it would be interesting and thought-provoking to share my own viewpoint here as the expert for this chapter and to share my experiences of the consultation:

Many agents from around the world, including several of the biggest names in the industry, arrived for the first agent consultation with FIFA in Zurich in 2018. They held high hopes and anticipation for the opportunity to have their voices heard in front of the major stakeholders in the game; FIFA, FIFPro, UEFA and the European Club Association amongst others. Whilst agents are not currently stakeholders in football, they play a large part in the industry and this seemed like the chance to come face-to-face with the decision makers in football and influence the future for agents. The importance of the consultation was reflected by the attendance of Pini Zahavi, Rob Jansen, Giovanni Branchini, Richard Motzkin and Mino Raiola. The general feeling towards football's stakeholders was a satisfied and hopeful one. It was an encouraging sign that the stakeholders in football were allowing agents to express their concerns, worries and feedback on the proposed regulations for agents that the lawmakers were set to bring in.

Although some agents were against any regulation at all, most agents, including myself, agreed that new regulations in the industry are needed to raise the ethical and professional standards of agents globally. The motivations behind and fundamental aims of the changes in regulation were also agreeable. Outcomes such as increased transparency, licensing, education, enhanced player welfare and stability as well as a centralised system to monitor transactions are all concepts that will improve agency and protect our rights (such as claiming commissions from clubs directly through FIFA) and football as a whole. For example, foreign players' incomes are protected and ensured by FIFA, this should now be the same for agents and their remuneration. However, for the regulations to be effective and successful in their aims, they must be reasonable, fair, legally correct and feasible to implement. For this to occur, agents themselves must be involved in the process of developing the new legislation. In 2018, the agents that were invited to Zurich were under the impression that the consultation was for exactly this; for them to express their opinions and help inform FIFA and other stakeholders of the best ways of implementing new regulations on the industry.

From the second meeting onwards, rather than the two way dialogue that should occur during the consultations, it seemed that FIFA had already decided on the regulations and were simply telling the agents what was going to happen. There were no actual decision makers in attendance. However, they continued to publicise the meeting as 'collaborative consultations'.

The pattern continued in the future meetings but FIFA seemed even less willing to collaborate with agents. Despite the promise that agents would be able to meet face-to-face with football's authorities and stakeholders again, future meetings involved only representatives. This meant that even if they did listen to any of the concerns raised by the agents in attendance, there was unlikely to be any changes as the information and solutions had to be relayed through to the decision makers who were unlikely to listen to second hand accounts.

At my final meeting in January of 2022, after I had made my intentions to leave clear, I was promised that if I remained part of the consultations then I would be able to meet with decision makers and stakeholders at the final consultation in February. I trusted my instinct, stepped away from my role at ProFAA and my fears were confirmed when no stakeholders were in attendance at the next meeting. The reason given for this was that they decided they did not want to confront agents directly. This was problematic and confusing as it was assumed that agents and the stakeholders were going to work in conjunction towards a positive outcome.

It remains to be seen what exactly the impact and consequences of these new regulations are yet to be seen. I believe there will be ongoing legal battles for the foreseeable future before an eventual overall compromise is found to almost all aspects of the new regulations. Throughout this book I hope that we can provide you with the skills and knowledge of how to be an ethical and successful agent, regardless of which regulations govern us.

There are several unanswered questions that are yet to be explained by FIFA and football's decision makers. I would like to pose these now as my concluding thoughts and something that may help your brain engage and think through whilst you read the remainder of this book. Personally for me, the consultation and the new regulations seem to fail to address these queries:

1. Why are the stakeholders not directly involved in the consultation process?
2. Why are agents that represent clubs capped at 10% commission whilst player agents at only 3%?
3. Are agents that represent clubs more valuable?
4. Is it time to separate club agents from player agents? Are club agents more consultants so they should not be regulated in the same way as player agents?
5. Why are the regulations solely directed at regulating agents rather than including limitations for club officials such as sporting directors who can currently earn and pay themselves bottomless bonuses?
6. If you cap agents, shouldn't you also cap the entire football economy? For example, players income, coaches income, club officials income...
7. Why are they claiming to consult agents worldwide whilst less than 1%, many of which are not fully established and inadequate representatives?
8. Are they planning to use the "consultation" with these agents against others once the matter is disputed?"

Further Reading

- FIFA Agent Regulations: https://digitalhub.fifa.com/m/1e7b741fa0fae779/original/FIFA-Football-Agent-Regulations.pdf
  https://www.fifa.com/legal/football-regulatory/agents/news/new-fifa-football-agent-regulations-set-to-come-into-force
- Regulations on the Status and Transfer of Players: https://digitalhub.fifa.com/m/1b47c74a7d44a9b5/original/Regulations-on-the-Status-and-Transfer-of-Players-March-2022.pdf
- Law in Sport: New Agent Regulations: https://www.lawinsport.com/news/item/fifa-to-introduce-new-agent-regulations-and-limit-their-commission-from-transfers

- Blog: https://erkutsogut.com/the-new-fifa-agent-regulations-explained/

Chapter 3: Getting Into the Agency Business

"There is no correct or incorrect way to become a football agent"

Introduction

We will begin by saying that the journey to becoming an agent is far removed from many professions. To become a doctor, you study medicine and then begin practising; in law, you study a law degree, complete a training contract and begin to practise as a solicitor or barrister; to become a plumber you learn the trade before you begin and the same goes with carpentry and other professions. Contrastingly, there is no set route to take to get into the agency business. This chapter will outline a variety of possible ways of getting started in this industry that may set you on the right path. However, ultimately it is the ones who are willing to dedicate themselves to the industry, put in the greatest amounts of graft, learning and work, that will prevail in the end. Importantly, remember that this industry may require a significant volume of patience at the start. It may be slow to begin with but focus, ethical practice and hard-work will pay off and you will reap the rewards in the end.

Internship or Direct Job Application

A common way into the footballing business is through applying for an internship or job at one of the larger agencies, either towards the end of your studies, or after completing them. Some of the agencies listed in the table at the end of this section (and other agencies not listed too) will run internship schemes in which they can employ from. Although these are naturally competitive, applying to as many as possible and trying to demonstrate your potential worth to them is pivotal. It is important to remember that gaining experience in either the marketing or legal department of these firms can prove to be just as valuable in the long term as working immediately alongside an agent.

It may be the case that the contacts you make during your time at these companies turn out to be crucial in your future career in the business. Even if you don't stay on after an internship or short mentoring agreement, it is crucial that during your time at an agency, you endeavour to grow and enhance your network and contacts in order to acquire as much knowledge as possible as well as being beneficial in the future.

An important point to note is that whilst the larger agencies may offer official internship schemes or 'grad-role' positions, it is still possible and sometimes a greater option to find an opportunity with a smaller, boutique agency. They may not advertise official roles but by using platforms such as LinkedIn and putting yourself out there by making phone calls, attending conferences and growing your network, you may be fortunate enough to be offered a form of internship or mentorship.

The greatest advice would be to bear in mind that these smaller agencies, even with just one or two clients, will be looking for individuals who can add value to their company. If you are able to demonstrate this whilst talking with someone, they are more likely to be willing to offer you some kind of role which will help you gain priceless experience as well as you helping them in some way. This is important to consider when you structure messages and have initial conversations with individuals already in the business. Under no circumstances should you take a phone call or meeting for granted. Always go into them well-prepared and knowledgeable of who you are talking to and how you might be able to help them. Each one is a chance for a new opportunity to arise so do not waste them! This is a crucial life-lesson for networking.

Erkut's Example

My own personal story demonstrates the power of adding value to these companies. I was in the middle of my law studies but wanted to gain some experience in the football agency industry. I had the audacity to seek a meeting with a top agent in Germany at the time which lasted all of five minutes. However, I came away from that first meeting with an idea of adding value to his work. For the next year, I wrote and produced a monthly magazine which I sent to the agency. The magazine contained lots of crucial legal points to consider in football agency and demonstrated to the agency that my education in law could be of benefit to them. After an entire year of perseverance, the agent who had originally spoken to me for five minutes requested I assist the agency with a legal case which we won. Following this, I began an internship with the company but I continued to show the value I could add and, at the request of the agent himself, I continued with my monthly magazine.

If you are unable to find an opportunity in a football agency, do not be afraid to get experience elsewhere in the football industry. Finding an internship or role with a sports-focused company in marketing, the commercial side, broadcasting, or with a club can be just as valuable. If this is what you find yourself doing but still have ambitions to one day transition into becoming an agent, make the most of such an opportunity to develop our network as this may come in very useful in the future. For example, if you are able to work within a club for a period of time, you will learn plenty about the football industry but more importantly, you will be spending time face-to-face with club officials, players and other important figures that may be able to help you as an agent one day.

Football agency	Clients represented
GROW (Formerly Family & Football)	Mesut Özil, Kieran Gibbs, Kerem Aktürkoğlu, Eren Elmali, Amadou Dante
Gestifute	Cristiano Ronaldo, Ederson, Bernardo Silva, Rúben Dias, Darwin Núñez, Diogo Jota, Fabinho
ICM Stellar Football Ltd	Jack Grealish, Kalvin Phillips, Eduardo Camavinga, Ibrahim Konate, Ben Chilwell, Yéremy Pino
CAA Base	Heung-min Son, Richarlison, James Maddison, Raphael Varane, Trevoh Chalobah, Kyle Walker
Wasserman	Aymeric Laporte, Harvey Barnes, Federico Valverde, Curtis Jones, Nathan Ake, John Stones
Rafaela Pimenta (Formerly Mino Raiola's clients)	Erling Haaland, Matthijs de Ligt, Marco Verratti, Gianluigi Donarumma, Paul Pogba, Donyell Malen

Elite Project Group	Jadon Sancho, Bukayo Saka, Roméo Lavia
Lian Sports	Federico Chiesa, Leroy Sané, Kalidou Koulibaly
Rogon Sportmanagement	Roberto Firmino, Joelinton, Marcel Sabitzer
ROOF	Kai Havertz, Sadio Mane, Serge Gnabry, Marc-André ter Stegen
Unique Sports Group	Reece James, Dayot Upamecano, Anthony Gordon, Marc Guehi, Tyrick Mitchell
Pini Zahavi	Robert Lewandowski, Christopher Nkunku, Yannick Carrasco, Pierre-Emile Höjbjerg, Aleksandar Mitrovic
Octagon	Roberto Martinez, Tajon Buchanan, Gianluca Busio

Source: Transfermarkt (correct as of October 2022)

A Contact in the Industry

Knowing somebody who is already connected to the footballing business is obviously a fortunate advantage that you should make the most of if you want to get into the industry. You may also be able to get yourself into such a fortunate position as a result of successful networking. A contact like this can range from a club employee (like a manager or sporting director) to an existing agent to a friend of a friend who knows someone else! It doesn't really matter how you know them and how they might help you, as long as it is done in good faith. When you're first introduced to this contact, certain things can be advised about how to present yourself:

1. **Be willing to learn:** anybody who thinks they are already the perfect agent (or thinks it is easy to become one) will immediately be caught out by any established agent. You have got to show that you are ready to learn and prepared to enthusiastically and thoroughly complete whatever task may be helpful to them, however small it may seem. This will

prove to them that you are willing to dedicate yourself to learning and developing as an agent and will result in them trusting you with greater tasks further down the line.

2. **Be professional:** whilst you want to convince this contact of your passion, you don't want to come across as overly eager or demanding. Agents are busy and often have little time, so make sure your words are smart, targeted, and you say what you want to say concisely. If you want this contact to give you the opportunity to shadow them and take you to meetings, they have to be confident that your presence will be of benefit and not of inconvenience. One way of helping you demonstrate this in a short meeting with them is to prepare well and carry out due diligence so that you are adequately prepared for discussion and what areas might appeal to the person you are talking to. This helps to present yourself as professional.

Attending Youth Games

A good way to go about getting your first client could be by attending youth and lower league fixtures. Whilst you must always be aware of abiding by the rules and regulations surrounding youth players, often the first player you represent will be young and eager to work their way to the top divisions. Going to as many games as possible (and seeing a variety of teams) shows your desire to make your mark in the industry. We will address scouting and identifying talent directly in chapter 10 but additionally, going to these matches are a great networking opportunity. Remember that it is likely that other scouts, agents and most certainly, parents, will be at these games which creates a special opportunity to connect with them and broaden your network.

As tempting as it may be to speak with anyone and everyone, you should always remain patient and professional, taking your time to research in order to make informed approaches and conversations.

Be brave. For some, it may seem a daunting task approaching people at games and striking up a conversation. However, if you are well-prepared and attend these games regularly you are in a much better position to represent yourself well.

(Erkut) In the beginning, I was told, in no uncertain terms, by parents that they were not interested in speaking with me. I was often anxious and hesitant in taking the initiative in striking up conversations with people at games. However, I was determined to overcome the daunting environment and as I attended more and more games, my confidence in doing so grew and the way I conducted myself adapted to the context. It became an enjoyable experience and my network began to grow rapidly. It is all about learning the system and how best to make yourself known.

These games are unique opportunities to network that can be of great benefit. Whilst not all conversations can ever go as planned, it is likely that if you go about it in the right way, most conversations will end with swapping contact details or the roots of a relationship. These can bring benefits further down the line.

For example, stopping in order to speak with a member of an academy player's family at the game is a great idea – as the relationship with the family is integral. Do not be overly forceful or come across as intruding on their privacy. Instead, demonstrate your interest professionally and do not become a nuisance by needlessly prolonging a conversation or interrupting their enjoyment of watching their child play. Also remember, if you want to work with youth players, there are certain rules and regulations you have to follow. For example, in England, you must not engage in any contact with a player regarding 'intermediary activity' before January 1st of the year in which the player will celebrate their sixteenth birthday, and any contract with a minor must have a parent or legal guardian signing off.

NB: In order to get to youth games, you often have to request access through the clubs. That is why sometimes not registering before you get your first client can be advantageous, as the clubs sometimes restrict or cap the number of agents attending certain youth games. In requesting access, having contacts at a club that you have gained from your network may stand you in good stead to be able to attend.

General Business Person

Many successful agents actually transfer over from mainstream professions, perhaps specialising in areas such as law, banking, journalism, business, marketing or teaching. Jobs like these, as well as so many others, are a great way into the world of sports as a player (and their representatives at the time) will always need the advice of specialists, for example in legal or financial matters that a lawyer or banker can provide respectively. If someone in these professions has the right contacts and is willing to dedicate themselves to a change in career, agency is a very realistic option for them. The transferable skills learned in their previous occupation will help greatly in succeeding as an agent. One of the many cases of this is Jörg Neubauer, who started his career as a lawyer but turned into a prolific football agent, representing Leon Goretzka before his recent passing which WE will touch upon in chapter 26.

There are also many business people that work closely with sport, whilst not actually being agents. Often, a business person can take care of a player's sponsorships or commercial dealings (or at least give advice on this subject) while continuing their day-to-day profession. Some agents may start out whilst still in their previous profession. This means they can continue to earn a stable salary whilst slowly building up their work as an agent on the side. This could be an attractive option as there is less financial and time pressure. If everything goes well and they are able to recruit a couple of clients, it may then be possible to transition into agency completely, leaving behind their previous career and becoming a full-time football agent.

Conferences, Summits, Forums and Events

Each year, there are a variety of networking and educational events in the football business calendar that aspiring agents should consider attending if at all possible. Whilst not all of these will specifically focus on football agency, talks on marketing and finance within the sport can still provide crucial details that a good agent requires. The most well-known event organisers include the Football Agent & Business Summit, Leaders in Sport, Soccerex and the Wyscout Forum – these events (amongst others) are well worth going to. Events such as these tend to attract great speakers from a variety of sectors, and they can provide you with interesting and useful skills, information, and experience. If you are unable to attend in person, some events are streamed online. Also remember that there are many (sometimes free) webinars and educational sessions held online. These will often pop-up on LinkedIn so keep an eye out for some that may be worth attending.

The greatest attraction of these events, particularly now that they are back in-person following the COVID-19 pandemic, is the networking opportunity. You never know who you might meet and what opportunities might arise from networking at these events. Some events allow you to see the guest list before attending. It is good practice to look through the list of attendees and make a thorough assessment of some specific networking targets. This may involve identifying three individuals that you can deliberately prepare yourself to engage with or perhaps just setting a goal of gaining ten useful phone numbers across the event. The latter may be a better option if you do not know the names of the attendees. However, if you are able to see who each person is, this gives you greater leverage to research them and make the most of the opportunity of chatting with them.

Family Member or Friend

Some of you reading this may be in the enviable and fortunate position of having a son, daughter, husband, wife or other relative, or even a close friend, that is a good football player and may need representation now or in the near future. With regards to being the friend of a player, you may be able to work with them directly in an agency capacity from the start, but what is often the case is that the player will have an already established agent to begin with, and entrusts you with important everyday affairs instead. For example, you might seek commercial opportunities on their behalf, help manage their daily routines or even just fulfil small tasks for them and their family. This is particularly the case when the actual agent has multiple clients or lives in a different country.

Sometimes, this relationship between player and friend can develop into something much larger in the future, as you are often someone they trust and have known for a long time. This is how Erkut's good friend, Nassim Touihri (the agent of Lukas Podolski), got into the business as he started originally as a close friend of his future client, before he formed his own agency (Fair Play Career Management) and took Podolski with him. If you do have a friend in this position then it is worth discussing with them or their existing agent (if they have one), whether there is a possibility of you becoming involved in the management of their career. This can provide invaluable experience, even if you do not end up representing them.

For family members, it is a very common occurrence in football for a relative of the player to act as their agent. Whilst this may seem frustrating given the extremely slim chances of falling into this category, you should bear in mind that family members will nearly always seek and receive help and advice from more qualified and educated agents behind the scenes. This means that although you may not be listed as the official agent of a player, you can still play a pivotal part and receive commission from your work. This once again raises the notion of importance in developing good relationships with a player's family, even more so if they represent the player themselves. You can gain their trust and they may need your help in the future.

In chapter 8, we will go into greater detail of how to look after and represent your own family member as their agent. For the sake of this chapter, you should be aware that it is a possible avenue into the industry.

Buying an Agency

It is worth touching upon perhaps the least common (and most expensive way) to get into the footballing business. Namely, buying an existing and established agency. Although this is fairly rare, an example of such a takeover is not difficult to find in the news. In 2016, Chinese company *Wuhan Double Co. Ltd.* purchased the sports agency *Nice International Sports Limited*, in a deal that also involved a partnership with Pere Guardiola's firm, *Media Base Sports*. This is an entry route into the industry that is extremely financially demanding. However, it is highly effective if the funds are available and is a direct route into the business with a readymade client list available. Keep an eye out for companies that enter mergers and purchase sports agencies. Even if you are not at the top of the purchasing company (it would be amazing if you were!) then there still may be an opportunity to get involved.

Expert's View: Thomas Freismuth

From Intern to European CEO of GROW
Agency, formerly Family & Football

"My story is a bit different to most others; I began as an intern at Erkut's agency and within 4 years I have become the CEO of the European team. You may likely ask; how did that happen?

Originally, my dream was always to become a professional football player myself. I played as a goalkeeper in an academy throughout my youth but as is the case with many aspiring young players, I wasn't able to make it. However, my biggest passion in life was and remains as football, so I always wanted to work in the industry. After my dream of becoming a football player fell short, I was determined to find a way to still be a part of the world of the beautiful game. I would have worked in almost any area but there was one field I had decided I never wanted to step into. Surprisingly, this was agency.

I sampled various jobs in football to find out what aspects of the industry appealed to me the most and it quickly became clear that I was best suited, and most drawn to, the sporting side of football. Perhaps due to tendencies I still had and the childhood dream of being a footballer; I still wanted to have an impact on what was happening on the pitch.

The breakthrough for me came in my final year at university. I was very fortunate that during this final year we had a guest lecture. The speaker on this occasion was Dr. Erkut Sogut. I was captivated by his presentation to the students and took the opportunity to ask him if he would be willing to have a coffee afterwards to chat further.

From that day forward, Erkut and I have built a strong relationship and I would never have guessed the life-changing impact that having the courage to ask him for a coffee that day would have on me.

Soon after, I began as an intern (the main value that I could add was in analysing ownership structures for Erkut). Fast forward to now and I am responsible for overseeing and managing nine young agents and over 50 clients across the European football market. To begin with, I was lucky and I will always admit that meeting Erkut, who has taught me everything in this industry, was like winning the lottery. However, I maximised the opportunity that arose from this luck and I can honestly say that I have dedicated much of my life to the job ever since, working countless hours to improve myself and the agency in my current role.

The biggest surprise for me was that Erkut changed my mind regarding becoming an agent so quickly. He had told me right at the very start, "forget everything you have ever heard about agents. Do it the way you think is right." For the next two years and beyond, he has shown me that being an agent in the right and admirable way would allow me to have an impact on what was happening on the pitch and would be a fantastic career pathway for me.

Since then, we have grown in size, with many young, aspiring agents joining our team. There are three nonnegotiables that we would say encapsulate the values of our agency, GROW, and for us, we look for these principles in anyone looking to get into the business:

1. Be hard working and dedicated: football agency is a 24/7 business.
2. Trustworthiness and loyalty is a key attribute for a successful agent in our agency.
3. We also consider what unique value an individual can contribute to our agency (special skills, legal knowledge, languages, understanding of data, contacts, etc.).

My advice from this is simple; whenever you approach an agency, think about what you can bring to the table for them. Do not just ask for them to hire you but instead, you must make yourself attractive to them and a positive addition to their team.

Once you get your foot in the door the message is still simple; work your socks off. You must understand and be prepared for the fact that the first three years are the hardest. You will have a very limited number of client clients, a very limited network, limited experience, and most likely limited resources. But the hard work will pay off, you will learn as you go and in the end, it can be a rewarding job.

Perhaps another way to get into the business that is indicated in this chapter is to start your own agency although I think this is usually a very difficult task, unless you have a very good contact in a club or to a player to start off with.

No matter which way you get into the business, my final view on this matter would be to emphasise that to be a successful agent and to "sign a deal", you always need a PEN:

- **P**ersonality: you need to have strong personable skills and must work on them constantly. Ultimately, football is a people's business.
- **E**xperience: get as many internships or work experience roles as possible; go to as many events and games as possible; and learn different fields and departments as agency can be very complex and the more areas of football you know, the better you stand to tackle it.
- **N**etwork: as you will realise throughout this book, 'your network is your net worth'. A good agent will get to know people wherever they can and maintain the longevity of these relationships. As an agent, you will live from and through your network for the rest of your life."

Summary

- The most important thing to remember is that there is no correct or incorrect way to become a football agent, as the top intermediaries come from all sorts of different backgrounds.
- If you are a student or young professional, getting experience through an internship at an agency can provide you with great insight and kickstart your network development in the business – but don't think this is an absolute necessity in football, you may be able to gain experience and transferable skills elsewhere in the sports industry or beyond before transitioning into agency.
- For those already established in another profession, the world of football is within reach, as so many other industries such as law and finance have links to the sport.
- The underlying theme of this chapter is that no matter which path you take into agency, networking is imperative. This network allows you to find opportunities and accelerates your progress in becoming an agent.

Further Reading

- The Deal – Jon Smith
- Becoming a Sports Agent – Gary Rivlin
- Grit – Angela Duckworth

- Rebel Ideas - Matthew Syed

Chapter 4: Registering as an Agent

"Do not rush into registering" - Dr Erkut Sogut

Introduction

This chapter has had to be completely rewritten since the second edition. In the previous edition we discussed that FIFA had been meeting to decide upon the new regulations for football agents operating in the industry which we addressed in chapter 2 here. From the 9th January 2023, FIFA implemented the universal document of Football Agent Regulations (FFAR) that govern agents in all football federations on each continent. FIFA hopes that this document is comprehensive, as far as possible, and can help make the system more consistent and straightforward to govern.

We individually assess each component of what it takes to become an agent in separate chapters. However, this chapter is designed to simplify the process, breaking down, step-by-step, what is required to register successfully as an agent according to the new regulations. It acts as a summary of each part of the process and can be referred back to easily.

Step 1: Comply with Eligibility Prerequisites

An applicant must first complete a licensing application via the FIFA or National Association platform. Part of this process outlines the eligibility requirements that a candidate must comply with. This includes details such as possessing no criminal record and other 'proper persons tests'.

NOTE: These requirements must also remain to be complied with throughout the entire period of time that the individual operates as an agent. Failure to do so will result in a revocation of an agent's licence.

These eligibility requirements are set out below:

- No false or misleading statements within the candidate's application.
- Zero criminal charges and convictions regarding all matters.
- Must not be a recipient of a suspension, disqualification or striking off order by a sporting governing body or regulatory authority.
- No record of failure to comply with rules relating to ethics and professional conduct.
- Must not be an official or employee of FIFA, a confederation, National Association, League, Club or any body that represents the interests of clubs. (The only exception to this is where an applicant has been appointed or elected to a body of one of these entities in a capacity of representing the interests of Football Agents).
- Must not hold any interest in a club, academy or league.
- Must not have been performing the services of a football agent without a licence prior to submitting their application.
- Must never have been personally bankrupt or been a majority shareholder in a business that declared bankruptcy, entered administration or undergone liquidation.
- Must not have been a part of a sports betting company or organisation in the year preceding the application.

FIFA are responsible themselves for investigating compliance with these requirements.

Step 2: Pass the Exam

As discussed in chapter 2, FIFA's new regulations demand that individuals wishing to obtain an agency licence must pass the newly formatted exam, details of which can be found in the Exam chapter (chapter 5). For the purpose of this chapter however, a summary is below:

- Candidates that are confirmed as eligible will be invited to attempt the examination in their National Association allocated venue.
- Candidates will have to pay a fee to take the exam and provide proof of payment.

- The exam is open book and is structured as 20 multiple choice questions regarding six FIFA official documents.
- You must achieve a score of 75% or above in order to pass this exam (15 correct answers).

Step 3: Licensing Fee

Once the exam has been passed, the candidate will then be able to pay the annual licence fee to FIFA. Unlike before, this fee will be paid directly to FIFA rather than to National Associations. This is also useful as the fee is set universally rather than whimsically being selected by these associations. It is the responsibility of the agent to ensure that they pay this fee and can provide proof of payment upon request from the governing bodies.

Step 4: Receiving Your Licence

Once the above steps have been satisfied, you will be issued your licence. It is important to remember that this is your licence only and cannot be transferred to others. This will remain valid as long as the eligibility criteria is met and annual licence fees are paid. This licence grants you the capacity of conducting the services of a football agent and authorises you to enter into representation agreements with clients globally.

Voluntarily Suspending or Terminating Your Licence

If your career as an agent is not what you may have imagined and you believe that the best course of action is to step away from the industry and to explore other options, it is possible to voluntarily give up your licence. The request must be submitted to FIFA.

Any previous termination of a licence will mean that should you wish to requalify as an agent you must repeat the above steps.

Expert's View: Dr Erkut Sogut

"Registering as an agent can be an exciting prospect. I hope that once you have completed this book you will be motivated to continue your journey to becoming a football agent but more importantly, well-equipped with the tools and knowledge to be able to do so successfully.

I would recommend using this chapter as a reference point that you can easily return to for a precise step-by-step guide through the process of actually registering as an agent when the time comes for you. However, the most important advice I can add into this chapter is that, as with many things in football agency, timing is a vital consideration.

Whilst being officially titled as a football agent may be something that has always been or has become a dream, do not feel compelled to rush into actually registering prematurely. It needs to be a methodical and calculated decision as to when it is an appropriate time to obtain your licence.

Firstly, there is going to be the small matter of an exam to pass. This book should teach you that whilst learning the regulations and understanding how to ethically operate in the industry are imperative to pass the exam, they are also key aspects for you to get on top of them to actually work in practice and succeed in the industry. In my opinion, it is futile to register, pay the fee and take the exam until you are in a position where you are confident you will pass it and have the necessary attributes and knowledge to then work well as an agent. Remember, once you have registered as an agent, you are under the umbrella of the FIFA agent regulations and breaching these can cause permanent damage for the rest of your career so it is not worth the risk of registering prematurely.

Secondly, what is the need to register unless you are in a position to officially sign and represent a client? I find that the people who do the best when they register as an agent are the ones that are patient when it comes to actually registering. Many people, perhaps alongside their current jobs or their educational studies, will begin building their networks, attending games and learning to communicate with people within the industry. Out of this can arise an opportunity with a player or another possible client which would then require you to be registered. Hence, the principle of timing is important once more; to understand when you need to be registered and when it may not be necessary if you are unlikely to sign a client anytime soon.

Nevertheless, when it comes to registering, as I hope is the case for many of you who are inspired and empowered by the rest of this book, be prepared and dedicated. It is a significant step in one's life to make the move to register as an agent and although it will most likely be a turbulent ride, it will almost certainly be an exciting and enjoyable experience. And no matter what you do, protect your process always, before and after registering!"

Summary

- Making sure that you are legally registered as an agent is key, and there are harsh implications if the rules are not abided by.
- To become legally registered, there are several steps within the registration process that an individual must follow in order to successfully obtain a licence.
- It is vital for prospective agents to stay up to date with modern regulations and governance around licensing to ensure they do not breach their licence which may lead to revocation.

Chapter 5: The Exam and How to Pass It

"Education and preparation should be relentless"

Introduction

As part of the new FIFA regulations explained in chapter 2, agents must now pass an exam, similar to the pre-2015 requirements, in order to obtain a valid licence. This time around, the exam adopts a slightly different structure and delivery. The exam's altered appearance to the one that was scrapped in 2015, includes all of the multiple-choice questions being universally applicable, based only upon FIFA regulations rather than including national laws.

As we also covered in chapter 2 regarding the new regulations, agents that have sat an exam prior to 2015 are exempt although we would always advocate for updating your knowledge of the profession. An important point to note is that despite agents that have obtained a licence after the 2015 deregulation being likely to have built the foundations of their careers already, they will be required to sit the newest exam in order to maintain their licence and status as an agent. The deadline that FIFA have permitted for this transition period is October 1st 2023, after which it becomes a breach of the regulations to use an unlicensed agent's services. Be careful not to be caught out.

The format and Structure

Once an applicant has satisfied all additional criteria, such as a criminal record check, they will be eligible to take the exam for a fee disclosed at the discretion of FIFA. Remember that this time, the exam is only available in three languages; English, Spanish and French. This is because these are the most-spoken languages in football and agents must know at least one but preferably two or more of them in order to be successful.

An important aspect of the new exam that differs from pre-2015 is that agents will have to physically sit the digital paper at a desk at a certain location. Having to do the exam on a computer whilst in-person will help FIFA gain more control and prevent cheating. National Associations will provide venues for prospective agents to attempt to pass the exam in person and on a computer in a regulated and appropriate assessment environment. These have not been specified yet but it is important for you to be aware of your nearest location and how to register to sit the exam. FIFA will also set the dates and frequency of the exams for candidates. It is currently understood that there will be two a year in the months of March and September. The first exam will take place on the 19th April 2023.

FIFA has explicitly stated the permissibility of the following items:

Permitted	Prohibited
Hotspot device with sufficient internet connection	Mobile phones and devices that can be used for communication
Laptop or computer device with compatibility with the exam format	Headphones
Prescription glasses	Earplugs
Non-alcoholic beverage container	Any item that may be deemed as suspicious and capable of misuse to provide an unfair advantage for the candidate
Study materials	External websites used on the computer device
Disability or medical aids e.g. hearing aids or wheelchairs	

The agent exam will take the form of multiple-choice questions; there will be 20 in total to answer in 60 minutes. They will ask candidates to consider different scenarios and case studies and require you to select the single best answer to each question or situation. The exam will also be open book. However, as there is only an average of three minutes available per question, preparation and prior knowledge is a necessity. The pass mark is yet to be officially stated but it is expected to be 75% or 15 correct answers out of a possible 20. Prior to 2015, the pass rate of the FIFA exam was less than

20% and it is likely that FIFA will aim to simulate the same level of difficulty this time around. However, for those that commit themselves to the ambition of becoming an agent you can take it upon yourself to explore resources to enhance your knowledge and ensure that the exam will not be an obstacle to your career.

Note: the first sitting of the new exam will take place on Wednesday 19th April 2023 (application deadline: 15th March) before the second is held on the 20th of September (application deadline: 31st July). The exam will be held twice a year although the exact dates may vary in 2024 and beyond.

What is Included?

So far, FIFA have stipulated that the exam will consist of multiple-choice questions targeted at addressing six key regulations that they have implemented and case study application. Hence, when preparing and learning for this exam, as we will reconsider later in this chapter, it is important to scrutinise and to understand the following:

1. **FIFA Football Agent Regulations (FFAR):** As discussed previously, these are all the new regulations that have been implemented as well as those that are still relevant and applicable from previously. This covers everything from commission and representation contracts to representing youth players and exclusivity. It is expected that 15 of the possible 20 questions will be based on these regulations, whilst the remaining five questions are based on the below.

2. **Regulations on the Status and Transfer of Players (RSTP):** This is the most important of FIFA documents that outlines registration of players, contractual matters, compensation, third party influence and jurisdictions.

3. **FIFA Statutes:** Details the legislation and general rules and regulations for the operations of FIFA.

4. **FIFA Code of Ethics:** This outlines rules of conduct within football as well as the sanctions and disciplinary measures that can arise from it. It also includes the procedures and methods of adjudication in disputes.

5. **FIFA Disciplinary Code (FDC):** A wider and more intricate report regarding various disciplinary sanctions and infringements from doping and assault to forgery and

corruption. It also explains the various bodies and organisations involved in sanction procedures.

6. **FIFA Guardians - Child Safeguarding Toolkit:** Refers to education on the protection of minors and players.

Learning and Preparing

The exam will focus more upon a candidate's knowledge of the current football regulations rather than testing how you would act in a certain situation when acting on behalf of a player or a club. This is because FIFA wants to ensure that the next generation of agents will abide by international football legislation and hope to minimise any underground or unethical activity of agents.

To reiterate, differently to the pre-2015 exam, all questions will be universal. The previous exam consisted of 15 questions set by FIFA questions and then an additional 5 based upon national association regulations. All of the new questions will be applicable under wider FIFA legislation and set by FIFA themselves. As expressed above, it is expected that 15 of the possible 20 questions will be based on the FFAR, with the other five relating to the additional documents. This means that your preparation should emphasise learning about these regulations. Various resources such as regulation handbooks, publicly available FIFA documents and educational platforms on the matter are the best form of learning and preparation for the exam.

My best bit of advice for passing the exam is not to spend a few months learning everything you think you might need to pass the exam. Regardless of the assessment, a good agent will *always* keep up to date with changes in regulations regarding their profession and other important bits of information. Your knowledge on the industry should therefore be vast and comprehensive at all times. Once the exam has been passed, are you planning on never looking at regulations again? Absolutely not. Begin now by understanding the rules and regulations that govern this profession and then never stop. This profession is an ever-evolving career choice and a continual learning environment. Your education and preparation should be relentless and we can almost guarantee that this attitude will see you pass the exam.

This book should provide a solid foundation to help set you off on your learning journey. We have included several examples of the line of questioning that is to be expected in the exam below as well. This should give you some indication of the broad array of topics and regulations that FIFA will try to test you on. We hope that this triggers you to go on with your research and that once you have finished this guide, you will continue to educate yourself and eventually pass the exam and work alongside others in this awesome industry.

We would also direct you to Dr Erkut Sogut's LinkedIn page if you are interested in seeing more practice questions that he often posts onto the platform to help further with preparation.

Practice Questions

The questions below are not official questions set by FIFA. They have been designed and written by the authors of this book for the purpose of guidance and education.

Note: correct answers and explanations are at the end of this chapter.

1. Which age range covers when training compensation can be due to the club(s) at which the player spent their development period?
    a. 12-15
    b. 12-23
    c. 12-21
    d. 16-23

2. Of the parties listed below, which would be categorised as a third party by FIFA when investigating Third Party ownership?
    a. A football/soccer agent or agency
    b. An investment consortium fund
    c. Another club that the player hasn't played for previously
    d. A club that the player formerly was registered with

3. In a Representation Agreement that is made between an agent and an individual, the contract can only be for a maximum duration of how long?
    a. 5 years
    b. 4 years
    c. 3 years
    d. There is no limit but both parties must have given express and explicit consent and agreement to this

Answers

1. **b**. The correct answer is b (12-23). c (12-21) is wrong as this is only the age range for which training compensation is calculated but the sum calculated will be due every time a player transfers up until the end of the season of their 23rd birthday (RSTP art. 20). a and d are wrong as they only partially cover the range of when compensation will be due.

2. **a & b**. The correct answers are a (an agent or agency) and b (investment fund). Art. 18 of the FIFA RSTP prohibited Third Party Ownership private investors to acquire economic rights of professional footballers such as was the case with Carlos Tevez and Javier Mascherano when they signed with West Ham from Corinthians whilst their transfer rights were controlled by an agent.

3. **c**. The correct answer is c (3 years). The new FIFA agent regulations state that a representation agreement is only valid for a maximum of 3 years. After which, it will end and it is not permitted to have included an automatic renewal clause. Hence, the agent will need to resign the client on a new Representation Agreement.

Further Reading

Exam Blog: https://erkutsogut.com/the-new-fifa-agent-exam-explained/

Chapter 6: The Work of a Football Agent

"Your network is your net-worth"

Introduction

Despite there being a certain preconceived idea and perception that the football agent profession is simple, straightforward and a chance to earn a significant sum of money easily, in reality it is a highly complex career. It is certainly one of the most relentless careers and the football market never stops. Whilst you may be able to work from different places in the world and are not restricted in that sense, you may never be able to fully switch off and will have to keep one eye on your work or phone at all times. There is almost no fixed daily routine and each day will offer something different from every other day. It is an unpredictable and exhilarating profession that is certainly not for the faint hearted.

An advantage of working as an agent is that the effort, dedication, and hours you put into the profession directly correlates with the reward you get out of it. The busier you are the better. Attending every football game in the world is impossible, as is meeting every player; but the more work you do, the more clients and business opportunities you will gain and hence, more success, reward and income.

This chapter summarises the key areas and criteria for an aspiring agent to consider and meet if they wish to survive and succeed in the industry. Most of the points made in this chapter will be touched upon or developed into more detail in different stages of this book.

Understanding Football

Having a good knowledge of players, clubs and leagues is a very important and self-explanatory aspect of the profession. Understanding which type of player goes to what type of club is often overlooked as a skill, as agents must always think ahead. Agents that are able to do this best often quickly gain respect and build a reputation in the eyes of clubs and scouts. Monitoring the performances of certain players and clubs can be helpful, as well as keeping an eye on the appointment of backroom staff and club officials. You can never really know too much about football and the system!

There are some free and helpful tools to keep yourself updated on the latest in football that include Transfermarkt, ESPN and sports newspapers and magazines, whilst paid services like Wyscout, InStat, Comparisonator, LawinSport, Transfermarkt, Off the Pitch and The Athletic are also extremely useful. Making notes and jotting down ideas about players that you represent (or know the agent of) is certainly something that is advisable, as it may be relevant for a future deal. Similarly, doing a 'scouting report' or just noting down thoughts for potential players for a club that you have a contact at is also very useful, especially if you are to meet with a sporting director or club official. Even if they do not ultimately provide you with a future deal, it is good practice to analyse players, clubs and the industry to develop your detailed insight into football.

Networking

REMEMBER: Your network is your net-worth!

How can you prepare and send scouting reports to contacts at a club or go about recruiting and signing players without first having a good contact base and a list of connections across the footballing world? Clue: IT IS VERY DIFFICULT!

Networking in the football business is an absolute non-negotiable necessity. The bigger and better your network is, the more likely you are to find opportunities and to succeed in the industry. Whilst building a wide-reaching network may seem like a daunting task, there are many ways to do this, through sporting events such as the Football Agent & Business Summit, Soccerex and Wyscout forums, and just generally trying to be proactive. This could include attending games and targeting certain individuals in a professional manner.

You have to utilise your contacts well once they begin to increase in number, and find out what *you* can offer them to strengthen the relationship; business often centers around exchanging favours in a mutually beneficial collaboration. Use your knowledge of the football industry to identify gaps in the market, players without agents or players needing new clubs, and then try to work your way into a position where you can make a difference to one of your contacts. If you make a difference to them, the chances are that they will be willing to repay the value in the future when you need it. Some ways to think about that can help you provide value to your contacts are:

- Have access to information about clubs that is not publicly available.
- Have contacts that someone may need but they cannot obtain without you.
- Give the contact access to a new market where they may not be so well connected themselves. This could be in another national football association or perhaps in a commercial sphere.
- By directing or guiding them to a player, coach, opportunity or away from a problem.

Simply establishing and utilising a strong network is just part of the whole process. Maintenance and development of your network are the next steps that are equally important. This requires you to keep in touch with everyone, even when there doesn't seem to be a need to. This could be done by communicative methods such as email, messages and phone calls, but perhaps more effectively by setting up face-to-face meetings. For example, an invitation to a match day or organising a time to catch up at an office, hotel, restaurant or cafe´ is a good way of doing this. However, be wary of being annoying. Make contact again with your network in a productive manner, identify important things to talk about and prepare well. To repeat, try and find a way that you can help them and make their time meeting with you worthwhile and something they want to do again. The more often you are able to do this, the more likely you are to develop these relationships to a point where you can engage in business together and further utilise your network.

Erkut often says that a reputation can take years to build and five minutes to tarnish. This should motivate you to give your all to every meeting and never let yourself down. For every good impression you make and relationship you create, they will then speak positively about you to others, This is why networking has a cumulative effect. The more people you know and that have respect for you, the more additional contacts will be opened up to you through them and the pattern repeats itself.

To reiterate, the importance of building and effectively using a network in the football agency business cannot be underestimated

– it forms the basis of your everyday actions and will play a substantial factor in affecting the success you experience in this industry.

Networking can be summarised into three main aspects:

1. Establish.
2. Maintain.
3. Utilise.

One thing to bear in mind is that the simplest and easiest way of establishing a good network is to represent a top client. Top players are able to open many doors and if you are fortunate enough to represent one of the biggest talents in a market, clubs in that association and beyond in the wider market will be willing to meet and discuss with you. Of course, getting to this position requires a lot of hard work and a lot of networking beforehand but if you are ever in this position, it is a chance to optimise the potential network that becomes available to you.

Who Do You Work For?

The answer to this is simple... the CLIENT. Whilst you may see large football agencies boasting a vast quantity of clients, each player, club or other client will have an agent who deals with them directly. Nevertheless, a key distinction between agents is whether you work as part of a big agency or are more independent, and there are advantages to both. By being part of a large agency, you have the benefit of great resources, a pre-prepared and established wide (often global) network and enhanced player-recruitment power. Furthermore, as an employee, there would be certain employment privileges that you would be entitled to and have the security of a job and steady salary. Although often, commission is limited in such agencies and you are more likely to be employed on a retainer and bonus salary rather than directly related to the commission you generate.

Nevertheless, being independent from an agency certainly has its benefits too. You definitely have more freedom and perhaps don't have the pressure of having to be answerable to a superior. In addition, your hours and schedule can be more flexible, and could go about your business in a far more unrestricted manner.

The most preferable option perhaps, is to find an agency that is in the middle. They may already have a solid network, a robust clientele list and admirable recruiting power which can help you begin your journey. However, you may still be entitled to commission and are less restricted in certain things you are entitled to do for your player and the company.

It is worth spending time researching this and judging, based upon your skills and your network, which option you think may be best suited to your career path.

Location of Work

Being a football agent is a job that requires you to be active and thus normally involves much travelling. As already mentioned, those working as part of a larger agency will certainly have more structure to their routines, and consequently would have a desk or office to be based in. However, for those that are independent of a big firm or part of a smaller agency, your headquarters could be anywhere and everywhere and change every day! For example, in the UK these meetings occur in Knightsbridge, Marylebone or the private jet terminals at Luton Airport; whereas in Milan, these happen in the hotel lobby's; and in Dusseldorf these are more likely to occur in the airports hotels.

Regardless of where you are based or where some meetings may take place, personal interaction with your client is key, and therefore visiting them at either their house or the training ground, as well as accompanying them to commercial shootings should dictate where you work. The same goes with having face-to-face meetings with other professionals in the industry. Most agents will have a certain location in which they prefer to meet business people and other agents. Sometimes a candid, quiet restaurant or café can provide the perfect setting to talk over deals. Alternatively, high-end hotels or eateries are also popular amongst agents, particularly when hosting significant or foreign guests. It is up to you to make the decision on the most appropriate setting to make whoever you are meeting feel comfortable and appease their own wants and needs.

Qualities of a Football Agent

All football agents have their own style, and their own way of doing things. You will find yours as you learn and become a part of the industry. However, there are certain objective and desirable characteristics and qualities that many successful agents share, and that aspiring agents should try and develop.

Amongst the most important traits are **loyalty** and **trust**. In order for a client to allow you to negotiate deals on their behalf, they have to trust you and believe that you will endeavour to do what is best for them, and not act selfishly. A simple demonstration of this is to never ask a club what your commission will be first unless they specifically and directly ask you in which case you must let them know what you hope for. However, this comes last; after you have obtained the terms that are best suited to your client and ones that they are happy with.

You are the representative of the player and this profession demands that you seek to fulfil *their* best interests and desirable outcomes, not your own. Especially when dealing with younger players, this will help build the trust and gain the respect of their parents, who are essentially allowing you to work so closely alongside their child.

Some other useful qualities are outlined below but this is not an exhaustive list; every skill may be transferable to benefit your performance and professionalism as an agent:

- Football agents have to be **hard-working** and **willing to sacrifice**. No agent ever has it easy from the start; often the first three years are the hardest as you form your reputation and establish your name in the industry. You have to work as hard as possible in order to be successful in an incredibly tough and competitive environment. Make the most out of every meeting, every contact and every day. If you do so, this will put you on the right path to success as an agent.
- **Proactivity** refers to the willingness to go out and create the next opportunity for your client rather than waiting around for somebody to approach you can make a huge difference to the standard of service you provide! At the end of the day, the best agents are the ones that do as much as is logically possible for their clients; you should be the one making things happen. This doesn't mean you shouldn't let others in

however, as utilising your network and experts in different fields is a key skill too if it is outside of your expertise and is in the best interests of your client to do so.

- **Preparation** is key as we will reiterate throughout the entirety of this book. Your day will mostly consist of meetings with a range of different people, perhaps spanning various industries, and therefore it is for you to be ready for the day ahead. This includes the obvious requirements of being equipped with a phone and laptop (with chargers) as well as a notepad. Note that your phone may become an extended part of you. Picking up the phone to people swiftly and being a good digital communicator will always be a useful quality of an agent. Preparation also extends to pre-meeting preparatory research and keeping a copy, either digitally or in writing, of what has been agreed in your meetings to help you keep track of all your business. Remember, plans and agreements may change, it is your responsibility to stay on top of this.

- As with any profession; **preparation, organisation, adaptability,** and **flexibility** are also key factors for success.

Languages and Culture Adaptation

The majority of top football agents have the ability to speak more than one language. Knowing a second language automatically expands your jurisdiction within which you may conduct your services as an agent. Put simply, language gives you a better opportunity to do business in the country (or countries) that your secondary language is spoken in. Furthermore, before travelling to any other country on business, you should try and research the key customs and be respectful of the traditions of that culture. For example, in Japan you must always give and receive business cards using both hands and ensure the card is turned towards the receiver. Not following this protocol is seen as rude and disrespectful.

In general, travelling is a fundamental part of being a football agent, and you have to be prepared to spend time away from your home. But at the same time, this is an aspect of what makes the profession so enjoyable and interesting - you get the chance to travel all across the world and interact with such a variety of people. Language is a key addition that will help make the travelling life easier and more successful.

Matchdays

One of the most important parts, and often busiest, of each week are match days, occurring on the weekends and sometimes mid-week too, depending on the level which your client plays at. Depending on the exact nature of your relationship with the player, motivational conversations before the game can be greatly beneficial, and given the importance of your client's performance in aiding your job, every little to help them has to be done. Be aware though that whilst some clients may really enjoy and encourage your direct involvement in their on-field performance, others may not be so inclined and would rather you focus on their off-pitch matters and leave the football to them and their coaches.

If you are fortunate enough to look after a top player, the likelihood is that they will have access to a box. This can be utilised in order to invite special guests and family to watch your client. It is important to liaise with your client to ensure that they are happy with how you distribute the ticket usage. Alternatively, players at a lower level will still usually get free tickets which you can help to allocate and organise.

In either case, as the agent it would be your responsibility to organise the guests. Whilst some family members of the player will specifically request access to the tickets which is important to appease, it is also crucial to find the balance between them, and business guests. Allocating the tickets between friends, family, commercial partners, potential partners and other agents can be a difficult balancing act. Alternatively, as Mesut and Erkut did together at Arsenal; "we reserved a handful of tickets each game for children in need and would arrange for a personal meet and greet with Mesut. This was particularly important to him to give back to society and it was part of my role as the agent to facilitate and organise their attendance."

You should always keep in mind that this is your profession and you are in the business side of football; so try to treat these matchdays as potential gateways to further deals. Even though matches are 90 minutes, for the agents the matchday festivities will last the whole day and often the surrounding days too! You will have to meet with guests and get to the stadium a couple of hours before kick-off, and stay with them after the game too - these are great times to talk business and develop your network and create opportunities for your client.

In exceptional circumstances, guests may be flying in especially for a match. You should offer to meet the day before or after the gameday. As previously mentioned, games can be twice a week for your client, and as an agent you will probably also be invited to other player's boxes who have an agent that you're close with, or even the director's box - so make sure you're committed to long hours and work on your organisation skills!

A final point on matchdays is discussed further in Chapter 9. In summary, matchdays also provide a great opportunity to host charitable guests and offer them the opportunity to meet your client and other players after the game. As the agent, you must factor this into your planning and thinking.

Expert's View: Thomas Freismuth

"Every day is different. I found this out right at the start of my career. The tasks you may have to serve your client can often seem limitless and you can experience almost anything. Fundamentally, being an agent is more than a full-time job; for the best agents, the profession becomes a part of their life.

As much as we have tried, it is impossible to create a book that comprehensively covers every aspect of being a football agent. Similarly, it is impossible to answer all the questions that an agent or prospective agent might have. Part of the reason for this is that new questions will arise every day.

Let's consider COVID as an example. At this point, the rest of the world was unsure as to how life would continue and if there would ever be a football game again. Nonetheless, my clients expected me to be able to answer every question and inform them exactly what was going to happen next. Hopefully this demonstrates that you can never be 100% prepared for every situation or challenge that comes your way as an agent. One snippet of advice I can give is that, no matter what you are faced with, your mindset must be solution driven rather than problem driven. This will help you in most situations.

For my expert view on this topic, I think it would be useful to give you an insight into my typical schedule and tasks for a week. However, remember that no two days are ever the same in this profession, let alone two weeks!

Let's start with the weekends. I aim to watch 3-6 games either live or on TV that feature my clients or future clients that I am looking to recruit. It is common that I will re-watch some games using Wyscout.

This can mean a lot of travelling for me and, differently to the general public, Saturday will most likely be the busiest day of the week as most of my clients will have fixtures. I will message them beforehand with a piece of motivation or a simple good luck text and then after the game as well to give them bits of feedback and help them to reflect on their performance.

Hopefully my clients will avoid any injuries, otherwise I will then be busy helping them to get a quick appointment for an MRI or X-Ray if the club hasn't done this yet. In extreme cases, I may already be trying to find the best specialist for a certain type of severe injury.

Matchdays are a very good opportunity to network, so I often have meetings before or after the games, especially with foreign scouts. Furthermore, if they are in attendance, the match can provide a good moment to check in with the family and friends of the clients to maintain your relationship with them. You can also pick up a lot of useful information on match days, from scouts, from other agents and from family members of other players. Hence, committing yourself to be physically at the ground to watch live fixtures each weekend is vital. For both networking, and for information gathering. Being an agent means that you are in the information business, the more details you obtain and the faster you get them, the better for you.

During the weekdays I use the time for meetings or calls with clubs to build my relationship with them and to gather more information such as their transfer window requirements or specifically about my clients. I will also meet with players and clients throughout the week to support them and fulfil any of their needs which may include helping with football problems. As with almost every line of work, there is also an administrative side that I will address during the week which may include organising for clients, preparing presentations and planning trips and the weekend ahead. Perhaps you may even find yourself, as in this case, writing a book!

Football never stops, not even during the week. Tuesday to Thursday there will be Youth League, Champions League and Europa League games that I might also attend on top of the weekend's fixtures. It is often a good time to host directors and other contacts from the travelling away team in my home city when they are coming for an international game. These midweek commitments can make a significant difference to your network.

When it comes to managing the clients during the week this could be anything as I have previously mentioned. The list of responsibilities includes, but is not limited to; hospital visits, organising late night hotel bookings, checking and organising insurance policies, negotiating employment contracts and marketing deals, answering interview requests, managing requests or interest from clubs or agents, organising rehabilitation or appointments with a doctor, organising extra training for clients, finding the best nutritionist and sleep expert, organising flight tickets or holidays, and finding the right schooling or educational courses. I could go on further but hopefully this gives you a taste of life of the diverse life of an agent.

For younger players I have a strong focus on their development and like to arrange for them to work with specialists in cognitive training, nutrition and sleep for example. Additionally, I believe that the biggest impact that an agent can have on a player is their mindset. Hence, I undertook a course in sports mental health to learn techniques on how to motivate players and keep their mental wellbeing stable and sustainable. As an agent, I advocate for the fact that a strong mindset is one of the most important traits that is needed to make it as a professional football player. Through my own work in mental health, I have developed a concept called "spirit of champions" with my clients. The focus of this concept is to train and develop the right mindset to help them succeed on and off the pitch.

Of course, there are also a few examples of 'lazy' players that become footballers but in most cases, a highly-talented youth player will fail to make it if they lack the proper mindset and mental professionalism. I, like many others in this industry, have witnessed players that I would have bet my life on to become a superstar but unfortunately, due to having the wrong group of friends, the wrong environment, and an improper mindset, they have fallen well short of the potential they had. That is why I think that I can bring real value to my clients when working with them in regards to mindset and attitude and I would encourage other agents to prioritise mental training as a service to your clients.

Finally, to consider the work of an agent on a monthly basis; I would say that the most intense months are January and then May to August as this is when the transfer windows in most of the major football markets are open or you are preparing for their opening. For bigger transfers it can often take 8-12 months of preparatory work and negotiations with clubs so you may always be busy if you are in this situation. However, most agents will go on holiday in September as this is usually the calmest and quietest month of the year. Nevertheless, an agent will always need to take their phone with them and be prepared to deal with sudden issues, particularly if your client has just moved into a new house in a new location."

Summary

- Unlike most other industries, football is non-stop – you must remember that there is always work to do, and those that work hardest and smartest will often succeed the most.

- Generally, work in this profession is unpredictable, and that is why flexibility (in addition to preparation and organisation) is so crucial – particularly when dealing with numerous clients or having overseas business interests.
- There is really no set or fixed formula for meetings, working and activities. It depends on you as an individual, the person you may be meeting, and the situation you find yourself in.
- Despite the difficulties you may face, the fact that every day brings a new challenge to overcome is not only exciting, but also really rewarding and something you should relish.

Further Reading

- The Life of a Sports Agent - Luke Sutton

Chapter 7: How Does a Player Select their Agent

"Trust is the easiest thing in the world to lose, and the hardest thing in the world to get back" - R. Williams

Introduction

An important part of being a successful agent is to be able to understand the needs and interests of a client. In other words, you need to be able to think like the client in order to provide the services they want. This chapter, therefore, is important in approaching agency from an alternative perspective; through the eyes of a youth player and their parent or guardian looking to sign with an agent for the first time. If you are aware of this process and the elements which a parent and the player will look for, you are more likely to be successful in recruiting and signing clients.

Remember, the decision of signing a representation contract with an agent is a major decision for a player and the family, particularly if it is the first agent they are signing with as a youth player.

Why have an agent?

First and foremost, a player and their family need to assess when is the right time to have an agent. It is important to begin working with agents once there are extraneous off-field details that need to be managed and negotiated. The agent's role is to relieve the burden of this away from the player and to help continue the player's career progression in a calculated and directed manner. For example, if a youth player is highly-rated and already being spoken to by several top clubs, it is likely they will need an agent to ensure they obtain the best outcome from the situation. Similarly, a player that may have just been released by a top academy but is looking for opportunities elsewhere, in lower tiers or abroad, may require an agent to help them find the best option. However, some youth players who have already secured a scholarship and do not need additional assistance may not sign with an agent but may begin to build relationships with agents for the future. Your role as the agent is to identify which category a recruitment target may fall under.

A key factor in the process, as the guardian or the player, is patience. A common factor across any association is that the biggest mistake is to become excited by the prospect of having an agent and rushing into an unsuitable representation contract or with an agent that is not best-equipped to represent the player.

Stage 1: Making Contact

The initial stage of the process will begin with making contact with the parents or the player if they are not a minor. In some situations, the parents may come to you if you have developed a good and trustworthy reputation or perhaps if you already represent a client who plays with a player, they or their parents may have recommended you to them. In other cases, it is the agent that will scout the player as discussed in chapter 10 and decide to make contact. Remember, it is likely that parents and players will meet with and consider several options from big agencies to independent agents and you must not be seen to be rushing the process.

At this step we must raise a vital point. At no stage throughout the recruitment process should money or extortionate gifts exchange parties. This is a form of 'bribery'. Some agents may offer parents an immediate payment for their child to sign with them or some parents may even request it.

This is incredibly dangerous and must be avoided for many reasons. Firstly, if it is over a certain amount it must be declared to tax authorities as it is taxable. Furthermore, it can be dangerous for agents as it sets a bad precedent for future relations and the parents may move their son to another agent for more money. Remember, the aim of signing with you as an agent is to benefit the player and not the parents or the agent and bribery undermines this. The consequences that may result are not worth the risk and "selling" the player out to an agency that pays the largest sum defeats the purpose of finding the best agent that will benefit their career the most. Do not encourage such a practice as an agent.

Stage 2: Meetings

Over the period of time in which the player and his family find the right agent, they will meet with a handful of agents. For a youth player it may be more of a responsibility for the parents to deal with this rather than involve the player to avoid extra hassle for them. The age of 16 is an important part of a player's career development. They will often be set to begin the scholarship stage of youth football and officially signing with an agent immediately may not be necessary. However, some players may want to be involved as building relationships with interested parties at this age can allow a longer duration of time to best understand each offer rather than being forced into a rushed agreement immediately before the player may sign their first professional contract. Once again, as the agent, you need to be aware of which parties are more involved and ensure they are demonstrating astute attention to fulfil the wishes of the party without pressuring the situation.

During this period, developing an understanding between the family, the player and you as the agent is vital. This can happen through in-person or digital meetings. We will explain the criteria that interested players should look for in each agent in the next section of this chapter but the fundamental aspects are that the agent can be trusted, is the kind of person the player and their guardian want to work with, and that they have a clear and focused strategy for working with the player.

It is likely that the player and their family will conduct additional and sufficient due diligence and informed research to obtain and assist them in making the right important decision. This supplementary research can also involve things like speaking to other parents or other players who know you or may even be looked after by you already and hearing about the quality of services you provide. This is why reputation and dedication to each client is vital for agents.

Remember that football is just a part of what an agent can offer. The best agents will be able to show that they can add value in other areas such as through the player's educational pathway, by building their social media and other personal marketing or branding, support them mentally through injuries and the high-pressured scholar environment and generally help the player to become a well rounded and good human being.

Meetings to build relationships should continue throughout the selection process and even beyond. It is common sense that a player is more likely to make the best decision on an agent if they have met with you several times and have a greater understanding and insight into you as a person and as a professional. These meetings build trust and will often be a major factor in deciding upon the right agent. Once the representation contract is signed, you should encourage ongoing review and planning meetings to continue to ensure that targets are being met. These meetings can help you to demonstrate the value you are providing to the client and perhaps highlight areas where you could improve your services.

Stage 3: Filtering and Final Calls

As the process unfolds, it is likely that what may have started as a handful of agents gradually depletes to a maximum of two or three of the best options. This filtering process takes place by assessing the interested parties' compliance with essential criteria that the player and their family are looking for. Remember this process can last any amount of time; a couple of weeks, a couple of months or a couple of years. As long as the player and the family are informed enough and have seen and understood what you can offer during their time in contact then the time to sign with an agent may be appropriate.

An important point of consideration at this stage for families and players is to distinguish the roles between the agent themselves and the agency they work for. For example, in some cases, bigger agencies will use their top agents in the recruitment process. It is important for the player to establish they will be the main point of contact moving forward. As the agent you must be able to provide this information honestly and avoid misleading or offering false information to the recruitment target. Dishonesty sets an unfavourable precedent for the rest of the working relationship.

If it has not been the case before, the final stages of the process and the final calls should involve the player. After all, you will be the player's agent. The age of the player will affect the influence they have in the decision. If they are young it is the guidance of the parents that will take priority but as a player gets older they are likely to be more likely to know which agent is best for them. Regardless, involving them in at least the final calls will help them understand each option and the benefits and possible drawbacks of each one.

The final calls should be fully informed and developed discussion which gives the player and his family the chance to ask any final questions or express any other queries before making the final decision. The agent should be prepared to answer all of these in an encouraging but truthful manner.

Stage 4: Signing a Representation Contract

Eventually, without any sense of rush or pressure, the family and the player can decide upon the preferred option and enter into a representation agreement by signing a representation contract with the agent. However, when this stage arises, the parents or the player depending upon the age, will often recruit the services of a lawyer to review and offer guidance on the representation contract. Hence, as the agent you are liable for ensuring that the contract is legally and ethically sound and that it does not contain any clauses that could be surprising or off-putting to the player. You should have discussed these clauses with the family and the player during previous discussions.

Essential Criteria

A lot of factors that will be considered when deciding upon signing with an agent are subjective to the individual player and their family. It is part of the task of an agent to decipher which factors are the highest priority for each individual target. This is understandable as the values and principles of each player differs and will likely align with the values and principles of different agents. This will also differ in terms of backgrounds of course. For example, the nationality, language, religion or other personal circumstance of the agent may be an important factor that matches them with a player and their family. This is something that an agent needs to be aware of and discuss during recruitment meetings. There will then be additional considerations for them to meet to then reach the stage of representation.

Despite this element and extent of subjectivity, we believe there are fundamental, essential criteria that a player and their family ought to be aware of when judging prospective agents. The most important of which we have outlined below:

- **Trust:** An absolute imperative. A player and the family must be able to trust the agent. They must consider the integrity, motivations and intentions and ensure that they wish to represent the player in order to provide the best possible service and to be of benefit to the player's career. Any indication that an agent is more motivated by financial gain or otherwise is likely to undermine trustworthiness and professional integrity.
- **Priorities:** The generic term is an objective criterion to look for in an agent. However, this may materialise in different ways. The player and the family will assess the priorities that the agent may have in advancing the player's career. This may include factors such as education, off-field commercial opportunities, on-pitch development, mentorship and international transfers. The player and the family will have a good idea themselves of where they want an agent to add value to their career and they can judge whether the priorities of the agent and their professional strengths are consistent with this.
- **A Clear Strategy and Plan:** Even at a young age, direction and guidance for a player's career path is important. During meetings, the agent should be able to provide and outline a structured and targeted strategy for the career and can obviously identify where they will be able to enhance the player's progress and prove their value.
- **The Extent of their Involvement:** Once again, the expectations of an agent's involvement is subjective to each player but it is an essential consideration to be made. Some players would benefit most from their agent being in attendance at most of their games and having a very hands-on approach as a mentor figure for the player's career, this is more likely with smaller agencies for example who can provide a more personal touch. For others, they want their agent to leave them to the football side and to take care of business away from the game, only involving the player once it is relevant and a necessity. The player can gauge this approach through meetings with the agent and the agency they work for.
- **Professional Strengths:** As mentioned in point 2, in order to fulfil the priorities which a player is looking for in an agent, the skills of the agent are important. A player needs to

understand the extent of capabilities that the agent possesses. For example the player and their family may ask the following questions; Is the agent a qualified lawyer with a high-level knowledge and understanding of contracts? Do they have a financial background with a good understanding of money and handling finances? Were they previously a footballer themselves with an in-depth knowledge and insight into the game to be able to provide on-pitch advice? Has their background given them access to a vast network in football and with possible commercial endorsement opportunities? For some players, some of these things may not be important and it is up to them to decide which areas they are hoping their agent can add value in.

Summary

- If the agent is able to understand the process of entering a representation agreement from the perspective of the player and their family, it is more likely you will be able to understand what they are looking for in an agent.
- The process can last any amount of time, from weeks to months to years. During this time, it must never seem as though you are pressuring the player into making a decision, it is important that they decide to sign with you when the time is right.
- Often, each player will look for different attributes of an agent but aspects such as trustworthiness, honesty and loyalty are absolute non-negotiables.
- Agents need to demonstrate a strategy that is directly aimed at fulfilling the best interests of the player and adding more value to their career than other interested agents.

Chapter 8: Working with Your Own Family and Friends

"Loyalty makes you family" - Katie Reus

Introduction

Employing family members as agents was first brought into the public spotlight in 1999 with Nicolas Anelka's move from Arsenal to Real Madrid which was orchestrated by his brothers. In recent times, it has become increasingly common with players such as the now PSG trio Neymar, Mbappe and Messi all represented by their fathers. This was made easier after the deregulation of agents in 2015, as discussed in chapter 1, which removed the obstacles to enter the industry. The most well-known past and present examples are detailed in the table below:

Player/ manager	Agent	Agent–client relation
Sergio Ramos	René Ramos	Brother
Diego Simeone	Natalia Simeone	Sister
Lionel Messi	Jorge Horacio Messi	Father
Kylian Mbappe	Wilfried Mbappe	Father
Álvaro Morata	Alfonso Morata	Father
Mauro Icardi	Wanda Nara	Wife
Eden Hazard	Thierry Hazard	Father
Christian Pulisic	Mark Pulisic	Father
Danny Welbeck	Wayne Welbeck	Brother
Pep Guardiola	Pere Guardiola	Brother

Family members as agents may seem an attractive option for players but there are many issues that may arise. This chapter will also outline how family members may be regulated compared to regular agents under the new FIFA regulations in order to ensure ethical and legal compliance.

The Issues

In a perfect world, the love and trust between a father and son or brothers would mean that each party is acting in a way that benefits each other as much as possible. Unfortunately, this is not always the case. There is a risk in mixing familial relationships with professional business.

The combination may lead to big fallouts. Even family members can develop a hunger for money or power-grabbing from representing their relatives. For example, the agent of Marko Arnautovic, his brother, clearly stated in 2019 that Marko wanted to stay in the Premier League with West Ham as he wanted to compete with the best players in the world. However, months later he completely reversed his statement as he moved Marko to Shanghai for a transfer fee of £32million. The attraction of taking commission from the transfer fee as well as an employment contract worth £280,000 a week may have had something to do with the sudden change in heart of his agent.

The most infamous example of how an agent can create an issue for a footballer is in the case of Mauro Icardi. Mauro married his wife, Wanda, after having an affair with her whilst she was with a teammate of his at Sampdoria. He was banned from playing for his national team as a result of the scandal and her involvement in his career as his agent. Questions must be asked whether it is ethically okay for a player to involve an agent that has been at the centre of scandal and problems in their career.

The risk of failure is possibly the biggest issue. In reality, not all potential transfers and opportunities will materialise as the player and the agent may have expected. Sometimes in this situation, the player will blame the agent and in extreme cases, may leave the agent. This creates a whole new dimension of complication if the agent is a family member and could result in damaged familial relationships. Where emotions and relationships may play a part in any process, often it is best to delegate these perhaps to a lawyer or to another agent in order to avoid such undesirable consequences. The emotional factor is not prevalent with independent parties and hence, there will also be no bias or underlying motivation.

Regulating Family Members

FIFA's new regulations will see family members treated in the same way as all other agents. The regulations contain a clause that prohibits family members from acting as agents unless they are fully licensed as per the criteria set out in chapter 4. Importantly, this includes the requirement of passing the agency exam. This is a step in the right direction as it will ensure that family members receive a level of education and qualification before they are able to represent their relatives. FIFA emphasises that players should only use agents that have a proven level of aptitude in the industry and are qualified enough to serve them well.

This does not mean we are discouraging family members from caring for their relatives. Far from it, in fact. Needless to say, if you are a family member of a talented player reading this book then you are already taking steps in the right direction in learning the art of agency so that you can act professionally and successfully on behalf of your son, daughter, brother, sister, spouse or otherwise. So kudos to you for beginning your journey of developing as an agent.

It is important to understand, however, that you are not exempt as a family member or even as a friend of a player. You must ensure that throughout your career you abide by the rules and regulations for all agents. Transparency, as always, is vital. If a family member is representing a player, all transactions, commission fees and gifts should be recorded and visible to FIFA. Do not attempt to find methods around this and stick to a policy of ethical practice and rule-following. We assure you that those that do so, will endure a much more successful career than those that don't.

Being the Agent

Many aspects such as networking, negotiating contracts and seeking opportunities are the same as representing any other player that is not directly related to you. This is why it is important when representing relatives or friends to establish a distinct separation between familial relationships and professional activity in an agency capacity.

In some instances it may be more appropriate to outsource certain deals and opportunities to external parties and other trusted agents in order to avoid any kind of dispute or confrontation that may have sad consequences for your relationship with your relative. One of the easiest ways of avoiding this is to only prioritise their best interests. If you were an agent for another, unrelated player, this would be how to succeed as an agent for them and it is no different for family members. Forgot any collateral motivation such as financial reward and instead, focus upon working for them out of love. This kind of relationship is what can make a family-agent situation unique and special. You can be devoted to them as an agent on a level above a normal agent with a non-relative and working for them in this way will produce the most favourable outcomes.

Nevertheless, it is important to remember the possible issues mentioned in the beginning of this chapter. In some extraordinary cases, parents have been known to let emotions get the better of them and have verbally assaulted a sporting director, manager or scout for some form of criticism about their son. This is obviously a situation that should be avoided. Hence, whilst being the agent, often it is important to let an independent party such as a sports lawyer to lead negotiations to prevent the process and problem intertwining with emotion and family relationships. It is common practice to seek assistance from an expert or a professional to help in such circumstances.

Expert's View: Wayne Welbeck

Brother and Agent of Danny Welbeck

"I must state that my experience is not true for all that find themselves in a similar situation.

Every family has its own dynamics, unique characteristics, intentions and capabilities. When my brother Chris and I took the responsibility of managing our younger brother's career it was extremely uncommon for a family member to do so; in that regard we were trailblazers without realising it. What started off as managing our brother's career solely, grew into managing the careers of other players, from youth level to full internationals.

In my experience there have been many benefits to having a familial relationship with a client and also admittedly, some potential drawbacks. Nobody knows an individual more so than their family and footballers are not exempt from the human elements of life because of their job, wealth or status.

Communication is key with any client and in my case, this is easier with a family member because of our shared experiences, history, understanding and respect. I also know that this isn't always the norm in every family. It is also easier to identify when a player needs their space or wants to switch off from football if you understand them personally. In my own experience it has worked well and we quite quickly found a healthy balance between work and regular family interaction.

Nothing in life is a straight line and in football there are ups and downs. It's natural that when your family member is dealing with difficult situations such as long term injuries, you'll naturally feel that more because of your familial bond. Of course, I must add that it affects you when such situations arise with clients who are not related. The difference is that it doesn't impact your home life on the same level; your parents, your siblings and other relatives feel that pain too so you can't escape it.

On the whole though, my experience has been a great one and one that has brought much joy sharing the journey with that of my brother and other clients.

As a football agent you're in an extremely important role, bearing great responsibility with the potential to have a significant impact; both positive and negative. This responsibility has the potential to affect the rest of an individual's life, career as well and fortunes. I have seen family members mismanage players, the result of which has led to irreparable damage so it is important to identify that if a family member is to do the job, they have to have the right credentials, qualities, and capability to help guide the player in the right way."

Summary

- The opportunity of being the agent of a family member or close friend is a very exciting prospect but there are several things that an aspiring agent in this position must work on:
- You must have the best interests of your relatives and friends at heart.
- Act properly and by the rules in all situations. Whilst you may be in a fortunate natural position, you are not exempt or unique from other agents in the eyes of the governing bodies in football.
- Money must not be the motivation. Remember these people are close to you and you have a special relationship with them. This should provide an accentuated sense of duty of care.
- Separate emotions from your role as the agent. Business is business and family is family. Overlapping the two can make decisions and negotiations far more difficult and fraught.

Further Reading

- Jorge Messi: The agent father behind Leo's fortunes - The Athletic: https://theathletic.com/2029445/2020/09/02/who-is-jorge-messi-leo-bartomeu-barcelona-transfer/
- Neymar: Conversations With My Father – Neymar

Chapter 9: Working with Players

"Football is a reference business"

Introduction

Sometimes, it can be difficult to find the correct balance between managing the business and personal side of a player's life, as the two are so often intertwined.

Unfortunately, as with everything in the unpredictable nature of football agency, a comprehensive 'how to look after a player' guide would be impossible. There are numerous factors that affect the service that you ought to give to each client and what they want from an agent. This includes things like their fame and status, the level they are playing at, the extent of their off-field endeavours, their personal or family life and their independence. However, this is not limited only to player-based factors. The number of clients you look after and your own personal life affects the extent of the services and the number of hours you are able to commit to each client.

Working with Established Professionals

With a client who may already have a strong professional career and is well-known, it is important for you to make the most of both their footballing ability and their sponsorship potential, especially if and when they are at the pinnacle of their career. When dealing with an established professional, it can be really beneficial to propose and implement a long-term plan, as well as back-up options for security.

Although football is unpredictable, making connections with a range of clubs that could be a future transfer prospect for your player is an admirable habit for a good agent. The player will have a greater understanding of what they want from the rest of their career. Communicate well with them, be aware of where their interests lie and how long they might be around for before retirement. Remember, some players will never want to leave football and will carry on as long as they are fit enough whilst others will hang the boots up once their passion for the game dies off. The game is evolving and it is important for you to keep updated on where the best leagues for older players are. For example, historically the MLS has been a retirement home for top European names but an agent should be aware that this dynamic and reputation has now changed and it is also an exciting opportunity for youth players to develop before moving onto European Leagues. Perhaps in the future it will even compete alongside these leagues.

Regarding the personal life of your player, it is crucial to find the right balance. Whilst you may always have their best intentions and interests at heart, being an excessively controlling or overbearing agent is not an appropriate approach in most circumstances and particularly with established and mature players. They may have a young family at this point or just simply like to be independent as they begin to adjust towards a post-football lifestyle. Having an understanding as to the level of independence they would like is important. Ultimately, this is something that you will inevitably learn along the way and that it varies case by case, player by player.

Other factors in their personal life will need to be addressed by you as an agent to offer a holistic service to your client. Classic 'grown-up' worries like insurance, housing, taxes and more are also relevant to your client. Your role as the agent may not be to directly advise them on such matters but is certainly to ensure that they are able to access the right support from professionals and experts on these topics. Remember, part of the job description is to help the player be able to focus solely on their performance on the pitch and hence, to relieve them of any concerns or problems they may have off of it.

Working with the Friends and Family of a Player

As we detail further in chapter 11, the family of a player is always likely to be an important factor for them and consequently, for you as the agent. Developing a good relationship with them is always a significant benefit if you are to be successful in your work for a particular player.

Even footballers at the top level, not just youth players, can be heavily influenced by their family in terms of decision making and other footballing endeavours. For example, as an agent you should understand if your player may have reservations about a transfer away from their young family if they are unable to move with them. Or you may also be seen in a positive light if the parents of a player see you watching every game and you overtly try to build a strong relationship with them.

Below is a summary of the key points we would advise you to bear in mind for conducting yourself around the friends and family of a player, no matter how old they are:

- Demonstrate that you are trustworthy, knowledgeable, well-connected and good at what you are supposed to do.
- Interact and communicate directly with the family if appropriate and your client does not mind. Often they will want to be kept updated about any developments or opportunities as well as your intentions.
- Make an effort to have a vested interest in their lives. The collateral responsibilities of being the player's agent is that you should also endeavour to look after their family.
- Be aware and understanding that some players may want to keep their personal life very private and separate from football whereas other families may be very involved.

Working with the Spouse or Partner of a Player

In relation to working with families, when a player enters a serious relationship this may create a difficult situation in some cases so it is important for the agent to be aware. Remember, a spouse or partner is always going to be an influential figure in a player's career and life. Their opinion and their own desires are likely to be factored into and will influence the decision-making of the player. Having open and honest communication channels will make it more likely that there will be no issue at all with the player's other-half'. It is pivotal that you, as the agent, recognise the personal needs of your client and their partner. However, remember that your primary role is to communicate to the player and the spouse that it is important for them to make the most of their career whilst there is the possibility to do so.

Erkut can reinforce our point that partners of a player can be very influential based upon his own personal experiences with clients:

"In one instance, I have had a girlfriend and a mother invite other agents to games and attempt to sway the player away from my representation to sign with another agent who was offering different incentives. Fortunately they failed on this occasion but it showed how much of an influence they may be. In another situation, a player that I had moved from Germany to the UK championship had suddenly decided that he wanted to give up football and return to Germany. It transpired that his girlfriend back in Germany was encouraging him to give up his career in the UK to return to her, and he seemed happy to consider it! Thes examples serve to highlight how important it is for you to maintain good relationships with the important people around your client."

Mental Health

The extraordinary pressure and fragility of a professional football career is something that is hard to fully comprehend and appreciate until you are right in it. Particularly due to the astronomical wages of top players, there is a reasonable expectation of their performance on the pitch and their conduct off of it. Furthermore, players are in the public spotlight and those at the very top will make major headlines if there is an event. This could be positive or negative depending on the circumstances; from a hat-trick in a crunch game, to a 'disrespectful' celebration, to a groundbreaking sponsorship deal, to strolling out of a nightclub looking worse for wear or overweight. The pressure is relentless and this can have a significant impact upon the mental wellbeing of a player. There may be some underlying, stereotypical presumption in society that professional football players naturally have a robust mentality which is what got them to the top. But particularly as an agent, you should understand that this is not the reality; they are ordinary human beings and feel the same anxieties, pressures, nervousness and 'down days'.

Players are seen to be living the dream of a high percentage of children growing up, playing a sport they love in front of thousands of people. However, they are still young adults and the abnormal environment may cause some to experience mental struggles. Particularly in the knowledge that one challenge could end the years of hard work in high-pressured and highly-competitive environments and under the watchful scrutiny of the media, especially so in the era of social media, you as the agent must be aware of how your player is mentally as well as physically. Ensure they spend ample time with the club psychologist and be sure to check in with them and their feelings regularly, not just after a good or bad game! Remember that as mental health is rightfully considered as more important in modern society, clubs are employing staff specifically to protect players. You should connect with these professionals and work in conjunction with them to maintain your client's positivity and general happiness.

Another significant consideration for a client's mental health is when it comes to retirement. Whilst most players are in the knowledge that one day their career and their 'footballing lifestyle' will come to or be forced to an end, it is very common for them to struggle to come to terms with retirement once it does happen. It takes a considerable toll on the player's body and their mental health. Years of hard-work, commitment, devotion, healthy eating and high-pressure is suddenly removed. Inevitably, this is an important period of time to look out for a client's mental health and to be there to offer support as they adjust to their new lifestyle. One of the best ways of helping with this, as we discuss in chapter 26, is to have already established a second career for the client. This gives them something to look forward to and then to set their mind on once they leave their playing career behind; this can only be a positive benefit to them and their mental wellbeing.

(Erkut) An example of when looking out for the mental health of clients has been very important in my own work was when I made the decision to send a psychologist to the team hotel at an away game before the match. Despite the client's reluctance to openly talk and address the mental vulnerability and struggle they were feeling at the time, I managed to convince them to meet with the psychologist and the two-hour conversation that followed enormously benefitted the client going forward.

Thomas Freismuth is a specialist when it comes to the mental health care for our clients in our agency. His three key messages for players for protecting their mental wellbeing are as follows:

1. **Focus on controlling the controllables:** in football there is a large volume of external factors that a player cannot influence themselves. You need to help your client learn to ignore and dismiss these and focus everything on what they can alter and influence rather than feeling burdened by the things they can't.

2. **Extract the positives in every situation:** the client needs to be able to turn a narrative around and turn it into a positive situation. Even in events such as injuries and deselection from a side, there is only harm in feeling negatively about it and it is far better for the player's mental stability if they find happiness through identifying the positive consequences. It may seem difficult but there are always positives!
3. **Football is not everything:** a lot of the time, players can lose sight of perspective. Ultimately, there are more important things in life that football and losing a game cannot compare to these. At the time it may seem as though it is the end of the world for your client. They need to receive support and coaching that helps them to compute this and shift their perspective.

Racial Abuse and Discrimination Towards Your Players

Firstly to point out, in a sport where there is incredible racial, ethnic, sexual and religious diversity amongst players, fans and clubs, it is baffling that this is still an issue that has to be spoken about. However, a whole book could have been written on all the issues of racism and discrimination. For now though, we will focus upon how an agent has a role in protecting and supporting their clients against racial abuse.

Speaking openly with your client on the matter is imperative. They must be able to entrust information with you and you should advise them accordingly. This will include guidance as to how to react appropriately to racial abuse or other forms of discrimination and to ensure that the right process is followed in order for justice to prevail and the offender to be suitably punished. Whether through social media, during a match, or even in public, the sad reality of receiving and confronting racial abuse or discrimination can be extremely damaging for a player. You must be there to support them through trying to prevent such events affecting their performance and mental health whilst also helping them to address it in order to demonstrate to the world that it is not to be tolerated in football or in any circumstances in society.

An effective way of assisting your client in taking a deliberate stance against any form of racial abuse is to partner with charities and campaigns that look to combat racism and discrimination. For higher level players, their platform and public spotlight can be a tool to push for change and the extinction of racism and discrimination in football. Additionally, actively participating in football-wide initiatives such as a Rainbow-Laces campaign or taking a knee before the game can help your player join the fight against abuse. However, you must make sure this is not a futile notion and that the client meaningfully engages with the meaning and intention behind the initiatives.

(Erkut) One of the most difficult periods of my time as an agent was having to witness and live through the racial abuse my client, Mesut Özil, received whilst playing for the German National Team. It was an incredibly upsetting and distressing time for him, and as the agent you share their pain and want to do something about it. This fueled a passion for anti-racist sentiment that Mesut and I worked upon as part of our agent-player relationship.

Clients as Recruiters

Recruiting your first client may be the most difficult part. However, once you have this first client it is down to you and your aptitude as an agent to gain further clientele. Remember, changings rooms and team environments are talkative. Players will have conversations about agents and if you are performing your roles impressively on behalf of your first client, the word is likely to spread. Consequently, other players who have contrasting opinions of their current agents or do not have an agent at all may consider opening up a conversation with you to explore possible representation opportunities.

Information is key in this regard and the best scenario is that you are to rely upon your interaction and professional relationship with your client to inform you as to which teammates or friends are looking to change agents and you can take the next steps with their support. You should have a strong relationship with your client that means they will put in a good word for you with any interests you may have. However, do not force this. Some players may be willing to help whilst other clients will feel uncomfortable and awkward in doing so. Make sure you do not make them feel as though they are being used, this needs to be approached smartly and appropriately.

One of our favourite slogans to summarise this is that *"football is a reference business"*. Good references to others from the people you have served well will ensure future and continued success in the industry.

Losing a Player

It is our hope that reading this book and developing and following the attitudes, processes and habits that it promotes will render this section needless. However, the nature of football agency may mean that you may encounter a situation where a client decides to leave you. This could be either for another agent, a new venture or for family or friends who wish to look after them. The latter of these is understandable but could still present an opportunity for you. If you have a good network and have proven your worth as an agent, the player and their family may be keen for you to continue to work for the player in collaboration with them through a mandate contract.

The agency industry is competitive. In most situations, you should be flattered that other agents are wanting to pursue your client as it means they are desirable to represent. However, if you have carried out your services and responsibilities to the client ethically, dutifully and successfully, you should have nothing to worry about. Nonetheless, for whatever reason, a player may decide to change agent. You should respect the client's decision if they believe it is in their best interests and should take the opportunity to reflect upon your own work and if there are areas you can improve on with your other clients or for next time. Hopefully, your relationship is good enough with the player that you can ask for honest feedback and learn from and understand their reasons for deciding to change.

Losing a player is not a career-ender for an agent. Unfortunately, it is part of the industry and the profession. Regardless, you should try to understand why it has happened and consider it as part of the process of bettering yourself to become the best agent you can be. Prove to the player that they should never have left you!

The Size of Your Clientele

The question of how many clients an agent should look after is much-debated. Some of the biggest agencies have vast numbers of clients as well as large numbers of agents employed to look after them. However, some agents prefer to have smaller clientele capacity in order to best carry out and fulfil the extensive and holistic responsibilities outlined within this book. The table below highlights the main benefits and disadvantages of different clientele sizes:

Clientele size	Advantages	Disadvantages
Small (0-15 per agent)	You can commit more hours to each client You are able to provide a more personal service and help with day-to-day tasks Facilitates for a more comprehensive, holistic and diverse set of responsibilities Develops better relationships with clients Allows you to have specific criteria for recruitment and to target clients of a certain, preferred level and character Allows inexperienced agents to learn about the industry and improve themselves in all areas Enables you to attend lots of their games and visit them often Easier to focus on and understand the needs of fewer clients	Less earning potential unless you have a handful of top talents More onus on you to develop your network as less players to give you access into wider networks
Large (15+ per agent)	More clients can mean greater earning and	Less 'hours-per-client' available

| | income potential as the agent
May help expand your network more widely across a wider range of football
Allows you to specialise in narrower areas – i.e. more focus upon playing contracts and transfers without worrying about commercial deals etc.
Greater chances of one player reaching the top | Restrictive as to the amount of responsibilities you can take on for one client – i.e. will have to outsource commercial deals etc. elsewhere
Less selective approach to which clients you choose to represent
Difficult and particularly stressful for young agents as will have to learn quickly which may be detrimental
Harder to watch all of them play or to make time to meet up with them
Highly stressful as requests, demands and expectations come from multiple sources and vary greatly |

The graph below depicts these advantages in a more visual way. This may be easier to understand depending on your personal learning preferences:

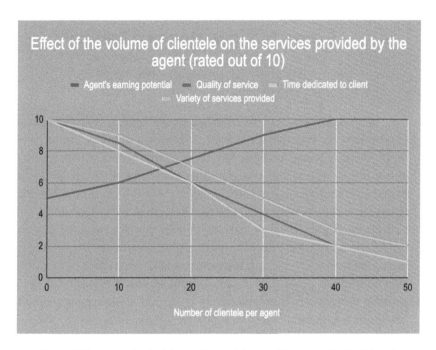

Effect of the volume of clientele on the services provided by the agent (rated out of 10)

Agent's earning potential — Quality of service — Time dedicated to client — Variety of services provided

Number of clientele per agent

It could be concluded from the table and the graph that having a smaller clientele list, perhaps limited to a maximum of fifteen, is the most advantageous approach to being the best agent. However, this is up to you to decide as an agent as both different methods have been done successfully in the past. It depends on what your ambitions are as an agent and the services you wish to provide to your client. It is important to think about this before you start amassing a list of clients and it is too late to stick to a smaller and more selective group.

Expert's View: Nassim Touihri

*Managing Director, Fair Play Career
Management, agent of Lukas Podolski*

"As an agent, it is crucial to have a good, strong relationship with your player. For me, this is established through trust and honesty at all times, and these are the most important characteristics of an intermediary who is successful in their field of work. Although this is easier said than done, in my experience there are ways of achieving this type of relationship with a player. You must always be willing to help them in their personal life when they come to you for advice, but at the same time, do not try to interfere in matters that simply don't concern you – finding the balance is key. Remember, not only do you have to protect your player from others, but you must also protect them from themselves, as they can endanger their own career at any point.

Regarding the business aspect of the player-agent relationship, you have to be constantly thinking ahead to the future and making smart plans. At the end of the day, as an intermediary you are responsible for all of your client's interests and you have to be managing both their football career and making preparations for their post- playing career – this is the sign of a good agent.

Personally, I was a little lucky in that Lukas Podolski has been my close friend since we were young kids at school. But at the same time, I had to work incredibly hard and my role today was not given to me because of this. Even when I did not officially represent Lukas, I was always by his side giving advice in both personal and contractual matters. Eventually, our relationship evolved into what it is today. As I said (and will always say), trust and honesty are the qualities that breed success in this business."

Summary

- You must always be aiming to find the appropriate balance between the business and personal aspects of your job – this is something only you can discover as you go along.
- A good way to try to ensure success is to always be open and communicate frequently with your client, as this proves to them your honesty and transparency.

- Do not underestimate prioritising the mental wellbeing of your player and support them throughout adversity, however it may be caused.
- The decisions that you make with regards to clients and other aspects of the profession are important, but at the same time they are not permanent – always be sure to review and improve the choices that you have made.
- Losing a player may be the best chance you get to improve yourself as an agent.
- Size of clientele is an important consideration to be made. There are advantages and disadvantages to smaller and larger lists.

Chapter 10: Scouting and Identifying Recruitment Targets

"Better a diamond with a flaw than a pebble without one" - Confucius

Introduction

Ultimately, after all the networking you may have done and the reputation you have built, it is your clientele that are the product of your dedication whether it is a player, a coach, a club or otherwise. From the outset this may be difficult and often signing your first client may be the biggest challenge, particularly if you are working independently and not as part of a wider agency. Once this first client is signed, the services you provide are of course important as if you serve them well you are likely to find that they refer you to teammates. Signing further clients may become slightly easier. However, you must still be proactive in sourcing and signing talents across the footballing market.

This chapter explains the overlap between agents and scouting that allows you to identify a player client that has high potential and is a suitable fit for you as a client. Scouting and a certain level of insight and knowledge into the abilities and potential of a player are a vital part of being a successful agent; from identifying youth talent to placing your client in a club that is appropriate for their playing style and where they will fit into the system used at the club.

Why and When to Scout?

When it comes to scouting potential clients, particularly in the beginning, an agent needs to be willing to dedicate sufficient time and to sacrifice weekends to watch the talent on offer. Put simply, the more matches you attend the better; your network expands, your understanding of the industry develops and the chances of finding suitable clients increases.

Our advice is to make a plan for each month of which games you wish to attend. Write down each one and work out how you will be able to attend. Perhaps at the start, this will likely be youth games such as under-16's, under-18's and reserve teams. Usually this will involve requesting scouting tickets at these clubs. This is where having a strong network in place and contacts at various clubs will be useful as they will be able to guide you on how to gain access, especially for youth games. For example, in the UK, there are strict safeguarding rules and regulations that mean, at almost all clubs, it is difficult to watch youth teams. Furthermore, at these youth games the players will not have names on their back and often, nor will there be a team sheet available so it is up to you to carry out your own due diligence to identify each player. However, in other football associations it is far easier to access youth games but you must be aware of this in each region you operate in.

Do not just attend any and every match simply for the sake of it. It is important that you go to a match with at least one distinct purpose. This may be for scouting or for networking for example. If you have a contact who has mentioned they are attending a fixture, it may be of benefit for you to attend and to build upon your relationship with them. Of course, there may also be a small selection of players, or maybe even just one, that you have discovered does not currently have an agent or is looking to change agent and could therefore be a potential recruitment target to you.

If you are attending for the latter reason, there can be many benefits of attending their fixtures. Firstly, you are able to watch and understand the players themselves and, using your own knowledge, formulate your own opinion on their potential as footballers and hence, as prospective clients of yours. Furthermore, at youth games, it is likely that their parents will be in attendance too. This is an interesting one as you do not want to appear 'stalkerish' or intimidating to them by approaching them inappropriately and putting uncomfortable pressure on the situation. However, by identifying the parents of the player, this can sometimes lead to an 'access point' in engaging with the player, expressing your interest in working with them, beginning to build a relationship and demonstrating the value you think you can add to them.

If you attend a few of their fixtures, one of the simplest yet most effective methods of doing this is to make notes on their performances and write brief scouting reports that shows them you are particularly interested in them and have the football nouse to be able to understand where they can improve and where you can add value to their career. Remember, it is impossible to obtain a full picture of the abilities and potential of a youth player based upon a single match. It is important that you observe them on more than one occasion to build a more detailed understanding and impression of them. One of the key bits of understanding that you can get from these fixtures is distinct from what you can get from watching videos of the player in games. We would recommend arriving at games early as you can often gauge a lot about a player from the way they behave before a match. The manner in which they warm up, are attentive to the coaches and prepare for a match in terms of body language, discipline and intensity can give you an indication as to their character and the potential they may have in their footballing future and in a healthy working relationship with you.

Another useful aspect of attending their fixtures is the possibility of interacting and networking with scouts and coaches that may also be watching. Through chatting with such professionals, you are also able to gauge an independent opinion on the players you are looking at. For example, the scout may be from a certain club and will have the player's name on their list of 'ones-to-watch'. This may be a useful indicator to you that the client has potential as a professional footballer.

The Art of Scouting

Scouting is a profession in itself and we could write a whole book on it alone. The top scouts refine their eye for talent over many years of experience and become experts in identifying youth stars that realistically have the potential to go on to play at the very top. Hence, to reiterate, it is vital that you have a strong network of scouts that can assist you along the way. Nevertheless, an ability to scout and understand a player's potential is part of the broad job description of an agent as well.

The difference between scouts and agents is that often the scouts will be observing players on behalf of clubs and assessing the scope for their inclusion in the future in their club's first team and academies. However, agents approach scouting from a slightly different perspective, to identify the best clients to work with. Usually this is centred upon their on-field potential as agents naturally want to represent the top talents. However, an additional consideration is their suitability to represent as a client. For example, deciding whether your unique and niche selling point as an agent aligns with their character including their attitude and personality. Perhaps there are other factors you look for such as commonality in terms of ethnicity, religion and heritage that tend to be the kind of client you represent as they are easier to personally relate to.

Scouting is a unique science. In terms of on-field ability, below we will attempt to outline and summarise key factors and indicators that should be considered and prioritised by an agent and particularly in the youth football context. It is important to note that this is not an exhaustive list and that a lot of scouting can be subjective but the general overview of identifying talent is universal:

1. **Relative age effect:** remember that at under-16 level for example, some players may have turned 16 eleven months prior to some of their teammates. Knowing when their birthdates lie and assessing the pubertal status as either early or late developers is a vital part of scouting youth talent. Do not dismiss a small but incredibly skilful and technical player based solely upon their physical attributes. There is a chance they may develop and surpass their teammates physically as well as technically once they have matured fully. Key indicators for this may be the size of their parents as well as their current body composition.

2. **Potential rather than performance:** in youth football especially, one game does not determine the quality and potential of one player. It is important to look for and spot small indicators that may suggest the player has an abundance of potential that could see him flourish in the near future.

3. **A 'weapon' skill:** A clever way of simplifying scouting is to narrow potential clients down to those players that have what may be referred to as a 'weapon' skill. In other words, the player may have a single exceptional attribute that distinguishes them from the rest of the players. This can be something like sheer pace, their set piece capabilities, incredible strength or a flamboyant and mesmerising dribbling ability. These are the kind of players that will be noticed by scouts and, whilst their all-round game is important too, a weapon skill can help them become a professional footballer.

4. **Necessary attributes:** for some positions, certain characteristics are non-negotiable. For example, goalkeepers must be agile and have considerable size, wingers often need to be fast and strikers must have a

notable finishing ability. Clients that may be of interest to you will likely have all of the necessary attributes as well as some additional traits that indicate potential for a future in the game.

5. **Unique characteristics:** some players are harder to come by than others. For example, it may always be worth making note of a left-footed, tall and fast centre-back as they are always in high demand. The same can be said for a top quality left-back as they are treasured at the highest level. Other positions such as strikers are difficult to find when it comes to players who may go on to play at the top of the game as there is an abundance of strikers across youth football and beyond. However, this is not to say that some academies may be capable of producing the very best strikers, keep a keen eye out for these talents.

6. Finding your own niche method is also a very important aspect of successful scouting as an agent. This is less of a point about identifying the talent itself but more about how you go about identifying it in your own niche way that can give you a talent identification advantage. Knowing where to look can give you a headstart against competitors. For example, finding gems where very few agents are looking immediately increases the chances of you signing the player before other agents even see them play. This may be at non-league level or in exotic countries, identifying underrated and unearthed talents that you can represent.

Expert's View: Max Legath

*Former Chief Academy Scout FC Bayern
Munich and now Head of Scouting at FC Basel*

"After working for ten years as a youth coach from U9 to U17 teams, in 2015, I got the chance to not only work with the most talented players, but to learn much more about the identification of young prospects. I would like to share some of my insights and experiences from scouting in the grassroots sector up to the first team, from local players in Munich to players from all over the world that are now plying their trade at the World Cup.

First of all, Scouting is not a magic trick – for me it is the combination of persistence, passion, meticulousness and the willingness to learn. The accuracy of your estimation and evaluation of young talents is going to increase within time and predictions will be more precise – and still then, you are going to fail at times. Every scout fails, you cannot get it right all of the time, and every scout makes mistakes. These instances are not commonly spoken about, but I can assure you that every scout and every sporting director gets it wrong between 20-50% of transfers that are completed. Our mission is to increase the probability of a successful transfer as much as possible. And this is the same kind of approach an agent should take; maximising the chances of recruiting a top talent.

Two key aspects that increase the likelihood are comparison and comprehensiveness. I would like to start with the comparison of players. For most people, it is not complicated to watch a football match and identify the best players on the pitch, performing in that match, standing out and making the difference, we would probably have the same handful of names at the end. But the art of a scout lies in those that are able to compare between different clubs and leagues; between countries and different phases of player development; between teams coached by a good coach that is dedicated to the development of young players and other teams that have a coach who does the opposite? Once all these points of comparison are accounted for, we might find that the selections of an everyday football fan watching a game, differs from the selections and assessments of top scouts. As an agent, if you are able to fall into the bracket that can answer the more intricate and 'hidden' questions of talent identification, this can be a huge benefit to your career.

Irrespective of any age category or country, my belief is that you will need about two to three years to understand a specific scouting marketing in its entirety. After this period you will have seen and collated enough evidence of players going through different stages of their development. Whether it is "football kindergarten" or the Champions League, only after a longer period will you really have all-encompassing knowledge of the market.

Defining your market is the first step for an agent and for a scout – my advice would be that it is better to make it smaller and clearer rather than jumping around. With disciplined and structured scouting habits, you will develop a detailed understanding of players in this field and be able to identify players that would be valuable, high-potential additions to your agency.

Scouting also helps you to build up a network, see the same people more often and develop useful relationships that will give you access to more information.

In 90 minutes you can observe so many actions of a player that can give you a good first impression based on his performance on that day. However, you must be aware that you could see a completely different player the following weekend. Therefore, following players and talents over a longer period of time and seeing them under different circumstances will make your assessment of a player more complete. The more information you gather on the player, the more likely it is that you will be able to give an accurate report on them and sensibly decide whether they are a suitable recruitment target.

All the best and stay hungry for football and talents."

Summary

- A knowledge of football and a scouting eye is very useful in identifying talent and potential future clients.
- Attending fixtures, such as youth academy games, will widen your network and provide the chance to watch the next generation of footballers to identify those that may be of interest as clients.
- Understanding which players have the potential to play in top leagues across Europe is a unique skill but there are several key indicators and attributes that can help you formulate your own opinion.

Further Reading

- The   PFSA:
  https://thepfsa.co.uk/?gclid=CjwKCAiAheacBhB8EiwAItVO2
  -5AYRVGGPI3aQC-ILHAhINyqipXbn5ai-yp3WNiMncNnA3W-
  l82AhoC-jQQAvD_BwE
- Anatomy of a Football Scout - Jon Cotterill

Chapter 11: Working with Youth Players

"A normal childhood can be sacrificed, but the opportunities that come with the prize of success are often far too good to turn down" - *David Jackett*

Introduction

Stemming from FIFA regulations, there are very strict rules concerning agents working with youth players and minors. National football associations have their own set of rules focused on protecting the young players, with strict punishment (for agents and clubs) if these regulations are not adhered to. It is the role of the agent to be aware as to the national association regulations governing the representation of youth players and ensure they comply with them as a priority.

With the growth of youth footballing talent around the world leading to more scouts, more interest and more transfers, there is an increasing need for such policies. For our interest, these regulations must be understood and adhered to by agents.

For agents, working with youth players is an exciting opportunity. Once they are of the legal age which allows agents to work with them, it is your job to help guide them through the early stages of a fledgling career in football. This chapter delves into the different methods and practices that should be adopted when looking after youth players.

Handling Youth Players

First and foremost it must be made clear that youth football is a volatile and tense environment. These players are not guaranteed to make a sustained living from football and some may not ever be a paid professional at all. When assessing opportunities for youth players agents must ensure that the player and their parents are aware of the low percentage of academy players that go on to play at the top level. Competition is fierce and the risk of career-ending injury is all-too-real. Education should always be encouraged for youth players to provide them with a secondary option should the worst case happen and their career as a footballer fail to materialise.

Some agents may choose to pursue recruitment in older and established players. Whilst this is a safer option, there is a greater risk and reward in recruiting youth players. Agents may have a good scouting eye and can identify young talent that has the potential to go onto play at the very top. It will be an incredible achievement for an agent to pick up a player at the earliest possible stage and go on to represent them throughout an illustrious career, however, it is not unheard of.

Network, as is the case in most areas of agency, is once again a valuable asset for an agent in recruiting academy footballers. Having a good contact base of youth scouts and academy coaches gives you access to inside information and the ability to catch onto word-of-mouth. If scouts and coaches trust you from the relationship you have built with them, they may share their insights and point you towards certain players which you can then attempt to recruit if they fit what you are looking for. In exceptional cases, some relationships can be built to an extent that the academy coaches may even point a player in your direction. However, it takes years of plying your trade as an agent in an ethical and successful way, and building an immaculate reputation, to reach the stage where someone believes you are the best option for a youth player's next steps.

Some youth players must also be kept grounded. At a certain age, youth footballers begin to think of themselves as 'footballers'. This can be dangerous. The feeling of being so close can overwhelm them and attributes such as their attitude and work rate begin to suffer as they feel as though they have already made it. An agent must spot signs of this and help to keep the client grounded and working hard to reach the goal of becoming a professional footballer and beyond. Many players fail at this hurdle but with the right guidance, an agent may be able to assist them in navigating through such a precarious period of time.

Even once the fortunate few young players that are offered their first professional contract begin the next step in their careers, agents have a responsibility to ensure the sudden disposable income and public limelight does not affect their performance or work ethic. The job is not yet done and there is always room for improvement. Whether the player begins in the development squad, on the fringes of the first team or is thrust straight into the starting XI, they must continue to better themselves and become accustomed to the highest level of football they would have played so far in their short careers. You as the agent should be by their side, taking care of off-field business, beginning to find sponsors and maybe even looking for loan or transfer opportunities that will be a benefit to their progress, whilst reinforcing the importance that they continue on the same trajectory on the field.

The tables below show the extreme cases of youth talent and value and why agents working with and monitoring academy players could be a worthwhile investment.

Most Expensive Transfers of Under 18s:

Player	Age	Transfer	Fee (£million)
Pedri	16	UD Las Palmas → Barcelona	15.75
William Geubbels	16	Olympique Lyon → Monaco	18
Pietro Pellegri	16	Genoa → Monaco	18.81
Jadon Sancho	17	Man City → Borussia Dortmund	18.53
Alexandre Pato	17	Internacional → AC Milan	21.6
Jude Bellingham	17	Birmingham → Borussia Dortmund	22.5
Eduardo Camavinga	18	Rennes → Real Madrid	27.9
Alessandro Bastoni	18	Atalanta → Inter Milan	27.99
Renato Sanches	18	Benfica → Bayern Munich	31.5
Wayne Rooney	18	Everton → Manchester United	33.3
Luke Shaw	18	Southampton → Manchester United	33.75
Fabio Silva	18	FC Porto → Wolves	36
Vinícius Júnior	18	Flamengo → Real Madrid	40.5
Rodrygo	18	Santos FC → Real Madrid	40.5

Source: Transfermarkt (correct as of October 2022)

Biggest market values of players 21 and under:

Player	Age	Club	Market Value (£million)
Pedri	19	Barcelona	81
Jude Bellingham	19	Borussia Dortmund	81
Jamal Musiala	19	Bayern Munich	72
Gavi	18	Barcelona	63
Florian Wirtz	17	Bayer 04 Leverkusen	63
Bukayo Saka	21	Arsenal	63
Alphonso Davies	21	Bayern Munich	63
Rodrygo	21	Real Madrid	63
Wesley Fofana	21	Chelsea	58.5
Josko Gvardol	20	RB Leipzig	54
Ansu Fati	19	Barcelona	54

Source: Transfermarkt (correct as of October 2022)

Financial Implications for Agents

A quick but very important point to note for agents who represent youth players is that you are not entitled to any form of commission until the client turns 18. In transfers or in salaries, it is prohibited for the agent to claim any remuneration from the player until this age. Furthermore, in most cases, when the client signs their first professional contract with you it will not be particularly lucrative and hence, your commission as the agent will be small in the first place.

The financial implication of representing youth players can be difficult. Healthy and sustainable commission is more likely to come later in the career of the client and it can seem like a long journey for the agent without a guaranteed successful outcome of actually making money. However, representing a client through the youth development stage and through their first professional contract can also be a financially invaluable investment. Building this relationship and trust and demonstrating to them that you are committed to benefitting their career can mean that if they do prosper later in their career, they are likely to stick by you and your rewards will eventually come.

Family of Youth Players

Even more important than with professional players, having a good relationship and working directly with the parents or guardians of youth players is crucial. In some countries, this is a legal necessity as a legal guardian has to sign off on the documents. Moreover, the parents are likely to have played a significant role in the footballing journey of their child so far. From introducing them to the game, to bringing them to training every day to buying their boots and washing their kit, they are usually an ever-present supporter for their child.

Some may be more involved in others. For example, some parents take a back seat and enjoy watching their child learn and improve through academy football whilst others will be heard shouting and encouraging from the sidelines of every game they play. There is a wide variety of involvement from parents but all are equally important to build a relationship with if you are hoping to recruit their child.

Parents are often cautious of agents. Particularly when they are still the legal guardian of a player and if the player is under-18, parents still take on the duty of care for the child and will understandably be wary of strangers wanting to become involved. Reputation is important for parents and they will seek the most trustworthy agents that they feel truly cares for the success of their child.

Do not be overbearing with parents. Make contact with them once you have decided the player is the right fit for you but then do not make the player or their parents feel pressured or uncomfortable. Begin to build a relationship and show them the value you can add to their child's career. Demonstrate that you are trustworthy, knowledgeable, well-connected and good at what you are supposed to do. A good way to do this is politely and appropriately inviting the family to meet away from football. This way you will be able to build an authentic relationship and begin to gain their trust.

Never promise something that you cannot deliver upon and do not try to bribe the families. At the end of the day, conducting yourself professionally and ethically will build your reputation and result in success. Gaining the respect and trust of parents is of paramount importance to this and when working with young players, it is a necessity in most cases that the parents give their approval. Occasionally, although the final decision should lie with the player, some parents will take it upon themselves to select the agent for their child. Hence, you must not underestimate the value of impressing both the player *and* their parents.

Extra Training and Education

Another aspect of working with a youth player that needs to be considered by the agent is their schooling and football development. For the football side, of course, the academy they are a part of will provide the majority of football education. They will train with the academy and develop their skills through the club. However, you should always be willing to and in a position to offer your player additional support by outsourcing extra, supplementary training to another independent coach. This can help your player hear different views and advice for the areas in which they need to improve. Communicating with the youth prospect you are representing and understanding whether this will be of benefit to them is an important part of working with young players as an agent.

Football training is not the only necessary form of education that a youth player should be concerned with. It is perhaps unexpected that a football agent also ought to be encouraging and supportive of the client in their academic development and education. It is far better for an academy player to also perform strongly at school and to ensure that if the professional football dream doesn't materialise as they might expect, they will feel as though they have other options. Finding a healthy and productive balance between improving on the football field and finishing their school studies is vital in this regard.

Social Media, Sponsorships and Boot Deals

How many instances over the last few years have old social media posts come back to haunt professional athletes?

You may think it is overkill to say that players should begin to build a professional social media platform and personal brand as a youth academy player but it can only ever be a benefit to them in reality. A youth player that posts photos from training or matches will begin to develop themselves commercially without even realising. Brands will already look upon this well. Boot deals and other endorsements may come more easily in the future to players that have a long-standing, professional and well-established social media presence.

For an agent, you must help a player to understand that how they present themselves on their social media affects how other people, including scouts, clubs and brands perceive them. Avoiding photos of parties, alcohol and any inappropriate behaviour away from football is a useful starter for enhancing their online image. As they begin to grow their social media presence, you as the agent can begin to reach out to small brands and companies that may be willing to collaborate with young talent that has future potential. Whilst football is without doubt the priority at this stage, social media is something to be wary of and can be built well, despite their age.

Expert's View: David Jackett

Global football consultant and Wasserman agent

"Youth football is its own sphere, network and world. The modern game views young players as both low-risk commodities and high quantity 'investments' with the potential of great reward for the successful few.

A magnifying glass has been placed on youth football like never before, due to amplified worldwide passion from fans. This is coupled with increased access for a supporter to simply be able to follow updates on the other side of the planet. The demand for content overspills to 'who is the next young home-grown star of the team? 'This globalised modern world brands young footballers as prospects, ensuring a 'bandwagon' surrounding the next big star from all angles. Millennials have now subconsciously bought into the rising star philosophy through social media. This creates a very different perception to the apprentice reality of today, with old academies being challenged to adapt their teachings in increasingly lucrative and consequently deceptive surroundings. It is this evolution which will not make more players earn a living but will bring out the best in existing domestic talent who, from the age of twelve, face international competition with more basic upbringings at elite clubs.

The underbelly of the beautiful game raises questions about each child's journey by writers, coaches, parents and players. Roles are blurred. Injuries occur. social pressure. Passion overspills. A normal childhood can be sacrificed, but the opportunities that come with the prize of success are often far too good to turn down."

Summary

- The most crucial point regarding youth rules is to always act on the side of caution. The first port of call when trying to find the necessary regulations should be the relevant association's website, and contacting a representative is greatly advised.
- The punishment for not following the rules correctly can be extremely serious. Breaking the law, especially when concerning minors, must be avoided.

- This period of a client's career can be very significant. The agent should provide a service that enhances the client's development and places them in the best possible position for a successful career.
- Education is still vital and you should emphasise to clients that their career as a professional footballer is extremely fragile. By continuing to work hard at education, should the worst happen and their career is cut short, they will still have prospects in other areas of life.

Further Reading

- A Review Of FIFA's Minor Application Guide - LawInSport: https://www.lawinsport.com/topics/item/a-review-of-fifa-s-minor-application-guide-for-u18-international-transfers
- FIFA Protection of Minors Guide: https://digitalhub.fifa.com/m/2130eb84c31cf4e4/original/lb2t6bqgmi2a1x1pr5xs-pdf.pdf

Chapter 12: Being an Agent in Women's Football

"There are certainly promising prospects ahead for those considering an agency career specialising in women's football" - Carol Joy & Jacquie Agnew

A Rapidly Growing Game

As is currently the case in many sports, the women's game is on the rise. Since the establishment of fully professional leagues across the world, including the Women's Super League in the UK in 2010 and the increasing popularity of the US national team, the game has changed dramatically.

An increase in governing-body recognition alongside greater initiatives and resource allocation to further expose and boost the women's game are leading drivers of its ongoing growth. Women's leagues across the world are becoming more marketable and far more robust business and sporting entities that now appeal to enthusiastic companies and lucrative sponsorship opportunities.

Since its establishment in 2010, the Women's Super League (WSL) in England has become fully professional and now includes 12 teams. The WSL offers player salaries between £20,000-200,000 per year. Having an entirely professional league has consequently improved the overall standard of football and improves the game in its entirety. Even the league below, the English Women's Championship, is mostly professional with only a handful of players at the lower end needing supplementary jobs for income.

There is a similar pattern in leagues across the European continent and beyond who are rightfully choosing to invest more interest and financial backing into the women's game. The United States, Australia, France, Spain, Sweden, China and Japan are among the other most professional women's leagues globally with other countries that are well-renowned for football such as Germany and Italy forming fledgling women's top-tier and semi or fully professional teams.

Part of the professionalism of the women's game extends to the football clubs as well as the players. Teams now employ several full-time coaching staff, medical teams and background staff as well as investing in better infrastructure and facilities. The consequential improvement in the standard of women's football is reflected by the increasing attendances at games and the growing number of sponsors investing into the sport.

The Financial Impact

Many of the women's leagues across the globe are now named after major sponsors. This indicates the increased commercial attention and exposure that women's football has been receiving and has significantly boosted the financial success of the game. For example, in 2019, the WSL signed a three-year sponsorship deal with the British bank Barclays that has been valued at around £10million, including a £500,000 prize money pool for the league champions. BT Sport and the BBC have also taken on broadcasting duties and have played a role in extending the reach of women's football to wider, global audiences. Selected games are now shown in over 12 countries and BT Sport pledged to show games in over 1000 pubs in England.

Wider external investment has boomed. Companies can see the growing popularity in women's football and view it as an opportunity to boost their visibility to the market whilst identifying a chance to improve the company's claims of inclusivity, diversity and equality. Women's football has become very appealing to the innovative brand marketing strategies used by big sports sponsors.

The external and internal investment in marketing, sponsorship, commercialisation and promoting the women's game has paid dividends. Since 2017, the average attendance of top-level women's football games has tripled to around 3000 with the big names attracting far more. Atletico Madrid vs Barcelona attracted a crowd of 60,000 to set a new attendance record for the women's game. The impact has also been seen on a global level with the 2019 Women's world cup final recording global viewing figures of 11.7million – this is a monumental increase from the 1.7million who watched the 2011 version! FIFA also doubled the prize money for the competition to $60million in recognition of the increased financial viability of the game.

Viewing and attendance figures are also an interesting reflection on how the women's game has improved. The UK is different in that 60% of crowds are men at women's games whilst in the US the gender demographic split is even and in Europe it is mostly female.

The growth of women's football and the status and popularity of the players has had a profound 'role-model' impact on young girls and women globally. This can only benefit the sport in years to come as more and more females become involved in football and help grow the game further.

The growth of European women's football is demonstrated clearly in the table below. Although it clearly shows a large disparity between the men's and the women's game, particularly for the World Cup, it shows that women's football is experiencing significant growth and expansion:

FIFA World Cup Prize Money Comparison:

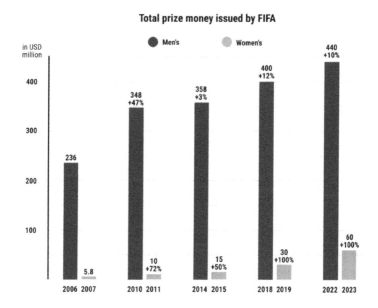

(Source: FIFPRO, 2020 Raising Our Game - Women's Football Report)

What this Means for Agents and How to Look after Female Clients

Ultimately, it is important for an agent that the business they engage with is financially viable and supports their livelihood. Previously, agents may have only worked with women's football players on commercial deals as this is where income from commission could be generated whilst the employment contracts were not enough to be sustainable from commission. Furthermore, the general commission available to agents in the women's game is usually around 5% which has made it less of a financially sustainable option for an agent. However, with the rising value of employment contracts and transfers, agents are now more likely and able to engage with female clients and will help to negotiate and source their playing contracts. Both the commercial and the football aspects of players is now an attractive source of commission for agents.

These changes have created a fresh and intriguing opportunity for football agents to venture into a different world that demands a slightly different approach to men's football. Some modern agencies have established themselves with the sole focus of embracing the women's game and a rising volume of women are entering the currently male-dominated field of football agency. The biggest agencies such as CAA and Wasserman have female-specific departments that look after their female football players. This is now a financially viable area that agencies can grow.

Being an agent in the women's game is in many ways the same as in the men's game but it also has its own unique demands and skill requirements. It is an exciting prospect for agents to engage in women's football going forward as it is a market that will continue to increase in popularity and attractiveness to football fans, sponsors, broadcasters, investors, media and on a global scale. For agents this can pose an enticing opportunity for us to challenge ourselves and our skill sets and apply them to a unique industry in a slightly different and adapted way but to attain the same objectives; to optimise the on and off-field potential and maximise the success of our clients.

On and off-field opportunities are emerging with increasing frequency as the women's game continues to grow. In 2020, the Danish forward, Pernille Harder, broke the world transfer record for a woman with her £200,000 transfer to Chelsea. Salaries are also ever-increasing and provide an exciting prospect for agents. As of 2022, the salaries for men and women in the US national team have been made equal in line with US Employment Law as a result of the USA women's team's case. This indicates the extent to which women's football is gaining greater traction, influence and power within the world of football and is still viewed as a growing and developing entity. However, this is only applicable on a national level and club salaries do not reflect the same principle. Nevertheless, it has become an industry that could offer lucrative rewards for football agents as it continues this exponential expansion. Beyond the possible income source, it can also provide an exhilarating challenge for agents as the role of an agent in women's football requires slightly adjusted approaches, techniques, methods and applications compared to player representation in the men's game.

As with the men's version, agents venturing into women's football must provide a full 360°, holistic service to their clients. Their responsibilities go far beyond just negotiating a football contract. The branding and marketing of a client is absolutely imperative. An agent must be able to utilise their client's commercial potential and help them create a marketable brand or 'identity'. This also includes finding a suitable sponsorship path such as with clothing brands or big boot deals. Most importantly, the agent needs to make their clients self-aware about their status as role models for young girls and women.

The current generation of women's footballers and those to come are technically and media-savvy. Social media has enabled them to directly access fans and brands to leverage themselves above purely being just a footballer, something that is of equal importance in both the men's and women's versions of the game. Agents have an influential pivotal role to play in guiding their commercial success and effectively utilising the digital age. Any agents venturing into the women's football market should have a comprehensive and applicable understanding of the power of social media and how to grow the commercial presence of their client to generate sponsorships, media publicity, revenue and to create a personal, globally-appealing identity.

The vital aspect of female commercial opportunities that agents needs to be aware of is highlighted by **Misha Sher**, Global Head of Sport at MediaCom:

"Brands turn to female athletes to leverage tentpole cultural events. We'll see a lot more female athletes featuring in marketing, but we'll also see a lot more collaboration and co-creation between athletes and brands. So rather than a transactional relationship where brands are basically just utilising the athlete's image, they will move much more into 'narrative-aligned', powerful, impactful storytelling with these female athletes about something that people deeply care about because the opportunity to connect and engage is much bigger than advertising; it's a cultural conversation."

An example of how a female footballer can do this is perfectly illustrated by the US national team forward, Alex Morgan. Alongside her agent, she has established partnerships and contracts with more than a dozen corporate business partners and sponsors that align with her character and personal identity; including global industry powerhouses Coca-Cola, Nike and Volkswagen. It is important to note that her salary from football alone is a fraction of her overall income at $460,000 whilst she has amassed an annual income of several million dollars through endorsement deals.

Agents must understand that it is imperative that their clients, whilst it is important that they are successful on the pitch, also utilise their position to generate additional income streams as there is greater opportunity and money beyond just the football. As the exposure and following around women's football continues to grow, their status will be increasingly malleable and a greater volume of opportunities will arise for the client. Agents must have a knowledgeable and detailed insight into the character of the client and her ambitions in order to accurately assess, encourage and negotiate the opportunities that are best suited to furthering their personal career and success. Their success is the main priority, not yours as the agent. But look after your client properly and appropriately and you yourself will flourish.

Another thing to bear in mind for representing women's footballers is the globality of opportunities that might arise and how to approach them. The International Women's game is highly regarded and continuing to boom in popularity, as shown by the extraordinary noise and hysteria around the 2022 European Championship. However, the top women's leagues and footballing status is found in countries from each corner of the world. Whereas the men's game is dominated by European football from England to the likes of Germany, Spain and Italy, the women's game has become well established in widely dispersed regions from Australia to the US to England to Scandinavia to China. This means that having a well-established global network and working on relationships with people from the other side of the world is an integral part of being a successful agent representing female footballers.

It is our responsibility to be proactive in identifying the suitable opportunities around the world and to avoid being narrow-minded and short-sighted in our approach. Remember that with a current lack of scouts and recruitment staff, clubs will be more reliant upon trusted agents. The women's game is currently more agent driven and you should be able to use your own network and knowledge to find and offer a good service to the players. The difficulty with this is that it is harder to find information. For example, there is no TransferMarkt for female players and scouting information is also lacking.

The best agent in the female game will have contacts across the globe and will actively seek a diverse range of opportunities for their client globally to ensure that they achieve and experience the greatest career possible. It is a taxing and demanding aspect of the job but it is the most rewarding and an investment of our time into it is vital if we are to be successful agents and serve our clients appropriately.

What Do the Statistics Show?

The data reinforces the narrative that women's football is growing and the role of an agent is increasing simultaneously. In 2022 there was a 42.9% rise from 2021 in the number of transfers involving an agent acting upon behalf of a club. Representing a club is covered in more detail in chapter 15 but for now, this statistic is useful in demonstrating how an agent's role in women's football has increased in recent times including beginning to involve agent's on behalf of the selling club since 2020:

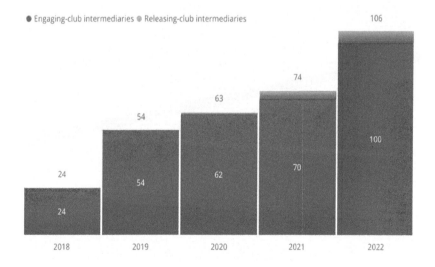

For player agents, their involvement in a proportion of all international transfers is actually higher than in men's football. Player agents were involved in 340 international transfers in women's football, amounting to 22.3% of all transfers whilst only 15.3%

of transfers in the men's game involved player agents. This increase in the use of player agents is shown below:

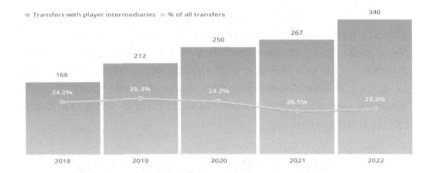

Source: FIFA Intermediary Report 2022

Expert's View: Carol Joy and Jacquie Agnew

*Pro Talent Sports Elite Women's Football
Career Specialists*

"At Pro Talent Sports, we often use #excitingtimes in our social media as a way of highlighting the here and now in the women's game, together with the possibilities of the future. There are certainly promising prospects ahead for those considering an agency career specialising in women's football.

Becoming an agent in the women's game can be very rewarding indeed, but is likely best viewed as an investment; the returns not only through fees and commissions, but also the satisfaction of pushing the professionalisation process on and being a part of these #excitingtimes. The direction of progressive travel for the women's game is clear, but whereas the men's game is already a mature market, the women's is still a fast-developing one.

Clubs and governing bodies have only recently acknowledged the need to recognise where sportswomen differ from men: for example FIFA now requires employment contracts to include minimum maternity paid leave and the right to return.

And such contracts are often shorter than men's (one to two years is common at present) which can impact a player's transfer decisions. Also, although salaries are rising, (and are very good at the top elite levels) many female players still seek additional income sources.

A good agent will recognise that personal chemistry will play a major part in how agent/client issues are handled and managed. We advise prospective clients to do their research on us before we meet. Meeting will then help establish for both parties whether there is likely to be a good working relationship. It is equally important that prospects understand the level of engagement needed for us to work well together.

A good agent will also prioritise building and maintaining good networks with other key professionals active in the women's game. This can help navigate the changes of personnel that are a feature of the landscape. For example, a change of manager with a different playing style can sometimes lead to significant changes in a squad. Familiarity with the set of managers who are already involved in women's football (or are likely to become so) can positively affect the pace of a negotiation with a club.

An agent who can draw on knowledge of and experience in the women's game will be well-placed to evaluate options for players, as well as demonstrate player value for any potential contract offers.

Wanting to help players make the most of their playing careers is at the heart of an agent's work and one of the most satisfying aspects; doing so in the women's game is also contributing to the making of sporting history."

Summary

- Women's football is in a fantastic and promising period of transformation; it is a rapidly expanding and exciting sector for football agents
- Whilst some responsibilities and duties might differ from the men's game, the fundamental principle that the client's interests are the top priority remains the same
- Remember, it is your job to keep up to date with rules and regulations and be aware of where this is different in the women's game. There are currently variations in terms of registration and transfer regulations.

Further Reading

- Football She Wrote - Various Authors
- A Woman's Game - Suzanne Wrack

Chapter 13: Representing Clubs

"Protect your process" - Dr Erkut Sogut

Introduction

In this chapter you will come to understand the difference between agents that only represent clubs (club agents) and those that represent players (player agents) as well as the reasons behind why clubs use agents for themselves.

The Role

There is a significant difference in the day-to-day work of a club agent and a player agent. Whilst they are both bracketed under the same licence, their actual responsibilities are far apart.

Ultimately, club agents are brokers. They do not have to take on the variety of tasks that a player agent has to do as they do not have a duty of care or responsibility for a player. Instead, they are directly representing the club. A club that is looking to sign a player will often not go directly to the agent of the player. Instead, they will provide an agent with the information of the player they're after and an offer that they can take to the player's agent. This usually occurs because the clubs do not know the agent of the player and strictly the clubs are not allowed to approach a player directly if he is under contract at another club unless his contract expires in the next six months. Hence, if the club can bring in an agent from their side it makes sense to use their services to protect themselves from any wrongdoing.

Many of these 'club agents' are very experienced and used by the clubs after establishing themselves in the industry, developing strong relationships with clubs and creating a network that gives them the ability to benefit a football club. However, the issue lies with the fact that interestingly many of these club agents are friends or relatives of officials in the club. The sporting director, head of recruitment, board members, president and even the coach can influence which agent the club uses.

It is a common strategy that is regularly seen in transfer deals in the world of football. It has become the norm for a club to have a specific relationship with one or, at most, a handful of agents that they will bring into every deal. This presents a significant opportunity for you as an agent. If you are able to develop a strong relationship with a club and their officials such as the sporting directors, you can hopefully reach a stage where they can place full faith and trust in you and position you as a favoured agent for their dealings. There are many benefits and perks that come with such a trusted position such as the club sharing key information with you like which players are considering changing their agent which allows you to approach them.

Building Relationships with Clubs

It is unusual for an agent to begin by solely representing clubs, although this may change in the future as we will explore in chapter 30. Usually, an agent may eventually be asked to act on behalf of a club's best interests once they have proved themselves as a reputable and capable player agent. Through dealings with player clients, agents will come across a broad scope of club officials and representatives during times such as contract negotiations and transfers for their players.

An agent that conducts themselves properly and morally during these meetings will gain the respect and trust of the club. This is enhanced by only suggesting players that are suitable and appropriate for the club and their needs and treating the opposing parties fairly. This creates the impression that you are an agent that knows what they're talking about and has the capability of helping their club in the future.

Remember the reasons why a club might be consulting you as an agent. Sometimes it may be because they want to sell a player and need the help of an agent to find them a new club that will buy them out of their contract. In other instances it could be that the agent has the ability to drive the market value up for a player in different global markets. Often, when acting for the buying club, the club will use you to contact the player as mentioned previously if they lack information, the contact details of the agent or even struggling with a language barrier. Another possible reason is for an agent to act on behalf of the club as a 'favour' to the board such as the Sporting Director or the Owner. This can be done to enhance your reputation and relationship with a club.

Once you have established your credibility as a potential candidate for the club to use on their behalf in future deals, you must then grow and maintain your relationships with the concerned members of the club. Be sure to stay in contact with them and follow the best networking processes to ensure they continue to trust you and to strengthen your link with the club. This will open up an array of opportunities for the future and become a new and exciting facet of your career as an agent. This is readdressed in chapter 14 which discusses relationships with and representing club officials and coaches.

What to Look Out For

Being an agent on behalf of a club can certainly present an exciting opportunity and allow you to see a transfer from a unique perspective as an agent. However, it does come with risks and dangers that as an agent you must be aware of and consider when entering into a deal on behalf of a club, much the same as when acting on behalf of a player.

It is possible and may occur more often than you think, for club officials to include family members or friends in deals. This may jeopardise the negotiation you are a part of and corrupt the proceedings. In some instances, these relatives and friends are receiving kickback payments. This is an unethical practice and something that you should avoid being a part of. Additionally, this may mean that you receive less commission than you deserve as the money ends up with other people. Being involved in such deals can damage your trustworthy and moral reputation as an agent and will have a detrimental impact on your future business.

Please also note that it is vital to understand the new regulations covered in chapter 3, in the section regarding the multiple representation restrictions that have been implemented by FIFA. The only situation in which multiple representation will now be permitted under the new legislation is acting on behalf of the BUYING club and the PLAYER. When operating on behalf of players and clubs you must ensure that you are not in breach of these laws or this will also harm your reputation.

One final point to consider on this topic is if you are on the other side of the coin and a club agent approaches you inquiring about your client(s). Often, they are fishing for mandates for your players and will give the impression they have a concrete and guaranteed plan and opportunity for the client. After conducting a thorough check yourself and adequate due diligence you may consider agreeing to a mandate if the opportunity is in a market where you are not so well connected and would ordinarily need help anyway. You can then directly collaborate with the club's agent although it is advisable to agree with them that their commission will be paid directly from the club rather than splitting your own commission with them.

The Stats

Representing clubs has never been more of a prevalent opportunity for agents. This is reinforced in FIFA's 2022 intermediary report which showed a 22.4% increase from 2021. 7.6% of all transfers involved an intermediary acting on behalf of the buying club. This is shown in the graphic below:

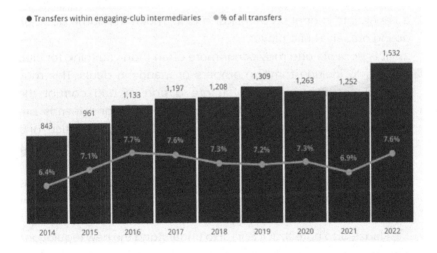

● Transfers within engaging-club intermediaries   ● % of all transfers

Source: FIFA Intermediary Report 2022

Significantly, the report also goes on to say that almost 60% of high value transfers (over $5million) involved a buying club agent. Currently, the national associations that use and spend the most on club agents for the highest proportion of transfers are in England ($188.8m), Italy ($72.1m), Germany ($45.9m), Spain ($35.6m) and although the fees are not as high, a high proportion of transfers in Denmark and Austria involve an agent representing the buying club.

A similar figure was reported for agents acting on behalf of the selling club if the player is not a free agent. This is a practice that is most common in Italy, Serbia, France and Colombia. Of the transfers that involved a fee, 6.1% had an agent acting on behalf of the selling club as shown below:

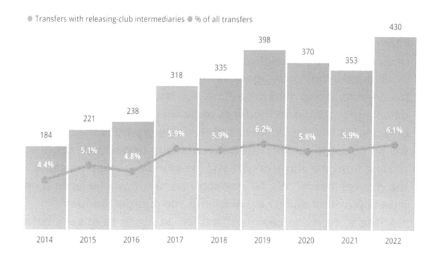

Source: FIFA Intermediary Report 2022

It is also encouraging for agents that the level of expenditure of clubs upon agents acting on their behalf whether buying or selling is returning the the financial levels pre-COVID-19-pandemic as shown below in USD:

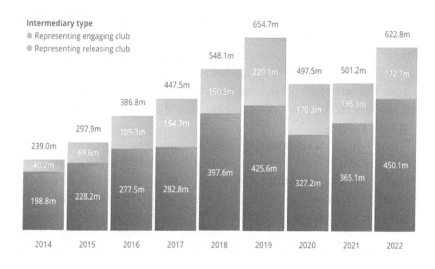

Source: FIFA Intermediary Report 2022

Expert's View: Toni Ortega

Real Betis Football Operations Director

"A transfer deal from a club's perspective has many considerations that must be taken into account by an agent (although they not always are). For an agent to work with a club in the long-term and for further opportunities as a trusted intermediary, you must show that you are thorough and professional and can see the perspective of the club in a negotiation.

In the beginning, an agent must ask themselves a few questions to understand and determine if the club is the best fit for the player's development and an opportunity to grow further (both for the player and agent). Will the player fit into the style of play of the club? How will he adapt to the city? How has the club traditionally dealt with players from the same origin? Will the club be a stepping stone for the player's future? Will he develop new skills? Will he learn a new style of play that could help him jump into a larger league?

Those are some key questions for an agent to answer before proposing a player to a club. In order to judge these factors accurately, the agent must understand the club's vision and management before starting a negotiation. Of course, the most important aspect is the sporting department of personnel; who are the key decision makers on players movements? Who is the manager/coach and how long have they been with the club? How qualified are the staff? Then there are also significant components such as the training facilities; the variety of nationalities in the squad; the historic performance of players from the same origin as the client and the compatibility of the player's best qualities with their teammates and the team's on-field structure. To have a better chance of impressing the club and eventually landing the deal, the agent needs to demonstrate that their client satisfies all of these questions sufficiently, which will indicate that they will be a success at the club.

As negotiations progress, it is also fundamental to understand how the squad is structured; the style of contracts; if there is a salary cap or similar; and what is the average salary paid in the league, to players in certain positions, of a certain level and relevant to where the club is positioned in the table. The majority of this information is not publicly available, and requires in-depth research and exploration on the part of the agent; acquiring the details from private conversations or by previous experience. Knowing these details will help agents act in good faith, be professional, and sustain a long term relationship with clubs. The football sector is relatively small, and business works in small circles. For example, whoever may be in front of you in a negotiation to buy a player, may be selling a player to you in the next negotiation. Hence, clubs appreciate honesty, transparency, and patience as desirable traits of an agent to build a long term and productive relationship with them. At the end, it is a marathon and not a sprint race that the best agents are aiming to win.

To conclude, an agent must treat all clubs as long-term partners and act in good faith. Negotiations and deals with people who clubs trust and know will conduct sufficient and professional due diligence on their own part, are far easier, efficient and often more successful than those that fall below this standard."

Summary

- Being an agent for a club is a unique and specialised area of being a football agent. There are several key steps to take and points to note:
- Remember that at the start, you are likely to be representing players so you must always prioritise their best interests.
- However, acting in a proper, efficient and trustworthy manner is likely to help you gain the respect of clubs and club officials which you can utilise in future.
- Aim to maintain the relationships and have an acute awareness of the footballing market that may allow you to identify a certain deal or manner in which you can offer your services to a club.
- On the back of strong relationships with club officials, clubs may seek your involvement in deals directly. It is then important to adapt your approach in order to best serve the interests of the club as a different type of client from a player.
- Even if you do not act on behalf of a club during your career as an agent, valuing the importance of relationships with club officials must still be a significant priority as they will help you in providing the best deals for your player clients.

Further Reading

- The Obstacle is the Way - Ryan Holiday

Chapter 14: Working with Coaches

*"By representing coaches at football clubs,
you will always have a link to that club"*

Introduction

Although this book centres around the player–agent relationship, the representation of other individuals within football is becoming increasingly pertinent and important. More and more top coaches, or managers as they are sometimes referred to, particularly in the UK, are receiving professional advice from intermediaries, with some specific agencies specialising in managerial representation. For example, Project B (the company that represents Jürgen Klopp, amongst others) showcases this new aspect of agency as they focus not on players, but those in management and board positions. Whilst the skills required to represent such clients are similar, there are some important differences to note.

Being the Agent of a Coach

Much like football players, coaches need professional representation. The majority of top coaches will have agents who are tasked similarly to player agents; namely to identify potential opportunities in the market and to make the deals materialise. Even though coaches are less likely to sign lucrative sponsorship deals, there are still opportunities to be successful through the contracts that they sign with clubs. Whereas with football players there are strict rules and regulations on representing them, there are actually no such fixed guidelines or practices that have to be adhered to with coaches. Currently, FIFA has no set guidelines for the services of agents to coaches. However, despite there being no fixed limit on commission, it is generally assumed that the agent is entitled to around 10% of the gross salary as a reward for their work on negotiating the contract. The likelihood is that representing coaches will soon be regulated as part of FIFA's ongoing reforms so it is an area that is important to follow if you are interested in representing such clients.

One of the most important areas where an agent can add value to a coach's career particularly is through media work. For coaches this is a vital area to master. Coaches are recruited based upon their reputation and often the public's perception of them. Generally, clubs are more lenient towards coaches that come across well in public-facing situations; they may get a few more games to redeem themselves whilst coaches that are not so strong in this area may be sacked without this opportunity. Therefore, it is a key responsibility as the agent to help your coach client to develop and improve their reputation. One way of doing this is to acquire the services of an independent expert that trains the coach in different successful methods of interview preparation and performance. Press conferences and interviews are the best opportunities for coaches to impress the club, the fans and the players and the value of them cannot be underestimated by you as the agent.

Ultimately, as with any client you work with, the role of the agent is to find and secure the best opportunities. For coaches, agents need to proactively seek possible opportunities for job interviews and offers in any market where the client could succeed and is willing to go to. A common question for this is when to go about seeking an interview for your client. Put simply, should you offer your client before the current manager is sacked but it is looking possible? Or do you offer the manager after they have already been sacked? In reality, there is no right answer that is applicable 100% of the time. It is more of a case by case solution. The agent ought to be proactive in finding and identifying clubs where there may soon be a managerial vacancy and then formulating how best to move forward to position their client as an attractive replacement. One distinguishing advantage that an agent can have for this situation is a strong relationship with the club. This can be enormously beneficial as you can obtain information regarding the club's stance on the current manager and consequently, you may be able to offer your client at an earlier and more appropriate time. This kind of club relationship can give you that vital edge over competitors.

Advantages of Representing a Coach

In addition to the negotiated commission, there are other major benefits as a result of being the agent of a football coach. If you represent the coach, it gives you the opportunity to utilise them as an important figure at the club to compliment the services you provide to your player clients. It is a more straightforward pathway into a new club for your players but should only be done if it is the right option for them rather than for convenience reasons.

This practice is one frequently capitalised upon by lots of agents, most successfully so by Jorge Mendes. He has acted as the registered intermediary for both the player and coach in many transfer negotiations at certain clubs. The most documented case for Mendes is Wolverhampton Wanderers which is now particularly well populated with Portuguese players after Mendes brought them to the club during the managerial stint of Nuno Espirito Santo who was also his client. Additionally, during José Mourinho's head coach role with various clubs many of Mendes' clients were brought into the squads. This included the likes of Diego Costa, Paula Ferreira and Ricardo Carvalho to Chelsea; Ricardo Quaresma to Inter Milan; and Angel Di Maria and Ricardo Carvalho to Real Madrid.

The bottom line is, by representing coaches at football clubs, you will always have a link to that club, even when they leave. Furthermore, this advantage is closely coupled with the fact that the coach (if you are their agent) can easily introduce you to other key employees at the club, which can strengthen your position if you already manage a player there. For example, if through the coach you can improve your relations with other important decision-makers and board members, it is more likely that your player would be treated favourably, perhaps in terms of getting picked for the team or when discussing a new contract.

Unfortunately, this also creates a potential issue. Often such a situation can be criticised as a conflict of interest if there are one or more players at a club that have the same agent as the coach. As mentioned, the coach will be significantly more likely to select the players of their agent and if this becomes public knowledge, it can lead to criticism of the coach and of you as the agent. Usually, a coach wants to win to keep their job and will pick the best side, but if they experience a bad run of form and the press and fans are looking for a problem to highlight that might be the root cause of the issue, selecting the players that are with the same agency can be a straightforward opportunity for them. One way to avoid this as the agent is to abstain from publicising your representation of the coach. Representing the client can be kept more private and discreet than if they were a player and this can be an advantage if a situation arises that could be questioned as a conflict of interest. If the fans of the club and even the press are not easily aware of you representing the coach, it is less identifiable as a problem. This can be a clever way of helping your client improve the longevity of a coaching role at a certain club.

A modern aspect of working with coaches is commercial potential. Previously this was non-existent but in more recent times, the most iconic coaches such as the likes of Jurgen Klopp, Jose Mourinho and Thomas Thuchel have their own commercial partnerships and brand endorsements from clothing to watches to shaving cream. This means that for agents, representing the world's best known coaches opens up another avenue for commission from commercial contracts, of which will also be 20%.

Young Youth Coaches

In modern football, young coaches are becoming increasingly used by top clubs around the world, and therefore it is important to try and establish good links and connections with these promising coaches. Usually, young coaches will start their career by taking charge of the lower youth teams between the ages of under-16's and under-18's, and slowly work their way to the U23 team or second team, depending on the club's system. It is sometimes the case that when the coach of the first team is sacked or leaves, the board may look to these coaches, who understand the set-up of the club well already and may have experienced success with the reserve team. They can be given the responsibility for the first team as perhaps a 'caretaker coach' to begin with but may be able to prove themselves worthy of the permanent role. This is the same for the assistant coach, who can also temporarily (and then permanently) fill the vacant managerial spot if they do not leave with the coach. Hence, it can be beneficial to have good relationships with young and promising coaches, as perhaps they will become the first team coach in the future and you will represent them.

Expert's View: Harun Arslan

*Owner, ARP Sportmarketing GmbH, agent of
Joachim Lowe and Hansi Flick*

"At first glance you may think that there aren't really any significant differences between representing a player and a club employee (such as a coach, coach, or director). After all, you treat both with importance as your client, and both entail work such as contractual matters and monetary terms. Whilst this is correct, there are some key distinctions that should be made.

Firstly, you have to take into consideration the age of the client. For a player (especially if they are young), the agent often takes up the role of an additional parent, whereas with a coach you ought to expect a completely different dynamic. Coaches are generally experienced personalities, and top-level coaches work in a highly complex environment. A coach is expected to always stay focused, and every single word or action performed reflects on the club that they are contracted to. Although it is in the interest of the club to protect their employees, the relationship with an agent carries a special function. You act with the necessary distance to give neutral advice in all circumstances and provide clarity in difficult situations, making tough decisions easier. In many ways, the agent of a club employee is like a good friend – you are there to provide unbiased support with the best intentions.

In addition to making sure your client gives off a 'good image' to the public, working in this area of football will subject you to important contractual and career decisions, as well as establishing a strong network to be utilised in the future. In the current game, on-pitch failure usually leads to the dismissal of coaches, managers and other club employees, thus making your job exceedingly important."

Summary

- Although it may not seem as rewarding or lavish as being the agent of a high-profile football player, representing senior club officials can be greatly advantageous as they often open doors and allow you access to the team's transfer dealings.

- Many agents (and agencies) opt for a mix between players and coaches in order to get the benefits of being close to both types of client. You need to learn the slight variations in skills and demands of each different role and be able to provide a professional service to your coach clients as well as the players if you choose to represent both.
- You must always be aware of the intentions of coaches and officials. They are likely to have 'closed- door' relationships with many intermediaries in the hope of getting the best possible deals for themselves. Your network, as always, is key.

Chapter 15: The Art of a Transfer

"No two deals are ever the same"

Introduction

It is likely not a surprise that a book on how to become a football agent has a chapter dedicated to transfers and the intricacies, processes and challenges that come with them. For now, we will look solely at permanent transfers. In simple terms, this is where the buying club will pay a 'transfer fee' to the selling club and the player will change employer. The following chapter will consider variations of this in loans and free agent agreements.

The important question for the purpose of this book and for you as the reader is where exactly the agent fits into the transfer and what roles and responsibilities they are tasked with. An agent, or agents, is or are a necessary piece of the transfer puzzle. More often than not, a transfer and agreement cannot take place without the valuable input of an agent to mediate and negotiate the situation until a deal is reached. Whilst the public may only see the end product and a nice photo of the player signing a contract and posing with the shirt of their new club, it is the work behind the scenes that is important and that we will cover in this chapter.

Preparation for the Window

Football agents often joke that the transfer window has no start and no end. Although the dates set by the national associations give you the actual dates at which transfers must be finalised, the preparatory work and negotiations take place well before completion date and often before the transfer window has even begun. It is rare that any deal (even if it is completed towards the end of the window) hasn't been the subject of talks between the agent of the player and representatives of the club for weeks, if not months.

It is crucial for you as the agent to constantly monitor the needs of clubs in case a player you represent (or could obtain a mandate for) fits the requirements and criteria. An important part of being an agent is understanding the market well and knowing which clubs might look for specific players and you are capable of finding and representing the right candidate. If you can build a reputation with clubs of being an agent who only offers meaningful options rather than anyone and everyone, you are much more likely to experience success.

Preparatory research can simply start from looking up when key players are 'out of contract' or knowing which teams are lacking personnel in certain areas of the pitch and in different positions. Additionally, you should be aware of the financial situation of the club and how much they are likely to be willing to spend on a transfer and player wages.

A personal example of this for Erkut was in 2016 when he brokered the deal for Shkodran Mustafi to transfer from Valencia to Arsenal for €41million. This was the outcome of originally meeting the father at the 2014 Brazilian World Cup. We developed a good relationship which continued after the tournament. Through Özil, he also had a good relationship with the Arsenal hierarchy and eventually a fantastic opportunity opened up. Two centre-backs were injured at once and he was in a position to be able to approach them regarding Mustafi. He met with Arsenal in San Jose and then with Valencia twice once they had expressed meaningful interest. Valencia originally said no until Arsenal produced an amazing offer that they could not refuse. This all came from the networking he had done combined with the preparation and proactiveness in spotting and capitalising upon an opportunity.

Remember, transfer windows can often be the pinnacle of the work that you have been putting in all year round so their importance must not be underestimated. However, you must remember not to rush, be impatient or be forced into any deal, and always keep in close contact with clients as your top priority is to understand what they want out of it.

The table below outlines the dates for the 2022/23 transfer windows that occur in each major national association and the kind of heights these deals may reach. Note that these dates are subject to change each year but will usually be around the same:

Country	Pre-season window	Mid-season window	Record transfer(s) (€million)
England (FA)			Jack Grealish: €118m

	10th June → 1st September	1st January → 31st January	Romelu Lukaku: €113m
			Paul Pogba: €105m
Germany (DFB)	1st July → 1st September	1st January → 31st January	Lucas Hernández: €80m
			Matthijs de Ligt: €67
France (FFF)	1st July → 1st September	1st January → 31st January	Neymar: €222m
			Kylian Mbappé: €180m
Spain (RFEF)	1st July → 1st September	2nd January → 31st January	Ousmane Dembélé: €140m
			Philippe Coutinho: €135m
			João Félix: €127m
			Antoine Griezmann: €120m
Italy (FIGC)	1st July → 1st September	2nd January → 31st January	Cristiano Ronaldo: €117m
			Gonzalo Higuain: €90m
Portugal (FPF)	1st July → 1st September	3rd January → 2nd February	Darwin Núñez: €34m
			Raúl Jiménez: €22m
Netherlands (KNVB)	9th June → 31st August	3rd January → 31st January	Steven Bergwijn: €31m
			Calvin Bassey: €23m
			Sébastien Haller: €23m
United States of America (USSF)	31st January → 24th April	7th July → 4th August	Gonzalo Martínez: €15m
			Thiago Almada: €15m
Turkey (TFF)	17th June → 8th September	12th January → 8th February	Jardel: €17m
			Dani Güiza: €14m
China (CFA)	1st July → 31st August	15th March → 15th April	Oscar: €60m
			Hulk: €56m

Russia (FUR)	1st July → 8th September	26th January → 22nd February	Malcolm: €40m
Australia (FFA)	22nd June → 13th September	12th January → 8th February	Riley McGree: €1m
			Shane Smeltz: €1m
Argentina	16th May → 7th August	23rd January → 22nd February	Lucas Pratto: €11.5m
Brazil	19th January → 12th April	18th July → 15th August	Gabriel Barbosa: €17.5m
			Alexandre Pato: €15m

Source: Transfermarkt (correct as of November 2022)

Note: these exact dates may vary each season but will usually be around a similar time.

A final point on preparation is to ensure that 'trusted relationships' are in place. These are key to successful transfers and hence, it is important to establish meaningful relationships with the board of clubs before the windows open. If the parties are able to trust you, they are more likely to find agreement with you for your player than with any random agent.

The Strategy of the Agent

Your understanding of your clients intentions and desires are vital in cultivating your plans as the agent in seeking opportunities. These can be outlined into four categories:

1. **Your client wants to leave:** the reasons for this can vary. The most common motivations behind seeking a transfer away from a club include falling out with the coach; not receiving enough playing time; simply wanting a new challenge; or seeking higher wages. It then becomes your duty to find a new club that fits in with what the player has in mind. Of course, it is rare to find a team that perfectly matches your client's expectations in terms of geographical location, league position, etc. and who are also in a financial position

to make the dream a reality – but this is where you show your worth!

2. **Your client's team wants to sell:** this results in a very similar situation to the above scenario, as you'll again be looking for a new club for your client. However, in this type of situation, several issues may arise. It is important to protect your client from being alienated by their current club whilst they are still there, despite knowing that the club wishes to sell them.

    a. The decision should not be taken personally; it is just football, and your player is being gifted an exciting opportunity to play elsewhere. The worst thing to do would be to breach their current contract and begin to underperform; this only makes a positive and desirable transfer more difficult to find. Remember as well, if the player is in their last 18 months of their contract, the club may feel pressured into selling them as it is the last opportunity to make good money from a transfer fee for them. Your bargaining power in this case is stronger as it is the club who wants to sell. Using this to your advantage can reduce the transfer fee for the player so that more clubs would be interested in buying them or they may even give the player a payout for their departure. Timing is always important in negotiations but in this case time is on your side more than ever so should be used wisely.

3. **Another club wants to buy your client:** you should always present your player with the offers that are proposed for them, as they have a right to know. Often as the registered agent of a player, representatives from the buying club will seek to contact you and alert you to their intentions to buy your client. This may also give rise to another opportunity for you to act on behalf of the buying club if they trust you enough and you can make the deal happen for them.

    a. The role of the agent is vital in this situation as you are the 'middleman' or the broker between all the parties. Although the clubs will sometimes not directly involve you for negotiations between themselves, you are the direct line of communication as the mediator for the deal and you need to gauge from each party where there is room for manoeuvre and compromise and adjust accordingly.

4. **Being proactive in promoting your player:** clubs around the footballing market should already know who your player is by the time you are able to offer them. It is important to use your network and your contacts to offer annual or even monthly updates on the success and performances of your client. This will mean that the club already knows that they could be a potential recruitment target for them and when the time comes, offering the client to them will not come as a surprise as a result of your proactivity.

Regardless of which of these four categories your client fits into, it is imperative that you communicate everything with them. You should develop a strategy based upon their needs and wants and ensure they are happy with the way you are approaching each situation.

Role of the Agent in a Transfer Agreement

Simply put, agents are fundamentally pivotal to the transfer process. You are the 'middle-man' between all parties and the deal relies on you to some extent. When a consensus has been reached by the buying and selling clubs over the exchange of the player, your role is to try and negotiate the nuances of the deal and get it over the line.

Perhaps the most common stumbling point for a permanent deal is the transfer fee. Your role is to structure the deal in a manner that appears favourable to both sides. They need to feel as though they are benefitting from the agreement that is being made. This is where negotiation skills and being able to read situations well is key. You need to understand and calculate the 'reasonable figure' that the buying club has in mind, and what the selling club would accept as a bottom line. As mentioned above, this negotiation regarding the transfer fee will generally take place between the clubs and you are not directly involved beyond the role of a mediator.

More often than not, an individual transfer is part of a much wider set of deals that are taking place. If a club is losing one of their top strikers because they want to leave, then it is likely that they will have targets in mind to replace him plus some spare budget that they will receive from selling their top striker. Consequently, they would want to ensure that any possible incomings are probable before committing to a sale. It is important to be aware of other ongoings in the clubs and it will help you judge the position they are in to sign your client. Put simply in a practical example, if club X has just signed a 24-year-old centre forward on a 5-year contract for a transfer fee of €50 million as the highest paid player in their squad to lead their front line ahead of two other uninjured top strikers already at the club, they are unlikely to be willing to spend a significant fee on your 27-year-old client that plays in the same position.

In general, all transfers are different; scenarios vary from league to league and club to league. Hence, whilst preparation is a non-negotiable, much of the process is also about being able to adapt to situations quickly and spot the opportunities as and when they arise. There will be several times where the deal looks almost certain to have fallen through, but the smallest event could re-energise talks, and you have to be ready for this. Agency is an industry where the cliche 'expect the unexpected' should not be overlooked.

A point to note here is that if a club seems to be ignoring your calls or efforts at communicating, remain professional and patient. Especially during transfer windows, sporting directors and other board members can be very busy and it can be a challenge to stay in constant dialogue with them. Try secondary emails and perhaps a message inquiring when may be a good time to speak. Be persistent but not overly pushy to the point where you can become annoying.

Mandates

Everything discussed thus far is in relation to you as the agent in transfer negotiations with a client that you exclusively represent (as signified by a Representation Contract – see Chapter 21). However, you can also be involved in transfers for players that you don't work with every day, or you may not even know! The players themselves, their agents or a contact of theirs may contact you if they believe your network and reputation may help them get a deal. If you are interested then you are able to sign a mandate which allows you to represent the player for a specified period of time and often in a restricted jurisdiction. A mandate is simply contract giving authorisation for an agent to represent the player, given their current agent or, if they do not have an agent, then the player themselves. This is usually done if an agent or you may need help from a 'local' agent with better connections at certain clubs or in certain markets. Mandates can take the following forms:

1. **Mandate from another player/agent:** depending on what exactly was agreed, a mandate means that you would handle just the player's transfer for the stated period of time (normally one transfer window) to a certain league, club or country. This is beneficial for both you and the full-time agent of the player. Firstly, it gives you an opportunity to make a deal happen that you wouldn't otherwise have had, whilst not having the workload of looking after the player to a full extent. It is also advantageous for the player and their agent because they may not have the network or connections to clubs to make a transfer possible. Mandates mean the deal can still occur without them necessarily being at the forefront of negotiations. In these deals, the commission is normally split as specified on the mandate agreement itself. This is normally a 50% direct split which is paid from the club to the agent but is subject to change. These deals are important to be aware of and can give rise to many additional opportunities for you as the agent.

2. **Mandate from a club:** whilst these types of arrangements are rarely disclosed to the public, clubs will have certain agents they trust and will seek out to help them with particular deals. Essentially, the club would give you a mandate for a target; often either a specified player or region/league, and there would be a split in commission with the player's full-time agent if you can help the deal materialise. Be aware that in modern football, the majority of clubs have someone appointed as Director of Football which reduces the frequency of such mandates.

Overall, mandates are certainly a worthwhile consideration for an agent. An up-and-coming agent and player may agree on a mandate for a transfer as a trial period for future representation, as it is sometimes thought of as a test of the ability of an agent. If this happens to you, make sure you maximise the opportunity as it can set your career on the right path from the very beginning. However, an important point to note on the matter of mandates is that they are often a risky commitment for an agent. Our advice for mandates is to only take one on if there is a high probability of completing the deal. It may not be worth the risk of damaging your reputation if you fail to make the deal materialise as you had promised. Don't go fishing for mandate opportunities, make sure you are selective as to which ones offer reasonable chances of success.

A point of caution for mandates is, of course, the risk of reputation damage to yourself as an agent. You may have very little control over the player and in extreme circumstances, after long periods of negotiation and work, the player may suddenly opt for a different option that you didn't even realise was a possibility or in the works. But if it is your own client that you have more control over, mandates can be more useful and secure as you can help your client find opportunities in markets where your own connections are not as strong.

Transfer Fee

When reading about transfers in the news or on social media, it may be reported that a footballer leaves, for example, for a fee of €100million. Of course, that's a substantial sum of money but, despite how it is reported, transfers aren't as simple as just one club sending over a lump sum of money in exchange for a signature. Newspaper headlines and easy-to-read reports do not consider the complex intricacies of a transfer such as performance-based add-ons, instalments and wage packages. For an agent, however, these are the important parts to know and understand how transfer fees are structured:

1. **Performance-based add-ons:** if player 'X' moved from club 'Y' to club 'Z' for an agreed €100 million, this does not necessarily mean that fee is guaranteed to be paid but is usually stated as the maximum figure of what it could reach. A reasonable percentage of the fee is likely to be subject to the performance of the player (i.e. number of appearances, goals, personal accolades, etc.) or the performance of the club (promotion, relegation, league position, etc.), meaning the final fee can vary significantly. You may hear pundits describing this as "signing player A for an initial fee of €85million which could rise to €100million".

    o   An example of this may be read in the employment contract as follows:

- In further consideration of the transfer of the player's registration to Manchester United, Manchester United also agrees to pay to AS Monaco, subject to and in accordance with the terms hereof, the following contingent sums:
- The one-time sum of €10.000.000 (ten million euros) in the event that the player scores 25 (twenty five) goals in First Team Competitive Matches for Manchester United during the period he is under contract with Manchester United.

2. **Instalments:** nearly all transfer fees are exchanged over an extended period of time rather than having the large fee paid at once. Using the same transfer structure as above, perhaps only 50% of €100 million is paid immediately upon completion. On the first anniversary of the deal, another 25% may be transferred, and the same again on the second anniversary. This makes financial balancing and protecting stability easier for clubs.

3. **Wages:** if a club is willing to pay a vast sum like €100 million, then clearly it is an elite player in question. Newspaper reports rarely refer to the wages the players will earn as part of the overall package that club 'Z' (the buying club) will pay. If player 'X' is to receive a weekly wage of €150,000 on a four-year contract, then this is an additional €31.2million that club 'Z' is spending as part of the overall deal. This adds on essentially another third of the transfer fee, making for a total investment of €131.2 million. The agent needs to consider the wider implications and overall asking expenditure of the buying club when assessing if the deal is worth pursuing.

4. **USA Transfer packages:** The MLS differs from other leagues when it comes to finances. When recruiting, clubs will have a 'transfer package' in mind. They will have budgets for each position. For example, club A may be looking for a left back for $500,000 and a right wing for $750,000. Importantly, this 'package' includes the transfer fee itself, the player's wages and the agent's fees. In order to obtain this information, you

need to have a network in place that you can utilise to find out which clubs need which positions and their budgets.

An important point to consider is also the timing of the transfer which will influence the fee. The following graph which was included in a recent FIFA transfer report shows the percentage of transfers that take place for a particular fee based upon the time before the end of the transfer window. This shows that the highest proportion of transfers takes place early in a transfer window and you will need to be aware of the spike that also takes place towards Deadline Day:

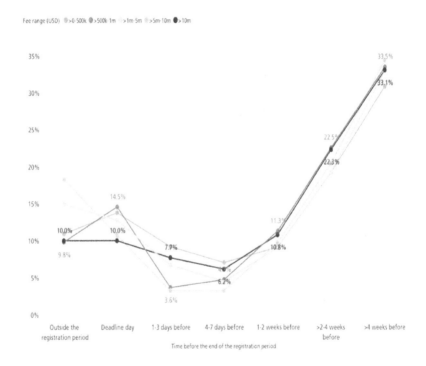

Source: FIFA 2020

There is no escaping the reality that transfers are complex business deals. *Not* included in the pay structure we have mentioned so far is what you would earn as the agent. Remember, although the Representation Contract is between player and agent, it is nearly always the case that the club ends up paying the agent their commission fee (as shown in the table below). A good agent will never seek to pursue a deal with the club who simply offers the highest agent commission. Instead, the agent finds the best option for the client, negotiates the transfer fee, finds the right personal terms for the player; and then finally, will agree upon their own commission. The player's interests are always prioritised. The right time to negotiate your commission differs and we discuss further in chapter 17. However, it is an important factor as too late may mean you either lose out on commission or the deal breaks down because of your commission demand whilst requesting it too early can upset the club if they feel you are only interested in your own economic benefit.

Spending on _club_ intermediary commissions in 2021 ($USD):

Country	Buying club (million)	Selling club (million)	Total (million)
England	118.8	14.5	133.3
Italy	55.6	17.8	73.5
Portugal	23.8	5.5	29.3
Germany	63.8	20.5	84.3
Spain	28.4	6.4	34.8
France	11	19.3	30.3
Netherlands	1.4	14.2	15.6
Russia	12.8	0	12.8
Turkey	8.6	1	9.6

Source: FIFA TMS – Intermediaries in International Transfers (2021 edition)

Training Compensation and Solidarity Payments/Contributions

Article 20 of the FIFA Regulations of the Status and Transfer of Players (RSTP) states that:

"Training compensation shall be paid to a player's training club(s): (1) when a player signs his first contract as a professional, and (2) each time a professional is transferred until the end of the season of his 23rd birthday. The obligation to pay training compensation arises whether the transfer takes place during or at the end of the player's contract. The provisions concerning training compensation are set out in Annexe 4 of these regulations." (FIFA)

For agents, training compensation is something that you must understand as it is relevant when discussing transfer fees and will need to be accounted for in negotiations if your player is under 23 years of age. For the ages of 12-15, the training club will be owed a sum per year at the rate of a category 4 club. However, for the ages of 15 to 21, the training compensation owed depends upon the category of the club which trained your player. You need to learn and understanding the categorisation of training compensation clubs as outlined below:

Confederation	Category I	Category II	Category III	Category IV
AFC		$40,000	$10,000	$2,000
CAF		$30,000	$10,000	$2,000
CONCACAF		$40,000	$10,000	$2,000
CONMEBOL	$50,000	$30,000	$10,000	$2,000
OFC		$30,000	$10,000	$2,000
UEFA	€90,000	€60,000	€30,000	€10,000

Source: theplayersagent

Example: Vinicius Jr's move from Flamengo to Real Madrid

1. From the age of 10, Vinicius Jr. was an academy player for Flamengo before making his professional debut aged 17 for his youth club in the Brazilian top flight.
2. At 17, in theory, he was signed by Real Madrid which in reality didn't come into effect until he was 18 – the minimum age for an international transfer.

3. For the time spent coaching Vinicius since the age of 12, they could also claim training compensation. In Serie Á, a category 1 division, this was a sum of $50,000 per year of training from the age of 15, and $2,000 per year from the age of 12-15 ($6,000), as per the category 4 requirements. This results in an additional $156,000 that was owed to Flamengo as part of the deal.
4. This fee is due within 30 days of Vinicius registering as a Real Madrid player. Any disputes are resolved by the Court of Arbitration for Sport (CAS) in their Dispute Resolution Chamber (DRC).

There are also three instances where training compensation is not due which you may need to be aware of:

1. If the contract with the selling club has been terminated without a just cause
2. If the player is moving to a category 4 club from a higher category
3. If they reacquire amateur status as a result of the transfer

These scenarios nullify the payable transfer compensation.

Whilst solidarity payments are required to serve a similar purpose, there are distinct differences with training compensation. Firstly, solidarity contributions are calculated for the ages of 12 to 23 rather than until 21. The solidarity payment is also only relevant if a transfer fee has been paid. In other words, a free agent that is signed will not entail a solidarity contribution. However, if a transfer fee is paid, 5% of the overall fee will be due in proportion to the club or clubs for which the player played during their 12-23 'youth development' stage. It is likely that in the new agent exam, FIFA could ask a question which gives a scenario of a player moving between a few clubs during these years and hence will require you to calculate how the 5% is distributed and the sum of money that each club is owed.

The key points to note for solidarity contributions is that between the ages of 12 and 15, the club(s) will be owed 0.25% of the overall transfer fee per year. From thereafter, for the eight years up until the age of 23, the club(s) will be owed 0.5% of the overall transfer fee for each year the player was with them.

Training compensation and the solidarity payments are mechanisms that are used to ensure that the club which has trained the player during their youth development is adequately benefiting financially from their future success.

The Personal Side of a Transfer

If one considers football to be like any other profession, then transferring clubs (like switching jobs) can require moving to another city or even country and is a major decision and significant change to a player's lifestyle. If this is the case, then multiple things need to be taken into consideration, especially if the player does have to go abroad. Will your client have to learn a new language? Should they buy or rent a new house? What is their personal/family situation? Will their family come with them? Do they need a work permit? Do they need a new car?

All these questions and more are necessary to consider carefully. Changing teams (even if you don't end up moving to a new country) is an important and often challenging phase in anybody's life. In order to overcome the anxieties or challenges that may be faced, having a good relationship with your player and their club is crucial. The overwhelming majority of top clubs will have people in place to help out incoming players that are new to the area and are labelled as 'player care' or 'player welfare' officers. They will help settle them into the region, learn the language if necessary, and make sure they are looked after. However, the agent still plays a role in this process. It is also your duty to safeguard your client and guarantee their well-being and comfort. Making sure you yourself speak the language of the country that your client is playing in can be very important. If your player needs your guidance or assistance you should be able to provide it adequately, or for particular specialist requests, be able to outsource help to professionals.

Similarly, given your duty to help your player, it is also important to ensure their family's needs are looked after. Depending on what relationships your client has, relatives may choose to move with them to help also settle them in. As the agent, your awareness of the importance of the client's family will help you produce the best outcomes for your player and accelerate their settledness in a new club.

A helpful method we would suggest using during the decision making process of which clubs may be the best options for your client is to use a three pillar system outlined below:

1. **Sporting factors:** this refers to details regarding the playing time they are likely to have at the club; their suitability to the league and the style of football; the coach they will play under; and the club's infrastructure, development and future aspirations and strategic plan.
2. **Social factors:** this is the more personal side that is concerned with lifestyle changes such as where the client would live, how far from home they will be, the quality of life for them and their family and of course things like language, culture and general lifestyle are worth considering, especially if it is an international transfer.
3. **Economic factors:** no transfer would happen without considering the financial implications of the offer. This pillar emphasises the attractiveness of an option based upon salary, bonuses and other important financial considerations.

An example of how this may look in practice:

The example of how this system can be utilised in a real life case is outlined below for Mesut Özil's move to Fenerbahce:

Sporting	Social	Economic
He was likely to have a high proportion of playing minutes The coaches, players and fans knew him well The style of football was something Mesut was going to be able to easily adapt to	Mesut was a childhood fan of Fenerbahce It was always his dream to return there, it was a fan decision made with his heart With a few years left in his career it was the best time to fulfil his dream	It was less money than other offers but the money was not important, social factors outweighed this

The 2021 Transfer Landscape:

Country	Incoming transfers	Outgoing transfers	Spending ($ M)	Receipts ($ M)
England (FA)	784	885	1,386.2	548.8
Germany (DFB)	448	476	451.9	523.0
France (FFF)	405	570	511.8	543.3
Spain (RFEF)	581	686	347.8	342.4
Italy (FIGC)	406	457	667.7	540.4

Source: FIFA TMS Big 5 Transfer Window Analysis for 2021

This means that for agents there are various ways to be involved in this high-value and high-volume occurrence of transfers. We will look into the details of this for agents representing the clubs in chapter 13 but there is also a high prevalence of agents acting on behalf of the player, hence they are known as 'player agents'. The graphic below shows the involvement, in a proportion of all transfers, of agents in relation to the salaries of the player demonstrating that player agents are more frequently used in transfers with higher player salaries:

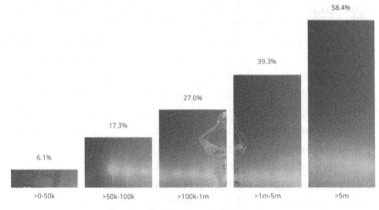

Player's total fixed remuneration (USD)

Source: FIFA Intermediary Report 2022

Expert's View: Nick Robinson

Founder and CEO of International Sports Consulting

"The global football calendar has evolved in such a way that there's a transfer window open in the major leagues for 8 out of 12 months of the year. Understanding the nuance of these windows is important to increasing your chances of being successful. For example, the January window in England tends to revolve around clubs who are conceding too many goals looking to add players to sure up their defence, or, if they're not scoring enough, looking to add players with a high goal scoring or assist ratio; it is generally not the window where clubs add "squad players", or players with future potential.

Similarly, clubs will look for players who can hit the ground running, and metrics currently considered by many clubs to increase the chances of this happening are a). previous or current experience of playing in the league (reduces the adaptation period) and b). that they are currently playing well (scoring and with no recent injury record). Finding these profiles, that are an improvement on their current squad, and at affordable levels (consider also that clubs tend to have spent their budget in the summer window, few have the foresight or financial wherewithal to hold back allocation for the January window) can be difficult, so clubs increasingly look to the loan market for the solution, hoping to find the right fit for their club.

With a scarcity in suitable profiles, many clubs tend to be after the same player during this window, giving the agent an advantageous negotiating position. A few seasons ago, we came very close to negotiating a transfer to Liverpool FC on deadline day in the summer transfer window, which ended up not happening for various reasons; but in the early part of that season Liverpool weren't scoring enough goals and it was clear they needed to come back in for our player. A deal was agreed in principle between both clubs and the player by the beginning of November, and the player officially signed on the morning of the 1st January.

Contrast this high-tempo, immediate solution orientated agenda with the USA winter transfer window for example, which currently opens on the 31st January and stays open the 24th April. This is their main off season window and the clubs are doing the majority of their business for the season during this period. This is akin to the European summer window and is less about immediate fixes, clubs are looking to make a broader spectrum of additions to the squad during this period, some starters and others cover players, and are open to a few more unproven or untested options which would be considered to carry a higher element of risk. Understanding all of these different contributing factors and entering the mindset of clubs will help an agent gain mastery over the art of a transfer."

Summary

- This chapter has shown that permanent transfers are complex and an agent needs to consider many factors and facets in progressing deals towards completion.
- You have to be smart, shrewd and professional at all times when dealing with a transfer – if you have to, use your network to source other trustworthy agents or lawyers to help you.
- Remember, the best type of agents will see out a transfer from beginning to end – making sure that all parties can benefit, and maintaining the best of relationships even with the club that your player has departed from and even if your commission is not as high as you would like. The main emphasis is placed upon finding the best deal for the client.
- Following the market and endlessly updating your knowledge of each relevant country will help you spot the best opportunities for transfers and how you may be able to be involved. Reading material on Transfermarkt and other forums provides priceless insights into these markets.

Further Reading

- Done Deal - Daniel Geey
- Training Compensation for football transfers blog: https://erkutsogut.com/training-compensation-in-football/

Chapter 16: Loans and 'Free Agents'

"Think about the bigger picture"

Introduction

Whilst permanent transfers were covered in the previous chapter, two other types of common deals have yet to be properly addressed – loans and 'free agents'. Agents require knowledge of both of these if they are to succeed in the industry.

What is a Loan?

A loan is the temporary transfer of a player from one club to another. Such deals are so popular that some clubs (like Chelsea) have their own loan department where people are employed just to look after the loaned players and visit them during the season in order to check their development. A loan can vary in length as long as they meet the FIFA regulations and just depends on what the two clubs agree on, however, they are normally for the duration of the season (or for the second half of a season). It is very common for the 'parent club' to ask for either a contribution of the wages of the player, or for a sum of money for the duration of the loan time. Both of these scenarios would require you as the agent to be active in the negotiations. Lots of teams have a 'feeder club' in another country in which they loan younger or unused players to. Well-known examples of this include Chelsea's former relationship with Vitesse as the owners were close friends, and Manchester City's relationship with other members of the 'City Football Group'.

There are specific rules and regulations around loans in different national associations and across wider jurisdictions by FIFA or other governing bodies. For example, recently UEFA have implemented measures which restrict the number of loaned players a club can sign and loan out at any one time. This has been devised to try and prevent the wealthier clubs hoarding players although it has affected the structure and transfer system which clubs had previously relied upon. As an agent, it is important to be aware of any regulations regarding loans and any changes that occur.

Below, the most important new FIFA loan regulations are outlined:

- A loan can only be for a maximum of one year as must be fully defined and agreed upon within a written contract regarding the duration of the loan and the financial conditions.
- The loan must however be for a minimum of at least the period between two transfer windows and no shorter.
- Sub-loaning is now prohibited. This is where a player is already loaned to a club and is then loaned out again. This avoids complex situations and contractual difficulties.
- Under the new regulations, clubs are prevented from loaning in more than three players from a single origin club and consequently, can also not loan out more than three players to one club. For example, if two clubs have a particularly strong relationship and there is a common pattern of loan moves between them, this new rule stipulates that only three players can now move in one direction and no more.
- During the 2022/23 season, a club can loan out a maximum of eight players and this number will be reduced further by one player each season. Put simply, FIFA have set this regulation so that a maximum of six players will be allowed out on loan in the 2024/25 season. The aim of this is to promote competitiveness, youth player development and prevent player hoarding by certain clubs that have a reputation of having a large squad and are loaning out players year after year. For example, Chelsea are the most publicised example of this; often loaning out around 20 players every season so this may have a substantial effect on such clubs.
- The only players that are exempt from these new regulations are players aged 21 and younger and those that have been trained through the youth academy system at the club. The limitations do not apply to them to prevent restriction of free movement.

Advantages of Loans

From the perspective of a player and agent, loans can be of great use and benefit:

1. **Playing time:** if your client is given more playing time at another club, it could showcase their potential worth for the 'parent club' in the future, or increase their transfer value if you are looking for a permanent move elsewhere.
2. **International fixture lists:** using the USA's MLS (Major League Soccer) as an example, the season starts at completely different times to that of Europe, and therefore players can be loaned from the USA to Europe during their 'off-season'. A well-known example of this is Landon Donovan who, whilst at the LA Galaxy, was loaned to Bayern Munich and Everton whilst the MLS was inactive. This was beneficial for both LA Galaxy as it meant he stayed fit as well as Bayern Munich and Everton as he was a good on-pitch option to have. Moreover, for the player (and thus agent) it meant that Donovan became more a household name across Europe, increasing not only his footballing value and experiences, but in addition the scope for commercial deals too given his more global notability.

Options and Obligations to Buy

The supposed middle ground between a loan and permanent deal is often deemed to be the 'option to buy clause'. This involves a club agreeing to loan a player for a certain amount of time, with an agreement also being in place for a full transfer. This strategy is becoming more common for clubs as they can test the player out, without having the obligation of a permanent deal. Recent examples of this can be found with top European players, such as James Rodríguez (Real Madrid and Bayern Munich) and Douglas Costa (Bayern Munich and Juventus). Sometimes whether or not the full transfer takes place is down to appearance and performance-based clauses that were initially agreed – these would have been made clear, and it is for you as the agent to be involved in the deal-making process.

This method of transfer has also been adapted in recent transfer windows too. The agreement between Monaco and Paris Saint-Germain for Kylian Mbappé has been labelled as an 'obligation to buy' rather than an 'option to buy', with the latter club supposedly required to follow through with the deal after the loan period has come to an end. Either way, an agent must be aware about the possible use of both methods and the reasons for each. This often relates to factors such as cash problems, financial fair play and transfer limitations.

'Free Agents'

Free agency grants players the ability to sign with another club in what is known as a 'free' or 'Bosman' transfer. In other words, the buying club is not under any obligation to compensate the player's former club with a transfer fee. The signature of the player is instead obtained simply by agreeing personal terms such as wages, bonuses and other contract clauses. These are agreed upon solely in the best interests of the player and their agreeability with the contract proposed, it does not involve negotiation nor any other business with their former club.

As a player nears a state of free agency, they are able to begin to discuss options with prospective clubs once there is less than six months remaining on their current contract (although this time period can alter slightly in different national association regulations). If their current club has failed to find agreeable renewable terms with the player or are likely to release them, the player and his agent will seek free transfer opportunities. The agent is very important here to be able to understand and utilise the powerful position of the player whilst adhering to regulations.

This can be an exciting and lucrative time for the player as their wages and bonuses are likely to be higher as the signing club is not burdened or restricted by having to also pay high transfer fees. This allows the club financial freedom to attract the player by offering high salaries and the signing-on bonus is often higher than a typical figure that is invested into a player which the club has paid for the transfer of. We will discuss the impact of this in greater detail below.

For the current club, once a player enters the last year or so of their contract, their power decreases and they are in a difficult situation. They will only have one or two more windows where they are able to sell the player before they become a free agent and every other club will be aware of this too. Their negotiation and bargaining stance is weakened and this is accentuated if the player is likely to try to run down their contract to become a free agent and seek a higher salary and signing-on bonus. As the agent, you can help your player achieve this position but also need to be aware that it may damage relationships between the club and the player and maybe with you too. In some cases, clubs may refuse to play a player who is rejecting their attempts to offer contract extensions and this may make them less attractive for a future club if they have lacked game time. However, this is usually a safe approach if the client is a high-profile player that the club is unlikely to be able to omit from their squad without public objection from fans and the press. Your role as the agent is to be aware of the power you and your client can hold in this situation. Hopefully, the simple chart below demonstrates the point we are making here:

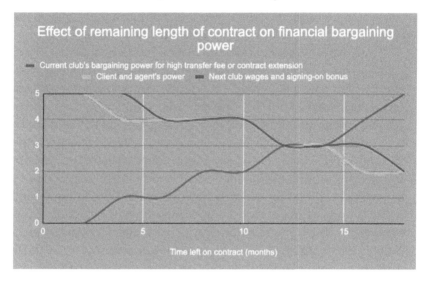

Free agents can also be signed outside of a transfer window in some national associations. This was the case in the recent signing of ex-Spain striker Diego Costa by Wolverhampton Wanderers in the English Premier League. Despite the English transfer window being closed, Wolves were able to sign Costa as he was a free agent. They benefited from this rule greatly having lost their two frontline forwards to injury in the previous week, they were still able to seek a top-level replacement from the market of 'free agents'. This rule means that players that are released from clubs are not stuck without opportunities until the window reopens and can still try to find a new contract elsewhere.

An important point on this to be aware of is that not *all* national associations permit signing free agents outside of a window. Although this can cause difficulty with restriction of trade laws, some countries such as Germany have prohibited registering and playing free agents after the winter transfer window and in Turkey you cannot register free agents at all outside of the transfer windows;

whilst in other countries it is possible. This defines the options that are available to you as the agent when seeking opportunities for your player if they are a free agent outside of a transfer window.

The Bosman Ruling

This is something that, as an agent, you will hear being referred to often. It is a significant legal case in football history and one that you would be expected to be aware of. For those that haven't, the Bosman Rule, and the case behind it are explained below.

In 1995, the European Court of Justice made a landmark ruling following a court case involving a little-known Belgian midfielder and a small club called RFC Liege. For a legal case and judgement that pitted two minor parties against one another, it had major consequences that are still felt within the modern football era today.

The case instigated the creation of brand new terminology in the football world; namely 'free agency' and 'free transfers'. The concept of free transfers and free agency have become commonplace since the ruling. It is vital for an agent to understand the impact, both positive and negative, that it has had upon the beautiful game. Importantly for our understanding of why such measures were brought into football, we will outline the 1995 Bosman Ruling for those that are not currently aware of the history behind the implementation of free transfers and free agency.

In order to fully understand the concept of free agency and free transfers, it is important to have knowledge of what is known as the Bosman Case. It was a historic legal battle that altered the landscape of transfers in modern football. As a consequence of the so-called Bosman ruling that resulted from the court case, free transfers are also referred to widely as Bosman transfers in recognition of the part that Belgian midfielder Jean-Marc Bosman played in helping future players move to a new club for free once their contracts expired.

The situation began in 1990 when Jean-Marc Bosman's contract with Belgian first division side RFC Liege had expired and renewal terms had not been proposed. Bosman was just 25 years old at the time so sought other options. His main target was a move to Dunkirk but an issue arose when the French club failed to meet the transfer fee that was being demanded by Liege. Consequently, RFC Liege refused to let Bosman leave causing his career to stall dramatically; his wages were reduced by 70% as he was no longer a part of the first team. As he approached the typical peak of a footballer's career, his progress was abruptly and unfairly blocked as Liege were demanding a transfer fee that was not obtainable.

Rightfully so, Bosman was frustrated and aggrieved by his predicament and decided to sue the Belgian Football Association and RFC Liege for restraint of trade. The matter was escalated to the European Court of Justice in Luxembourg who reviewed the case's compatibility with articles such as the 1957 Treaty of Rome which guaranteed the freedom of movement of workers and of association in the European Union.

The case of Jean-Marc Bosman seemed to infringe on these laws and hence, in December of 1995, the court concluded that RFC Liege had directly caused a block on Bosman's right to freedom of movement of labour and he received compensation of just €300,000. Furthermore, the court passed a new general law that granted the right to free transfer of players at the expiration of their contract as long as it was to another club in a European association. Clubs were no longer able to block moves and demand transfer fees. This exercised what is known as a court's 'rule of reason' as the new measures were brought into place in pursuit of the legitimate aim of free movement of labour that was justifiable from the perspective of public interest.

In short, the main outcome of the legal case was that the European Court of Justice effectively banned any form of restrictions placed upon players moving to another club without a fee once their contracts had expired. However, there was an additional judgement made that also prohibited any clubs or national associations placing restrictions or quotas on the number of foreign players from other EU associations being selected in teams. Prior to the Bosman ruling, this was common.

In European Competitions, there had been a system implemented that was known as the "3+2 rule". This meant that clubs were restricted to fielding teams that contained a maximum of three foreign players as well as two additional players that were originally foreign but came through the club's academy. These types of quotes were declared unfair and illegal and prevented thereafter following the Bosman ruling. Subsequently, teams were now able to field an unlimited number of foreign players from other European Associations.

Examples of Bosman Transfers:

Player	Country	Year	Transfer
Edgar Davids	Netherlands	1996	Ajax → A.C. Milan
Steve McManaman	England	1999	Liverpool → Real Madrid
Brad Friedel	United States of America	2000	Tottenham Hotspur → Blackburn
Sol Campbell	England	2001	Tottenham Hotspur → Arsenal
Henrik Larsson	Sweden	2004	Celtic → Barcelona
Esteban Cambiasso	Argentina	2004	Real Madrid → Inter Milan
Michael Ballack	Germany	2006	Bayern Munich → Chelsea
David Beckham	England	2007	Real Madrid → LA Galaxy
Andrea Pirlo	Italy	2011	A.C. Milan → Juventus
Robert Lewandowski	Poland	2014	Borussia Dortmund → Bayern Munich
Zlatan Ibrahimović	Sweden	2016	Paris Saint-Germain → Manchester United
James Milner	England	2016	Manchester City → Liverpool
Sead Kolašinac	Bosnia and Herzegovina	2017	Schalke 04 → Arsenal
Emre Can	Germany	2018	Liverpool → Juventus
Gianluigi Buffon	Italy	2018	Juventus → Paris Saint-Germain
Jack Wilshere	England	2018	Arsenal → West Ham United
Andrés Iniesta	Spain	2018	Barcelona → Vissel Kobe
Andy Carroll	England	2019	West Ham United → Newcastle United
Thiago Silva	France	2020	Paris Saint-Germain → Chelsea
Alexis Sanchez	England	2020	Manchester United →Inter Milan
Lionel Messi	Spain	2021	Barcelona → Paris Saint-Germain

David Alaba	Germany	2021	Bayern Munich → Real Madrid
Ivan Perisic	Italy	2022	Inter Milan → Tottenham Hotspur
Christian Eriksen	England	2022	Brentford → Manchester United
Willian	Brazil	2022	Corinthians → Fulham

Source: Transfermarkt (correct as of October 2022)

Benefits and Risks of 'Free Agency'

The advantages to representing a 'free agent' tend to be about money and freedom of choice:

1. **Money:** given that clubs do not have to pay any transfer fee, there is far more scope to negotiate a bigger salary for your client. Some of the largest wages known to date are those of players who moved as a 'free agent' or a renegotiation that took place in the final six months of the Employment Contract, where there is the possibility that the club could lose the player for free. Whilst many criticise players moving for monetary factors, ultimately it is your job to represent the player's wishes – and 'free agency' can often offer life changing amounts.

2. **Freedom of choice:** another fantastic benefit of 'free agency' is in essence the power to pick what club your client wants to go to. Because there is no negotiation between the two clubs, it means you can go directly to teams (and teams can also go directly to you). If your player has always had dreams of playing for a certain club, or in a particular country, then being a 'free agent' tends to be a fantastic opportunity.

Whilst the aforementioned advantages are clearly apparent, these do not come without some risks and downsides:

1. **Injury:** if your client suffers a serious injury towards the end of their contract, then this would be detrimental in finding a new club. Despite not being a big risk for a prospective club given the lack of transfer fee, there is no real need for a team to sign an injury player (who they would have to cover medical bills for) until they are fit and fully recovered.

Therefore, if your client suffers a significant injury and doesn't have a club, it could mean having to deal with rehab and recovery independently.

2. **Time:** the fact that most contracts nowadays are signed on a five-year basis means that waiting for a client to be a free agent is a lengthy process that could detract from making the most out of a player's career. If the initial contract is signed in a player's late 20's, then demanding a substantial paycheck over the age of the 30 is by no means always easy, and it is relatively rare that players actually end up staying at a team long enough to become a 'free agent'.

Expert's View: Loren Roman Garcia

Agent of Lucas Pérez

"In today's game, both of these types of transfer are really important to know about and use when appropriate.

Loans are great because of their versatility in allowing the player to move to another club and increase their worth without actually making any permanent decisions. Whether you're a youth player, a player stuck in the reserves or a player wanting a change of scenery, loans enable you this flexibility. With increased rules regulating clubs' spending, many permanent deals also take place in the form of a loan. The majority of 'options to buy' usually materialise into full transfers, or at least a transfer to another club interested after the (hopefully positive) loan spell.

The concept of free agency is so interesting for an agent. A player is free to go to any club they want to, and essentially becomes a bidding war for their services. Whoever can offer the best package normally wins the player. It *can* be such a great position to be in as an agent. But it comes with its risks. None other than Injury, the inability to find a willing club, as well as any unforeseen issues that can crop up."

Summary

- As have been detailed, both loans and 'free agent' deals come with their obvious upsides and must always be under consideration as an agent.
- For loan deals, just because the transfer isn't permanent it doesn't mean that you can be more relaxed or less scrupulous or involved in the decision-making process – you have to be on top of the deal at all times, even if the move is only for a few months.
- Even though 'free agency' can bring big money, you must always advise your player with best interests in mind. Don't selfishly advise a client to wait out years of a contract just so they can become a 'free agent' and get a more lucrative deal – always think about the bigger picture, and what is best for them.
- Erkut also explains loan deals on his Youtube channel:
- https://www.youtube.com/watch?v=YXY3H_egX1E&t=5s

Further Reading

- Explanatory Notes on the New Loan Provisions in the Regulations on the Status and Transfer of Players: https://digitalhub.fifa.com/m/785652de48694c8c/original/Explanatory-Notes-on-the-New-Loan-Provisions-in-the-Regulations-on-the-Status-and-Transfer-of-Players.pdf

Chapter 17: The Art of Negotiating

"In business as in life, you do not get what you deserve, you get what you negotiate" –
Chester Karrass

Introduction

Some agents can have many useful skills and attributes but when it comes to a certain point in closing a deal that is favourable to your client, it is the ability to negotiate that is tested the most. Negotiation is another topic that we could write an entire book upon. Having said that, there are many books available on the topic such as *Never Split the Difference* by Chris Voss which we would highly recommend. These books detail the intricate instruments and methods that can be used for effective negotiation.

No person will have the same negotiation styles and techniques as the next and it is something that is best learned through practice. Some of the best negotiators in the world span across various industries and deploy different methods and tactics to find a way to achieve the conditions they are seeking in any transaction.

In this chapter, we will attempt to explain and briefly examine some of the key concepts that are universally recognised in the sphere of negotiating. Extensive research and data collection by various top academics have revealed these tactics as fundamental to the majority of successful negotiation techniques. This chapter will also demonstrate the practical applicability specifically in the football world.

A Brief Outline of the Must-Knows of Negotiation for Football Agents

1. **Behave professionally at all times:** this is a straightforward concept to start. Put simply, to be successful in the long-term as an agent you cannot let the intensity and conflict of one difficult negotiation force you into portraying a bad reflection of yourself and your character. Whilst in some professions, the negotiator may only negotiate with the

relevant party once in their career, in the world of football it is likely that you will come across them again in the future. Even if you don't deal with the party again in the future, you must remember that football is a reference business and the likelihood is that any misdemeanour or bad representation of professionalism on your part will be heard about by other parties who may also be important to you in future. The major components of this are to always remain patient, be polite and well-mannered, conduct yourself appropriately, listen to the opposing party and demonstrate you understand their perspective, do not make unfair demands and overall, give a good account of yourself. There are a few key courteous principles to live by to ensure professionalism such as replying to the club within 24 hours each time.

    a. **Erkut's example**: "I once worked with a young agent who had a contract offer for a player but the agent failed to respond to the email of the Sporting Director for three weeks because the offer was too low. This was a big mistake that tarnished the relationship with the club as it was an unprofessional way of handling such a situation. Even if you do not like an offer, you need to act with respect and general nonnegotiable human manners."

2. **The BATNA concept:** often known as one of the most important attributes of a strong negotiator, is to always have a '**B**est **A**lternative **t**o a **N**egotiated **A**greement'. This concept has been shown to strengthen the power of negotiating. In other words, as the agent you should always prepare other options or a 'plan B' for your client. Even if the client wants to stay at their current club, this concept will help you. Having alternative possibilities for your client has several benefits for your negotiation position. Firstly, you are more confident going into the negotiation knowing that if all else fails, there is still a plan B in place. However, more importantly, it gives you leverage when negotiating. For example, if through your proactivity as the agent you have found several clubs interested in buying your client from their current club, it is important to let their current club know about it. These plan Bs allow you to demand higher and more favourable

financial clauses and otherwise as the club is under pressure to exceed the offers of the other clubs if they intend on keeping your client. Another strategy for doing this that agents deploy is to spread rumours in the press or on social media which strengthens their BATNA. Bargain power, after all, is all about a dominant position over and pressure on the other side. It is a subjective concept that you need to find a way of establishing and influencing in order to gain the advantage in a negotiation. Make sure that the outcome you strive for in these negotiations is the one that your client desires but remember that using BATNA can help you reach or exceed the expectations of the client.

3. **Getting to "YES":** this is often known as the Harvard concept and consists of four basic principles outlined below:

    a. Separate the person, the feeling and the problem. Removing emotion from the negotiation can prevent irrational decisions and objections and help you to better influence the other side.

    b. Don't become narrowly focused upon the position of the other side that they speak about externally. Instead, try to focus upon their underlying and internal motivations and interests and why they are making particular demands. Once you have sussed this, you will be able to pinpoint what exactly they really want and find a way to appease them.

    c. Behave cooperatively. It is important that you are not entirely selfish in negotiation as the other side will come to resent you if you do so and it is unlikely you will succeed in achieving your position. If you demonstrate a willingness to find options that benefit both sides then the opposing party is more likely to begin to agree and say yes to you.

    d. Establishing mutually accepted standards for evaluating possible solutions is the final key part in getting the other side to start saying yes. An easy way to establish this is by beginning with terms and demands that are straightforward and the other party is likely to agree to. You can then gauge from this the kind of approach that is needed to encourage them into agreement and how best to conduct discussions around potential solutions.

4. **Prepare:** as with many parts of being an agent, if your preparatory work is sound and sufficient, it is likely that you will be in a far better position to effectively negotiate, especially if you reinforce your negotiation with numbers, statistics and relevant data. This includes knowing your own and your client's interests and goals such as their expectations regarding salary, bonuses and release clauses; your plan B; an understanding of your counterpart which can be crucial in finding their internal interests and of course; devising a clear strategy including the next steps in each section of a negotiation. Additionally, your knowledge of the industry and which clubs are lacking certain positions and therefore will be more determined to find specific options will put you in a better negotiation position.

5. **The importance of time limits:** deploying time limits can be very useful for your position in a negotiation. For example, stating that you need a decision on a certain condition or demand can help to politely press the other party into appeasing such a demand if they wish to close the deal. This is why transfer deadline day and in the last days and weeks before a window closes, many deals take place as parties feel a sudden urgency to complete negotiations. Deadline day is crucial for an agent and can be the chance to get the very best deals and agreements for your clients. However, it is important to gauge how interested the other side is in meeting your demands. If they are indifferent about completing the deal then they are less likely to feel pressured under a time limit and more likely to dismiss negotiations altogether so be careful! If this happens the other way around, it is your responsibility to not succumb to time pressures placed upon you by the other party and to find ways of playing with and manipulating time in your favour. Remember that time can be an advantage, a disadvantage and a risk. Part of negotiating for agents is to find a way of respectfully and appropriately 'playing with time' to receive other offers or enhanced offers. You need to be creative but ensure that whichever way you do this does not upset the club and the officials you are dealing with; they cannot feel as though they are being used or played.

6. **Setting an anchor:** this is useful to deploy right at the beginning of the negotiation process. If you and your client

are clear on your own position and there are exact figures in your mind, state these from the outset to create an anchor. This will ensure that no time is wasted in negotiations as the opposing party will be able to judge your levels of acceptability with certain demands that you have laid an anchor for and this can accelerate the process to the point of agreement more efficiently. Knowing where to put your anchor is an important factor. You need to obtain information which is key to judging this such as the salaries that other players are currently earning. The best advice is to request for "as close to the limit of outrageous" without being disrespectful and insulting and ensure that you can justify your anchor with the information and understanding you have.

7. **Appropriate timing:** knowing when to ask for certain things is something that an agent needs to learn the art of. For example, if it is a contract renewal you're looking for, there are specific times that are a lot better to inquire about possibilities than others. The best scenario is that the club reaches out to you for this rather than you having to make a request but this can alter on a case-by-case basis. If your player has just had a few good games with strong individual performances, positive reviews from fans and coaches and is playing an integral role for the team, it may be a good time to inquire about a contract renewal and makes it more likely that you will be able to negotiate more favourable terms. Remember, the football landscape changes almost daily and impeccable timing can therefore be difficult but can make a significant difference to your negotiations. On the contrary, if your client is having a bad run of form and their performances have been below expectations, you need to find a suitable way of delaying contract negotiations in the hope that they will soon return to form.

The Negotiation Process in Football Transfers

Negotiation tends to take place in the latter stages of a transfer. Initially, the player is offered to the club usually via the sporting director, head of recruitment of the chief scout or the club may request the player themselves. The conversation and consultation with the club begins at this point but usually only with basic details such as the current contract situation and the initial transfer fee their current club is seeking. These initial conversations, particularly if they are international, will occur over email, the phone or more informally over Whatsapp perhaps. The club may outline why they are interested in the player and what their plans are moving forward if the player were to join.

Once you understand the position that is available and the role that they would play in the interested club, you should then communicate this with your client. Only do this once you are certain the interest is substantial otherwise your client may start to think you are wasting their time without anything materialising. However, if the interest is meaningful and notable then you should help your client understand certain things. For example, they will want to know the key personnel within the club, what the culture and lifestyle of where their new place to live is like, the training schedule and the club or coach's philosophy and principles. If they initially have an agreeable feeling towards the club, it may be advisable to visit the club with the player and to meet certain people or to speak with the players that the client may already know. It is your role at this stage in the process to ensure the client feels comfortable moving forward and sees a future with the interested party before beginning with the negotiation process.

Most of the time the initial negotiation meeting will take place in person to discuss and plan a rough idea of how the contract and offer will look and be structured. These meetings usually occur in secluded but convenient spots such as airport lounges, training grounds or hotel rooms. At this stage the most important clauses to negotiate first and foremost are the likes of contract duration, the type of transfer (loan or buy) and anchor salary requirements. This face-to-face meeting should end with an official written offer from the club to concrete the opportunity. Aside from the contractual details, a priority in this initial meeting should also be to inquire about the plan that the club has with your player and their perception and opinion on them. This can help you navigate through the negotiation if you have a greater understanding of your client's situation.

As negotiations continue, counteroffers will usually be proposed in dialogue over phone, email or WhatsApp or other direct messaging platforms. The goal at this stage is to deploy your personal negotiation techniques and the key concepts mentioned above to obtain the desired offer and the expectations of the player, or at least get as close to it as is possible. Remember, ultimately it is your client that needs to be happy to continually check in with them is of paramount importance! Never lose sight of this.

Another vital point to follow is that all of these discussions should be confidential and private and kept that way. The club has placed a level of trust in you and is willing to share sensitive details that should not be shared or forwarded to others. Treat it as part of the component of trust and confidentiality in a negotiation and hence, do not forward messages or emails leverage against other clubs to seek a better offer. This can be a tempting form of negotiation but will more often than not, damage the willingness of parties to comply with your expectations and requests as well as developing a fear that any information they do share will be shared with others that it is not intended for. Club officials speak with each other regularly and once this has come out, your reputation as an agent will be damaged.

As the process nears conclusion and agreement (hopefully!), the parties may meet in person again with the newest contract and offer. It is important to check that all the details that have been agreed and perhaps compromised upon from either party are accurately stipulated within the contract. Using a lawyer that specialises in contractual legal matters at this point is important and usually a necessity to ensure nothing is missed and no errors have been made. Once this has been cleared and confirmed, the signing date will be set and hopefully your negotiation skills have landed your client with a desirable contract offer that they will be very grateful for. Remember as well that at some point during the negotiation process, at an appropriate time, your own agency fee and commission needs to enter the discussion and be agreed upon without breaking down the rest of the negotiation or relations.

Expert's View: Dr Erkut Sogut

Has negotiated the Premier League record contract at the time in 2018 and the Turkish record contract

"Negotiation is one of the most integral and intricate parts of the agency profession. One thing I have learned during the years of an array of negotiations is that no two negotiations are ever the same. Agents need to learn to be flexible and creative, adjusting their style and approach depending upon the exact situation.

I mention creativity and flexibility as this can help you to negotiate alternative methods of obtaining what you are asking for. For example, a club may not be able to meet certain demands for a player's salary outright but the agent can find a way of using other approaches to ensure the demand is met ultimately. Remember, when you start out in negotiations, both parties will state their idea of how they envisage the outcome; hence, the purpose of the negotiations that take place thereafter is to find the position where these two ideas meet and everything is agreed upon. Your role as the agent is one of a 'middle-man', to liaise with both parties and to reach a result which is possible for the club and the player with which they are both happy.

The 2018 contract that I negotiated on behalf of Mesut Özil is a good example of how a negotiation plays out and what an agent needs to bear in mind throughout. The negotiations were drawn out over approximately 12 months from the point where initial contact was made with Arsenal to when everything was agreed and the contract was actually signed. It is always important that throughout the negotiations you are prioritising the best possible options for your client. In this case, Mesut had offers from around the world in the likes of Italy, France, the Middle-East and another club in the UK. As an agent I needed to understand his opinion on these interests and realise that his heart was set upon staying as a Gunner. This is very relevant to know and consider as it is a significant decision for your client whether to commit themselves to a contract and a club or, in the case of contract renewal negotiations, to become a free agent and move elsewhere.

Fortunately for me as the negotiator and deal-broker with Arsenal, I had a lot of different aspects and factors that I could point to and highlight as leverage in reaching a desirable agreement. For instance, Mesut had a social media following over double that of the club's, he was a brand and a powerful entity in his own right and this global outreach and commercial value was important for the club. This meant I could stress the significance of appropriately remunerating him for his image rights as a part of the deal. He needed to be paid more than the other players at the club as this was a unique factor that no other player would have been able to use as the same leverage. I was able to show the club how important Mesut was as a commercial as well as a footballing asset to them. My job was ultimately to identify every possible reason that merited our demands as reasonable and achievable in the eyes of the club. You are there to help the club reach a mindset where they see your demands as fulfillable and agreeable.

Throughout a negotiation you will most likely face time pressures and deadlines. The art of negotiating includes learning to manage these challenges and ensure that you remain in control of a negotiation. You need to be calm for the duration. Nervousness or anxiety from the agent can make instilling confidence and agreeability into the club more difficult. Furthermore, you need to be transparent and honest with both parties at all times. The family of the player and the player themselves can also be a source of pressure and may get restless if they think the negotiation is not progressing as they were hoping. Keeping an open and honest direct line of communication with them can help them understand the position the negotiation is currently in and the next steps. This is important as expectations and pressure could cause you to rush a negotiation and will damage the chances of success. Remember, timing is very important. Knowing when is the right and appropriate moment to make certain comments or demands is a key skill an agent needs to have. Hence, if there is any sense of apprehension or unnecessary haste, this is of detriment to your negotiation.

Put very simply, a negotiation begins with two different positions and through your thorough preparation, appropriate timing and clear, honest communication, you need to find a point of agreement."

Summary

- As you gain practical experience in negotiating with clubs you will usually pinpoint the negotiation techniques that benefit and suit you the most and that you find the most effective and influential.

- Always prepare a BATNA.
- Negotiating in football is unique but incredibly important for agents, understanding the right time to negotiate and the right time to compromise is vital.
- Remember that the sole aim of these negotiations is to reach an agreement with the opposing party that produces the best possible outcome for your client.

Further Reading

- Never Split the Difference - Chris Voss
- The Art of Negotiation - Tim Castle
- To Sell Is Human - Daniel Pink
- Surrounded by Idiots - Thomas Erikson

Chapter 18: Signing Day and the Completion of a Transfer

"It's not where you start, it's how you finish that counts"

Introduction

The most important days in an agent's year and across their career are the days when transfers are completed. This is when often months of hard work, negotiation and travelling culminates in (hopefully) a successful completion and the start of a new chapter for your client. The exciting opportunity you may have first mentioned to your client months before materialises into the next stage of their career, and you are the one that has orchestrated it.

This can be a satisfying and rewarding feeling for agents as the deal nears the closing stages. However, until the contracts have all been signed and approved, there is still work to be done. The day of the signing itself can be hectic, especially if it is under time pressure from a transfer window deadline. This chapter walks you through the most significant parts of each signing day that you are likely to encounter. However, no two completions will probably ever be the same and a key bit of advice is to always expect the unexpected.

Preparation

As with many things in football agency, preparation is always advisable when it comes to signing day. There are often many logistical parts to organise for yourself, for the player and sometimes for others. If it is an international transfer, the list of arrangements to be made can be extensive; including flights, transport upon landing, the hotel in which you and the client will stay, VISA requirements and any vaccinations that may be needed. Often, it is the responsibility of the club to pay and arrange for the accommodation for you and the player but it is your job to ensure that they have finalised everything and you are able to brief your client upon all the arrangements.

Your client also needs guidance on what they are responsible for. As the agent, your role is to minimise this and to relieve the client of as much stress as possible. However, often the client will need to know what exactly to pack and any details they need to provide. Sometimes your client will return home after the signing day but in most cases they will stay in a hotel for a few days or even weeks and they will need to be prepared for this. Once you have helped them with this, it is important to emphasise the most important aspects as well as making them aware of how exactly the process will take place up until the point of completion so that nothing comes as a surprise to them.

The Medical

You are likely to have heard discussions around a player 'undergoing a medical' as they seem on the verge of completing a transfer. This occurs once the player arrives in the city and at the club or a private hospital. It is usually conducted by a team manager, club doctor or another club official. Its importance varies from club to club and its format differs widely. The player will generally need to wear training kit and complete a list of mandatory tests.

In some clubs, there is a great emphasis upon the medical. Some clubs will rigorously scrutinise the player both psychologically and physically ensuring they are capable of performing at their optimum for the duration of their contract. They will analyse all aspects such as ligament stability, bone density, brain activity, their heart, the health of their other organs, physiological strength and more. For example, we have experienced a medical which has lasted two days and scrutinised anything possible.

Particularly with big transfers or players that have a history of injuries, clubs will focus more upon intense medical examinations to ensure there are no concerns. At other clubs, the medical will be more of a formality; the club doctor will conduct some very simple checks to confirm the player is not currently carrying any performance affecting injuries and will pass them if this is the case. At some lower league clubs, they may not conduct a medical at all but simply will rely upon a letter or email from the doctor at their previous club which declares that the player is medically fit to play and states that they would pass any medical checks.

Once the medical is passed and the player is deemed fit to continue with the process, the next part involves finalising the paperwork, a crucial part of the day covered in the next section.

Note: at this point it is important to understand that in some infrequent cases, a player may have already signed a contract prior to the medical due to time constraints and pressure to get the deal over the line. Critically, if the player then consequently fails the medical, the contract has already been entered into and remains legally binding if both parties have signed the contract. The failed medical fails to nullify the contract. Often the club will try to make the player sign the contract first and will delay their own signature until after the medical to avoid this exact problem occurring.

Attention to Detail

You, as the agent, and the client themself, will often sit face to face with some of the board members at the buying club. For example, the sporting director, the manager or the head of recruitment. It is likely some lighthearted brief conversation and welcomes will take place, followed by the more serious side of finalising the contract. Whilst the majority of preparation and checks will have taken place before, it is the responsibility of the agent to conduct a final check of the contract to ensure that there are no sudden or surprising details included that differs from what was previously agreed or were not discussed at all. To help with this, the agent should have printed off the copy previously sent by the club with notes from lawyers that they can then take a hard copy of to the signing meeting and directly compare the two to ensure every small and big detail is identical. Usually there is a mutual understanding that a club will allow sufficient time for an agent to do this.

You must then convey the key details to the player, but this should serve as a reminder as you will likely have had the conversation previously, occasionally in company with a lawyer. You should also ensure that you are not the first party to sign the contract and that the relevant club authority has already added their signature in the designated position. Then the club will specify where you and the player are needed to sign before the contract becomes legally binding and enforceable.

One thing that is vital for you to understand and to explain to your player is whether their salary that is given within the contract is gross or net salary. Gross being the salary they will be paid before it is taxed and the net being the post-tax wages. It is important for you as the agent to be aware that different clubs and different national associations tend to use gross or net salaries and sometimes interchangeably depending upon negotiation. This can be an enormously significant factor and the difference between a great contract and a horrendous mistake made that will detrimentally impact your client. The worst case we have seen with this was a player who signed in the UK and agreed to a salary that they believed was their net salary. The agent was unaware that the contracts in the English market stipulate the gross wages of the player. Consequently, the player agreed to a salary that was around 40% lower than what he, and his agent, had believed they were signing to. Be sure to check on this!

Remember, if there are any last minute changes it is vital that you do not feel pressured or rushed into finalising the agreement. You are well within your right to delay in order to consult a lawyer and review any relevant clauses that you may not have been prepared for. It is worse to sign a contract which ends up detrimental for the client than it is to rush into a contract that you have failed to prepare for adequately.

Paperwork will often include other relevant documents needed by the national association, the league, medical personnel, a TPO declaration, any forms from the selling club and a confirmation for the FIFA Transfer Matching System. All of these should be completed and signed with due care and attention and the responsibility for this lies with the agent. Furthermore, there are additional more minor details also to be agreed upon for the players benefit such as their shirt number and arranging the delivery of all their new kit.

Note: something to be very wary of is that you walk away from a signing with a copy of the completed contract as evidence that it is in place and is legally enforceable. You will need to request a copy from the club before you leave. This is particularly important in some places such as South-East Europe and the Middle-East where they may sign another player and then claim that the contract was never in place with your client.

The Aftermath

Of course, the immediate aftermath is the part to savour. It is the fruit of your work and you should feel deservedly content and pleased. This is where all the handshakes and smiles take place, followed by a barrage of photos posing with shirts, some marketing and promotional videos conducted by the club and some content created for your player to post on their own channels. If their family and loved ones are in attendance you should allow them to celebrate accordingly and understand your position as the agent.

It is also common in the few days following the completion, if not before, for the client to be given a tour of their new location of employment and introduced to all the club's staff from the chef to the kit man to the media and medical personnel. You should be beside them whenever they need your support, helping them in any way possible to settle into their new environment and to quickly quash any issues that arise. Some clients will like to get on with it but as soon as they have any queries or off-field bits that the agent can help with, you need to be continually available to help and to meet simple obligations like attending their fixtures if they want you to do so.

Of course, there are some life details that need sorting. Depending on the nature of the transfer, if it is long-term and international or short-term and local, your client will need satisfactory accommodation. You may be tasked with helping them find housing opportunities as well as advising them on details such as the nearest schools for their children, the lifestyle and culture in the area and sourcing a car dealership to help them and their families with transport. Taxes, banking, insurance and other everyday life requirements are also to be sorted and may come under the scope of your role as the agent. These roles may never stop and are all part of you adding value to your client and helping them to thrive and flourish at the club you have brought them too.

Case Study: Daniel James

Factors Outside of the Agent's Control

This transfer demonstrated that a lot of factors are outside of your control as an agent and that you must focus on the aspects which you can control to give your client the best chance of the deal getting over the line.

With 12 hours to go in the transfer window, Daniel James arrived at Leeds from Swansea City for a medical. The club believed that at this point, the deal was almost certain. The medical was passed and James, accompanied by his father, travelled to the famous Elland Road Stadium to sign the contract and partake in photographs and other formalities. At the concluding stages, Swansea's American based owners stopped replying after there was difficulty in agreeing the details of the terms of the transfer from Swansea.

With under an hour to go in the transfer window, the deal was still not finalised but nevertheless, Daniel James began to sign paperwork such as his employment contract to ensure that as much as possible was completed to avoid a rush towards the deadline. Leeds were eventually forced into a position where they applied for the fifteen minute extension permitted by the FA in order to 'finalise paperwork'. In reality, they were still waiting on confirmation from Swansea who had cited board problems as the difficulty. Eventually, the close of the window came and went and it had not been completed. Daniel James was to remain a Swansea player at least until the next window.

The difficulties caused and the ultimate failure of the agreement created a lot of sticky situations. Not least with the board at Leeds, but also with the disappointment of Daniel James as the player, who had been so close to a transfer he so strongly desired. In this situation, the agent must keep the player updated as much as possible but the reality is that sometimes everyone, including the agent, will be kept in the dark regarding boardroom politics and difficulties right up until the last moment. In a situation such as James' the player can be treated disrespectfully and as a 'commodity' which is not acceptable. In a professional and respectful way, the agent needs to protect the interests of the client and their status as a human being, particularly in such difficult circumstances. One way in which the agent can make a difference and speed up the process is by applying external pressure onto the clubs and expressing the player's willingness for a certain outcome.

The bottom line is, signing day can be a very stressful and occasionally extraordinary time. The agent's role is to relieve as much of this stress and angst from the client, allowing them to hopefully enjoy the experience and complete the signing without any issues. Sometimes, you may be forced to accept that things may not go the way you have hoped due to factors outside of your control. Nevertheless, by focusing on everything that you are able to influence as the agent and by putting in the appropriate preparation prior to signing day, the chances of difficulties arising are mitigated against and minimised.

Summary

- Signing day can be a rollercoaster. It can reach levels of stress and excitement that you may not be prepared for.
- You should approach each step of the process with calmness and focus and take the due care and attention to ensure each part is completed appropriately.
- Your client should be the main priority of the day. You must communicate well with them to keep them at ease and to create a welcoming environment for them at a new club. Remember, they may be anxious, apprehensive and stressed about such a change.
- Never feel rushed or pressured during the process. Try to maintain control and this will make the completion more straightforward for you and your client.
- Feel happy but do not feel a sense of 'job-done' once the signing is finalised. Take the suitable next initiatives to help your client settle into their new place of work and to succeed.

Chapter 19: Agents and Data

"Without data you're just another person with an opinion" - W. Edwards Deming

Introduction

The iconic Brad Pitt *Moneyball* film (2003) was a major contributor to the 'data revolution' that has been seen in sports across the world in the 21st century. It popularised the idea of collecting, analysing and using data to gain an advantage over opponents. Lots of books have also been written about the importance of the data concept and the place that it has within sport.

Football has adopted data analysis and it is becoming progressively integral to the game. Clubs, managers, scouts, players, financial departments and physios all use statistics to increase efficiency and performance within the football environment. In recent years, significant sums of money have been invested into the data sector of football clubs who employ an ever-increasing team of analysts.

One of the many ways in which data can be used in football is in player recruitment, Clubs such as Brentford and Leicester have reputations for 'smart-scouting'; identifying players whose underlying stats and performances are of considerably higher value than their cost. This kind of recruitment allows clubs to increase transfer returns, buying top class players cheaply before they fulfil their potential and then selling them for large profits. One of the best examples of this is Leicester's acquisition and selling of Riyad Mahrez. Using data in this way and for digital scouting means that clubs that may not have the budget of some of the biggest clubs can still compete at the highest level through smart, data-driven business. It is important, as we will demonstrate in this chapter, that agents understand the significance of data and how clubs use it.

Football can produce almost an infinite number of data sets. Both in training and in games, a player can be scrutinised based on the data they produce such as distance covered, expected goals, threat, interceptions and anything else one might want to analyse. Data is objective and measurable which is why it is such a useful tool in football.

Clearly, there is a vast variety of data usage in football. In this chapter, we will focus upon the ways in which data can be used by agents within their field of work and the future of data usage in transfers and contract negotiations. This is important as moving forward it is likely to make you more successful as an agent and provide a better all-round service to your client.

How Can You Use Data to Your Advantage as an Agent

The value of data analytics should not be lost on you as a football agent. Agents going into negotiations with a football club over a player would automatically be disadvantaged if they didn't have access to the data that clubs have. Clubs assess and use data to recruit players, so an agent needs the same data to 'keep up'. In order to give themselves an edge in negotiations they must have a detailed understanding of data and what it means. Raw data is pointless but once it is interpreted and analysed it becomes actionable and helps agents make better decisions. It is another facet and skill that can make you more successful as an agent if you are able to have expertise in data or at least a basic understanding is fundamental.

There are three main ways in which data could be used by agents:

1. **Recruitment:** agents can use data to help them in scouting and recruiting new clients. By analysing statistics they can identify players with the potential to be a success at the highest level of football. Lots of agents use digital data and analytics in their recruitment processes.When working with clients, you can also use data to improve the standard of the service they provide. Using data analytics can help to improve your client on and off the field from match performance to social media outreach.
2. **Transfers:** agents must use data to present a persuasive case around the value of their client to prospective clubs. Inputting this data into a succinct but detailed presentation can be a good way of advertising your player and the value they could bring to a club.

3. **Brokering:** for working on deals on behalf of clubs, agents should use available data to find the right fit for the buying or selling club. Analytics helps you make decisions on players and targets as well as evaluating the best monetary solutions for transfer fees and wages.

The number of data platforms available for football agents has grown substantially in the 21st century. *Wyscout, Comparisonator, Instat, SciSports, Statsbomb, Analytics FC* and other well-known platforms all offer a range of services for agents to subscribe to. You can pay a fee in order to access this data and to gain insights into the underlying statistics of clients, other players or even potential new clients. By comparing and contrasting statistics with other players, you are able to determine the 'worth' of their player. This knowledge can be used in negotiations to leverage clients and demonstrate to the club the value that they will add to the team as per point 2 above. This means that an agent that does this will be at an advantage in seeking higher salaries, bonuses and other fees.

Data is now considered essential in a transfer or contract negotiation. Agents should have a sufficient understanding and knowledge of data in order to improve the work they do for their clients. The statistics allow agents to see if the objective data matches their general feelings about a player and helps a club understand what they are paying for. If the data does not match, then the agent can use other statistics to solve the discrepancies and present a powerful negotiation to a club.

The Future of Data for Football Agents

The data revolution in football is set to continue. Digital scouting is becoming a preferable option over physical scouting, especially since the COVID-19 pandemic and as the quality and range of statistics available continues to improve, the use of data analytics will also rise.

It is expected that the ongoing development of data collection and interpretation will include algorithms and tools to predict the future success of players and clubs with increasing accuracy. These predictive models also turn data into practical guidance for future decisions. Agents can use this to their advantage to project their client's influence upon a club and the contributions they are expected to make to the future success of the team. This provides agents with even more leverage in negotiations, transfers and for finding new clients with big potential. It should also bridge the gap between agents, analysts and coaches as the understanding of data usage widens across the industry. Knowledge and specialisation in data by agents is becoming more of a requirement as football continues to modernise.

Could Data Remove the Need for Agents?

There have already been examples of how data and analytics that are collated by technological computer programs and analyst teams can be used in contract negotiations by the players themselves. Most notably in recent times, Kevin De Bruyne of Manchester City, one of the finest midfielders in the game, negotiated a contract worth an estimated £83million after bringing in data scientists as part of his team which saw him become one of the highest paid players in the league.

A drastic, sceptical suggestion to this example could be that there is no future for agents as data analytics and experts can be used instead to demonstrate to the club the on-field and off-field value that a player holds. However, there are two significant factors in this proposition which we argue make this an unlikely eventuality.

The four-year deal that 'data' obtained for KDB was not solely thanks to the analysts who presented the statistics. He still entered the contract negotiation with a team around him; his father, his lawyer and importantly, his two agents from Rockstar Sports. This is a telling indicator that players still seek the advice and knowledge of agents.

Whilst data played a vital role in helping the agents, alongside De Bruyne, to demonstrate to the club that he was worth forking out £83million (an extra 30% on what he was earning previously) for over four years, it was still the agents who played the pivotal role of getting the deal over the line. The bottom line is that footballers do not want the burden of responsibility for this aspect of the industry to lie with them. Their job is to focus upon performing on the pitch and even if they can call upon data to help with finalising contracts, there will always be a desire for agents to take on the responsibility of ensuring they are getting the best deal possible for their client.

Secondly to note on such a deal is that the level of data and off-field value that the data scientists were able to present to Man City were only possible because of the calibre and status of a player such as Kevin De Bruyne. It is far-fetched to think that, in the future, players that are in a lower division or even those not in the top bracket of top divisions will also call upon data and statistics. This would most likely not be the most realistic and cost efficient way of finalising a new contract and would fail to produce any significant advantage over what an agent could have done. Hence, agents will continue to have a major role and responsibility but must also incorporate a targeted focus upon learning how to use and utilise data to their and their client's advantage.

We will revisit this again in chapter 30.

Expert's View: Luis Kircher

Football Data and Match Analyst and
Consultant

"Too often in modern-day football, the focus is placed upon short-term success. The concentration on securing one's own job leads to administrative and little visionary action. The current processes in most of the world's clubs are extremely inefficient. In combination with widespread financial problems, this leads to repeated sporting and subsequently economic downfalls.

At the heart of every club must be a unified club philosophy that is and remains unchangeable at its core. For me personally, it is the key to sustainable and long-term economic and sporting success. Objective criteria and clear strategies – also in the transfer market – should become massively more important. The goal must be to avoid the risk of bad investments whilst increasing sporting quality at the same time. With the right know-how in the field of data analysis and scouting, professional clubs and agents can gain a competitive advantage while working efficiently at the very top level.

As an agent you always need to think in the best interest of the player, but you also must be able to see the transfer from a club's perspective. The club's goal is to buy a player undervalued at a price and sell him overvalued at a higher price.

And that is why player scouting and recruitment is probably the most important application of analytics. For example, a club that is 90% sure that the player has no fitness issues and is also 90% sure that the player has no personal issues produces a chance of 81% that the player is fine across both of these aspects. Then if you add in other aspects, this percentage decreases further and can become off-putting to a club. Other factors include things such as a player playing out of their best position, the manager doesn't rate the player, they aren't as good as the club thought, the club already has a player on the same level and of the same calibre. The overall chance of success goes down to a problematic level.

As an agent you can forecast and understand some of these aspects and prepare yourself, as well as the club with all relevant information based on objective data. Furthermore, if you are working as an agent on the club-side with the task of finding the right players, you can always use this mechanism from that perspective. Finally, and perhaps most importantly, data will not just increase the probability of you making the right transfer for your player or club, but also will have a positive impact on your reputation as a trusted agent.

As I always say: With every transfer, there is a chance that it will work. But, the probability of success is different. Data can help ensure that the balance of probabilities works in your favour as the agent and to produce the best outcome for your client."

Summary

- It is clear that data plays a now-essential role in football and is continuing to grow. The expansion of data usage and increase in available platforms and data sets will be significant in the future of football agents.
- The future of data statistics and agency is, we believe, one of harmony and mutual benefit. Agents can utilise data as a useful tool as and when it is appropriate and advantageous in reaching a more preferable and lucrative agreement for their client.
- Agents must learn to work with and understand the invaluable insights that data can give them into their client's performances and worth to a club.

Further Reading

- Expected Goals: How Data Conquered Football - Rory Smith
- The Science and Art of a Data Revolution - Christoph Biermann

Chapter 20: Working with the Press

"Nothing is quite so treasured by a football journalist as a strong, open, trusting relationship with an agent. " - Rory Smith

Introduction

More so than ever, the press has an incredible influence upon football and its players. Social media has given rise to the phenomenon of fake news and these stories are accessible at the tap of a button on our phones. News comes from all kinds of sources and freedom of speech means that they can write almost anything. Whether it is fiction or not has little significance for some journalists who are paid to create headlines that people will want to read.

The press also creates opportunities. For agents, as well as safeguarding and defending your clients in the face of negative media and news stories, true or otherwise, is imperative. As is developing good relationships with journalists and other professionals involved in the industry. It can be of benefit sometimes and makes protecting your client easier whilst also possibly helping to open up certain avenues you are looking towards.

Interviews and Media Work

Whereas with social media, a content-driven audience necessitates players to post frequently, interviews and media work as such requires a more nuanced approach. The story behind your client's rise from the dream of becoming a footballer to the reality in which they find themselves can only be repeated a limited number of times, so accepting every interview request that comes your way isn't the best thing to do. It is of course a positive to have your player in the public eye spreading positive messages but the last thing you want to do is devalue the worth of your player's comments or story.

Depending upon the calibre of the client, we would recommend that the agent does due-diligence and research on news platforms and chooses perhaps the most appropriate but well-known newspapers or interviewers in order to attract the biggest audiences.

In addition, timing is a crucial factor as well. If your client finds themselves in a difficult situation, telling them to go straight to the press to defend themselves isn't always the best approach. Let the situation simmer down a little, remove any emotion that may lead them to speak recklessly, and then make a decision wisely. Agents can also step in as a protective shield when this is called for. If there are negative circumstances surrounding the player, the agent can work with the press to reposition themselves as the 'scapegoat', diverting the blame onto them and alleviating it away from the player. If done properly and efficiently, the poor publicity will reflect upon the agent rather than the player. It is a necessary sacrifice for you to best serve your client. A well-documented example of such behaviour by an agent is from the late Mino Raiola who occasionally placed himself in front of his players to protect them.

Contrastingly, if the player is playing brilliantly and is grabbing headlines it may then be productive and beneficial to participate in interviews. Remember that the voice of your client being heard across news platforms will make them more relatable and boost interaction with fans. An agent must also make sure that whilst it is important for them to speak authentically, there must also be a level of media training to prevent any detrimental impact of interviews. Saying the wrong thing and the wrong time can, in extreme cases, even be career-ending. Interviews can take place in a number of different forms and different times, and in cases where an agent cannot be present (for example a pre- or post- match interview), it is even more crucial that the agent guides their player in how to conduct themselves in an appropriate way.

Newspaper or magazine interviews are of course much more under your control. Here, it is the agent's responsibility (or in some cases the appointed digital agency) to provide the player with prior knowledge of the questions to ensure that they are prepared to give positive and clear answers. This is why having last authorisation on the questions, as well as the power to dictate the article headline, is of paramount importance.

Another interview format is through social media channels; perhaps as a live Instagram or Facebook session or a Twitter Q&A. Especially in live sessions and Q&A's, there is a feeling of direct engagement and interaction with the fanbase which can be a positive thing. However, as these are often live, the player must also be cautious as once it is seen and heard by anyone, it is unrecoverable. Speaking badly about their club, other players or managers for example is an absolute no-no.

Global sporting news outlets and social media platforms

Country	Sports news outlets
England	BBC Sport, Sky Sports, FourFourTwo, LADbible, BT Sport, The Athletic
Germany	11 Freunde, Kicker, DW Sports, Sky Sports
France	L'Équipe, France Football, Le Monde
Spain	Marca, AS, Sport, Estadio Deportivo
Italy	La Gazzetta dello Sport, Corriere dello Sport, Tuttosport
Portugal	A Bola, O Jogo, Record
Netherlands	Voetbalzone, Voetbal International, Voetbal Primeur, FC Update
USA	ESPN, Bleacher Report, Sports Illustrated
Turkey	Fanatik, Fotomaç
Australia	SBS World Game, Fox Sports, The Daily Telegraph, Herald Sun
Brazil	ESPN, BolaVIP, SporTV, Gazeta de Alagoas, Lance!, RJsports
Belgium	HLN, het Nieuwsblad
Austria	Kronen Zeitung, Laola, SkySport
Switzerland	11 Freunde, Blick, SRF Sport
Mexico	ESPN, Marca, Depor, Mediotiempo, Record, Excélsior
Serbia	ArenaSport, SportKlub, Sportski Jurnal

This list is of course not exhaustive, and most mainstream newspapers have their own influential sports columns that are widely read. When choosing which news outlets would be most beneficial for your player to interview with, it is important to consider the audience which the organisation appeals to, in conjunction with the country or regions that it sells in.

For social media channels, the demographic of their audience and the type of news that they share is important to consider. Some pages are known for creating 'clickbait' stories and it is best to avoid your client involving themselves with such a platform as it is likely their words will be manoeuvred or manipulated in order to create a better story or headline. Targeting sports or football-specific pages is a safer way of ensuring the intentions of the journalists are purely for footballing reasons and aimed towards football fans.

Working with Journalists

Knowing which journalists to trust is something that all agents find difficult at some point and is a part of the profession that you pick up as you go along! As an agent, you will always get calls asking about the future of your clients, with many journalists cleverly phrasing questions in the hope of capturing snippets of information. Therefore, you always have to be cautious, as any mistake could be costly and you could harm your clients career or image. However, this doesn't mean that you should not pursue any relations with journalists, as they can be greatly effective in strengthening your stance as an agent when representing your client. Of course, relationships with journalists are *quid pro quo*, and they'll be looking to get some information back if they help you out – this is totally normal and just how it is in most walks of life! The following scenarios are examples of when journalists can be really important to you and your player:

1. **Your client wants to move club:** using your trusted contact to see if they know information that you may not (i.e. about the club's intentions, or other players moving). Similarly, helping spread word of the positive impact your player has and their on-pitch performances is something that can be done.

2. **Your client wants a new contract:** much like the above scenario, the media contact can be very useful. You could come out on behalf of the player signalling their intentions to stay despite outside interest, and thus help spike some urgency from their current club and maybe even force the hand of outside interest to raise their interest and offer if they are particularly keen on your player.

3. **Your client is launching a business:** off-pitch ventures are also newsworthy, and if you're trying to promote a new brand or business that the player has launched then using someone in the media to help share information and promote it. This may be an opportunity to do interviews or media work with a platform that is not just football-focused, depending on the nature of the business the player is launching.

4. **Your client is supporting a charity:** another newsworthy form of off-pitch activity is if your client is actively engaging with and raising awareness for charitable projects and campaigns. In order to enhance the positive impact your client is able to have upon the charitable organisation, promotion within the media will accentuate this and hence, the agent should make journalists aware of the valuable work the charity and the client are doing.

Expert's View: Rory Smith

Chief Soccer Correspondent, New York Times

"Nothing is quite so treasured by a football journalist as a strong, open, trusting relationship with an agent. That is no surprise. Journalism's prime currency is information, and there are few quite so rich in that as agents. They know if their clients are happy to stay or about to leave a club; they know which players are complaining about the manager and which remain loyal; they have their fingers on the pulse of what is happening throughout the game. Being able to share information with an agent should be the perfect way to make our work more accurate.

It does not always work like that. As a rule, journalists encounter three types of agents. The best are those who are willing to trust you, to offer an honest reflection of reality as they see it. Second are those who do not engage at all, who will not answer the phone, or simply offer a gruff 'no comment'. And third are those who, believing you need them more than they need you, choose to distort the truth to further their own ends.

Even at a time when many players prefer to access their fans directly through social media, there are increasingly few of the latter group. More and more agents recognise that journalists are not the enemy. In an age when players are as much brands as athletes, the media can help to present a true reflection of their clients; they can get their side of the story out in such a way that it does not look like propaganda; they can boost their profile. The cost is not high: just honest answers to a few questions every now and again."

Summary

- Interviews are a great way to boost the popularity of a player as well as impress existing and future sponsors. They serve to boost the profile of the players and a great public following translates to higher commercial value for sponsors.
- Agents must be wary of journalists but certainly should not avoid them altogether. The same value of networking is relevant in developing trusted contacts within the media industry. Do not share information that will ever harm your

client's career nor their relationship with their club, teammates, manager or fans, but you may want to selectively share information to utilise journalists to your client's advantage.

- The press and mainstream media carry great significance in society, and work in this field has to be conducted effectively and smartly.

- If you choose to do an interview, make sure it is with the right media outlet at the right time, and if you start to develop a relationship with a journalist, try to ascertain their loyalty and trust. Remember that they are paid to create good news stories so their intentions may not always be pure.

- Much like every other aspect of the profession, you should make sure your client is kept updated about future interviews and press work, as they will have their own ideas about how they want to be presented to the public. It is also your role to prepare them adequately for such appearances and help them represent themselves well.

Further Reading

- How to Win Friends and Influence People - Dale Carnegie

Chapter 21: Handling Contracts

"It is impossible to unsign a contract, so do all your thinking before you sign" – Warren Buffett

Introduction

Perhaps the most complex aspect of being a football agent is dealing with the contracts and negotiations on behalf of your client. Such contracts can be easily separated into two categories; those that are directly related to your player's career, and those that deal with the more personal side of their affairs. Even though negotiating stances vary between each individual depending upon your skills and knowledge, there are still certain things that have to be considered when dealing with contracts. Furthermore, it should be noted that taking the advice of a qualified financial advisor or lawyer is also a good idea and is sometimes a requirement. This is explored more in chapter 22.

This chapter will cover the following contracts that are important for football agents:

1. **Representation contracts** between agent and clients
2. **Employment contracts** made between a club and a player
3. Transfer and loan agreements
4. **Agency agreements** between clubs and agents

Representation Contract

In order to legitimately represent a player, there has to be a legally valid and enforceable Representation Contract between you and your client as well as, of course, being registered as an intermediary. This agreement, which is valid for a certain period of time until it needs to be renewed, is an extremely important part of the entire process.

The representation contract offers an element of legal safety and security for each party. If the contract contains all relevant information and requirements, it prevents either party acting wrongly within the relationship. Breaching such a contract can lead to termination with just cause and hence, protects the player if the agent does not behave in a professional manner as the player can then exit the relationship. Alternatively, it provides an element of protection for the agent contained within the exclusivity clause and prevents the player dealing with other agents.

In most national football associations, there will be a template layout of a representation contract. However, agents and agencies are able to adapt the clauses and include any additional obligations specific to the work that they do. Nonetheless, the majority of a representation contract is universal and replicated in each country. It is important to know that the common primary aspects of a representation contract that are likely to be generally universal under any national football association, but the details of which can differ, are clauses such as *Appointment, Duration of Representation* and *Commission and Agent Remuneration.*

Significantly, if the Employment Contract is due to end after the Representation Contract, the intermediary is still entitled to their agreed percentage.

Despite being a relatively straightforward contract, there are some basic things that agents often get wrong. The most common of these is to do with the names provided. If you work for an agency, you should always put both your name, as well as the name of the agency. If you are an independent agent it will just need your own name alongside the client. Also, despite sounding straightforward, do make sure both your name and that of your client are spelt correctly!

For example, the English FA (Football Association) requires that the Representation Contract has a maximum length of two years before it needs to be renewed. However, a common question posed is what if the player wants to leave their agent before the contract expires? Looking at this from the agent's perspective, there are some key things to consider:

- Firstly, if you're doing a good job, then this shouldn't happen! But of course, scenarios like these do occur, and you must remain professional at all times.
- When you initially agree to the Representation Contract, try to ensure it is done on the basis of exclusivity. Whilst this issue is contentious in countries like Germany which, by law, bans exclusive representation (although many German

agents do it anyway), this is not a law in other countries such as England and the Netherlands.

- Using the example of England where the Representation Contract is two years long, you don't have to wait until it is about to expire before renewing it. If you manage to get your client a transfer, new contract, or something of benefit, then it could be a good time to ask them if they are willing to renew it.
- If after all attempts your client still wants to leave you as their agent, try to make sure the next agent they sign with is someone who you can cooperate with and potentially share commission with on future deals.

Employment Contract

The contractual relationship between a player and a club is stipulated in the Employment Contract. This is something that is agreed when the player joins a club and will usually be agreed between the club and the player before the transfer negotiations reach advanced stages as these negotiations would be futile if the player then failed to agree on personal terms. The Employment Contract would normally cover a variety of different aspects between the two parties. For example, it may include clauses regarding a signing-on bonus as well as appearance or goal bonuses. Here, it would be for the agent of the player to negotiate on their client's behalf, in order to secure the best possible deal and that their client is appropriately remunerated for their services.

It is very common for much of a player's income to be significantly supplemented by performance-based bonuses and not only from their standard wage. For contracts with Premier League players, personal terms are set out in 'Schedule 2' of the standard contract; so everything from the basic wage to bonuses to compensation is agreed in this part of the contract. Under the Representation Contract as in the previous section of this chapter, as the agent of a player you will be entitled to commission and this is closely linked with the Employment Contract and the net or gross salary which the player earns.

Often, it is thought that players are the ones who pay their agent, but in reality it is commonly the club who do this. Clubs pay the agent the negotiated percentage on top of the wages they pay the player. This is often for tax reasons. As always, it is crucial for the intermediary to be aware of the rules set out by FIFA and the relevant footballing association regarding contracts as well as government tax regulations, making sure that all criteria and legal obligations have been followed and adhered to.

What to Check in Employment Contracts

It is important as the agent to be aware of key considerations in playing contracts. However, as discussed in chapter 22, often the best solution is to employ the services of a lawyer who specialises in contract law. Nevertheless, below we will outline the clauses that should always be checked and our thoughts on each one. Please note that this list is not exhaustive:

1. Ensure the same terms that were agreed upon appear in the same form and with the same details in the contract.
2. Triple-check the details of the player and the club, particularly for spelling mistakes, as simple as this may sound.
3. **Validity of the contract:** check for anything that stipulates how and why the contract may be terminated and if it may not be valid in other leagues or if the club is promoted or relegated.
4. **Duration:** confirm the length of the contract is correct and the exact dates upon which it starts and ends. Our advice for this is that if the player is younger and has high potential, the shorter the contract the better unless a release clause is included. Although this may mean less long-term financial security, it recognises the faith that the player will move on to bigger and better things and prevents them being unfairly tied down under a single long-term contract. In the case of an under-18 player, FIFA stipulates that they are only able to sign a contract that is maximum three years long for this exact reason. For older players, the longer contracts are favourable to prolong their career and add more job security.
5. **Contract extension options:** sometimes you will see reference to an 'option'. This often entails a 10-20% increase in salary and can be activated by the club prior to the

contract expiration. Our opinion on this is that they are often one-sided and to the disadvantage of the player, your client. Most cases allow the club to take advantage of the top players by keeping them at the club without the necessary pay-rise as you have less negotiation power. An option needs to be carefully considered before being agreed to in a contract.

6. **Salary:** the higher the basic salary, the better it is for the player, this part is simple. However, this section of the contract will also contain details of how and when the payment is due and this requires understanding. Particularly in some national associations, you need to ensure there is sufficient penalty in place in case the salary is not paid to protect your client's income. As addressed in chapter 17, it is vital that you check whether the salary is gross or net. Ultimately, the money that ends up in the player's bank account is what will be most important to them.

7. **Bonuses and increases:** further to above, there will often be clauses, as agreed previously in discussion, that outlines the bonuses and pay rises that the client will be entitled to. The wording here is important to analyse. For example, it needs to be explicitly clarified as to what constitutes an appearance bonus, whether it is playing 45+ minutes or simply coming off the bench. The clause in the contract will state something like: "the sum of £200,000 will be paid to the player upon each occasion (if any) that the player makes a minimum of 25 appearances in a season".

Contract renewals

When you read about players 'renewing' or signing a 'new contract', this is referring to the Employment Contract. Contract renewals can occur at any point before the expiration of the initial contract, and can be the result of numerous scenarios:

1. **There is interest from another club for your client:** if your player is the subject of an enquiry or bid from another team that is rejected, then this provides great potential for a renegotiation of the Employment Contract with their current club. Clearly, your client is in demand and another club felt that their value exceeded the current contract. Therefore,

this provides you with a perfectly logical argument for a renewal and a more lucrative contract. However, it is best to let the club raise this with you rather than have to request it yourself and will further strengthen your negotiation position as discussed in chapter 17.

2. **A breakthrough season:** if your client has greatly exceeded all expectations and is playing at a level that clearly surpasses their current contract, then this is an obvious opportunity for you. This often occurs when a young talent is given a first-team role and delivers some standout performances warranting a reconsideration of their deserved value.

3. **Teammates:** if your player's club makes a move in the transfer window and signs a player for a much higher wage, or renegotiates a current teammate's salary, then there *may* be scope for you to have your own discussions regarding your client. If you can reasonably argue that the difference in pay is far greater than the difference in talent and on-pitch (and also off-pitch commercial) value, then there could be grounds for a renewal. It is part of the agent's role to ensure their client receives what they deserve in line with the wages their colleagues are being paid. Sometimes it can be difficult to find out the salaries of their teammates but either your client will be able to find out for you or you can speak to your contacts who may know.

Transfer and Loan Agreements

Transfer and loan agreements are constructed and signed as the final part of moving a client from one club to another on either a permanent or a temporary basis. The contracts begin by outlining the details of the two clubs between which the agreement is taking place and by stipulating that the two clubs are agreeing to transfer the registration of the player from the selling club to the buying club.

Perhaps the most important clauses within the transfer agreement concern the transfer compensation that will be contractually due. This is more commonly known as the transfer fee and is split into two different components. The agent may have been a part of these negotiations, they definitely would have been if they were representing a club in the transfer. The first component is the fixed transfer compensation which states that provided the player and the club have signed an employment contract, the selling club will be entitled to a fixed sum to transfer the registration of the player.

The second and more complex side of the transfer fee is the contingent conditions. This will detail the additional compensation that is due to the selling club upon the satisfaction of certain events such as qualification for tournaments, winning trophies, gaining promotion and avoiding relegation or perhaps scoring a specific number of goals and playing a certain percentage of minutes during a season. For example, a player transferring to a club in England will warrant additional compensation to be paid to their original club if they help their new team qualify for the Champions League, win the Premier League, finish in the top 10, score 10+ goals and play over 70% of minutes during the season. The club may receive a set additional fee for any or all of these criteria, depending upon what has been agreed within this contract.

Another financial clause that is particularly significant in a transfer agreement is a sell-on fee that may be disclosed. This entitles the selling club to further compensation if the buying club transfers the player in the future for another transfer fee. This is often given as a percentage of the secondary transfer fee that will then be owed to the original club. In some cases, it is possible that the agreement will also contain buy-back clauses or 'options' that entitles the original club to reobtain the registration of the player should they so wish and for a certain fee. These are critical aspects of the contract that agents can use to their advantage if they manage them correctly and it can help both parties to reach an agreement that they are both satisfied with.

Loan agreements differ slightly in that there is technically not a transfer fee involved. The financial details contained within the contract will usually include a loan fee that is due from the receiving club and the salary demands that they are contractually required to cover whilst the player is under employment with them. This will also reference how bonuses and other financial matters will be addressed during the period of the loan. The 'period' i.e. the duration of the loan is also stipulated clearly within a loan contract and is something that will be discussed and negotiated by the two clubs and can range in length depending upon the circumstances of the player and the clubs. It must meet FIFA's loan regulations such as that a loan can be for a maximum of one year and a minimum of at least the period between two transfer windows. This is addressed further in chapter 16.

Other clauses in the loan contract that an agent needs to consider, understand and negotiate are concerns such as what happens in the case of injury and who is liable for the insurance of a player. In some cases, there may also be an 'obligation' or 'option' to buy clause which will only be implemented upon agreement of both parties. The clauses either make transferring the player permanently after the conclusion of their loan compulsory for the signing club or it gives them the option of buying the player for a disclosed fee should they wish to agree to this. If you are the agent of a client who has an option to buy clause in a loan contract; it is important to help your client understand that their performance on the pitch for their new club can have a profound effect on what happens next in their career but without exerting excessive pressure onto them.

In both loan and transfer contracts, it will be included as a requirement that the buying club is under the obligation to lodge the contract with the relevant national association, the FIFA Transfer Matching System and to log the details through the FIFA clearing house to ensure that it is legally processed correctly and does not involve any malpractice such as third party involvement.

Agency Agreements Between Clubs and Agents

Agents can also sign representation contracts directly with clubs in order to act on behalf of the club for identifying, negotiating for and registering players. This is very important for you as the agent as it is a good way of making money. For example, an agreement of this nature between a club and an agent will usually specify a duration of time that an agent will represent the club for in the transfer market. It is also possible that it will detail an exact kind of player that the club wishes for the agent to represent them for such as a striker or midfielder. In some cases the contract may also be for just one player that the club has already identified as a primary target for them in the next transfer window and will enter into a contract with the agent to help them to complete the deal. It is then your job as the agent to speak to the relevant people and convince the player to sign with the club. Throughout the duration of the contract it will be the responsibility of the agent to adhere to national association and FIFA regulations and keep a constant dialogue between them and the club, informing them of any relevant details and progress.

Often this agreement will be exclusive and the agent needs to ensure that the contract is favourable for them before signing the deal. It is also important to understand that usually once the club has signed the kind of player that you were contracted to seek, the representation contract will conclude but you will then be entitled to remuneration for your services for the duration of the player's employment contract.

For a representation contract signed between the club and the agent, ordinarily the agent will be entitled to a fee equivalent to a certain percentage (often 5-10%) of the player's salary for each season of their valid employment contract provided they remain at the club. Unfortunately, if the player then transfers again during this period and away from the club with which you are contracted, the contract and agreement is usually invalidated and you are thereafter no longer entitled to your remuneration.

The contract between the club and the agent should also detail the method through which the agent will be paid. It will be stipulated that it is the club that is liable to pay the agent and that the agent will not receive any payment directly from the player. The agent's fee will be paid in one of two ways. Either in a lump sum upon the completion of the deal and the point at which the player is registered with the club and hence, the representation contract with the agent concludes. Or, the club may ask to pay in instalments where the agent will receive part of their fee at a certain point in a season provided the player is still registered with the club and the contract is still valid. For example, if the player that registers through your services signs a four-year deal, you will usually be paid across two instalments in different transfer windows if the player is still under the same employment contract and has not transferred elsewhere.

One situation that may arise is if the agent has acted on behalf of the player and the club and therefore is entitled to a payment for his services to the player as well. Usually this will warrant a contract between the club and the agent. It will most likely be agreed that the services provided to the player will also be paid for by the club as part of the agreement as a technicality for tax reasons. The club paying the agent on the player's behalf will be included within the contract between the club and the agent and is a legal method of lowering the tax demands on the player. This can be a way in which you obtain an even better deal for your client and their net salary will be higher than if they would have to pay you directly themselves. In some cases, the club may cover 5% of the salary and pay this to you as a benefit of the player and then the player pays another 5%. If you represent the player it is vital that you inform them and help them to understand what they are required to pay as it has happened before where players are given a bill to pay the agent further down the line once they have signed the contract and it will come as a shock. The danger here is that the player may lose their trust in you. Agent-Club contracts can help you to relieve as much of this financial burden away from the player but you must ensure it is in accordance with taxation laws. If you do not know the tax regulations in a certain country then you should speak with a lawyer or financial adviser to avoid making a mistake.

This is a complex concept but an important one to understand. Put simply, if the agent acts on behalf of the player, the player will be taxed. So if the agent signs a representation agreement with the club instead then the club is technically solely responsible for remunerating the agent. The club is seen as 'hiring' the services of the agent and therefore the player does not have to pay any agency fee and hence, no tax. However, in practice, the agent is still realistically representing the player.

As you can see, it can be a difficult task to ensure that you are appropriately remunerated for your services as the agent. The best case scenario is that the club agrees to pay you as a lump sum upon completion of your work once you have brought them the player they had originally entered into a contract with you for. This avoids the risk that if the player moves you will no longer be entitled to claim the full extent of the fee that would have been due to you if the player had remained registered at the club. However, convincing and negotiating with a club to agree to paying it as an up-front lump sum can often prove challenging and you do not want it to affect the outcome of a deal.

Another way in which an agent may contract with a club is slightly different and is considered as a 'mandate'. For example, a club may be interested in a specific player and wishes to enter into some level of discussion with their current club and their agent to gauge whether there could be a possible transfer or loan in the near future. In this case the contract will stipulate that the agent's services are employed simply to begin discussions and to report back to the club regarding their findings. Importantly, this kind of contract explicitly prohibits you from signing any documents on behalf of the club and hence, you cannot reach advanced stages of a negotiation or transfer. However, this can be an interesting contract for agents should the opportunity arise as it can help you to build relationships with clubs and if there is reasonable chance with the player, you are likely to remain involved in the deal moving forward and will be paid for your services.

Expert's View: Daniel Geey

Sports lawyer, Sheridans

"For high-profile, elite footballers, there are a number of considerations when signing important football-related contracts. A robust Representation Contract which sets out the relationship between player and agent is vital. The Representation Contract will include the following elements which agents and players need to understand, including that:

- The contract is for the **maximum two years** possible under the rules, to ensure that players are not tied to an agent for too long.
- The contract **is exclusive** (as far as legally possible in particular countries) so that, during the length of the contract, no other agent can represent the player. If another agent claims to represent the player, and the first agent is then cut out of the deal and loses out on commission, it is likely that the player may be sued for breach of contract by his original agent.
- The agent has the power to represent the player when negotiating transfers, employment contracts and commercial deals. It is important for the agent that they can earn commission not just from on-field transfer and contract renegotiations but also from all commercial agreements (including, for example, an Adidas boot deal). This enables the agent on behalf of the player to **maximise earnings on and off the pitch**.
- The **commission rate** for negotiating a player's new contract or transfer can be between 3% and 10% of the player's total salary. However, when negotiating commercial deals (a boot deal, say, or a skin care deal), agents are usually entitled to receive between 15-20% of the value of the endorsement agreement."

Summary

- Given the legal importance of contracts, it is always advisable to have a strong relationship with a lawyer (or law firm) who you can trust in order to give you impartial guidance and help. See chapter 22 for more details on this.

- There are four common contracts that an agent should concern themselves with which demand different services as manifest themselves in different parts of the agency profession.
- As the agent, you will play an integral role in every negotiation and agreement that is made with regards to your client – it is therefore crucial that you check over every detail and leave nothing to chance.
- Furthermore, you should always keep your client well informed about every decision that you plan on making, as it is technically on their behalf that you are negotiating.
- Despite using a lawyer in many of these situations, it is advisable that you have your own extent of legal knowledge and contractual understanding to improve the standard of service you can provide to your client.

Further Reading

- How Do Football (Soccer) Contracts Work? | Field Insider: https://fieldinsider.com/football-contracts/

Chapter 22: Working with Lawyers

"Top quality lawyers are a necessity for a responsible and successful football agent"

Introduction

A common question that is asked is; "What is the difference between sports lawyers and agents?". In truth, there is a lot of overlap when it comes to representing a client in contract negotiations for example. Contract law is, after all, a major part of legal education and procedures. An important distinction is that agents are not limited solely to legal aspects of caring for a client. Nevertheless, a good or basic understanding of legal knowledge is important, we believe, to be the best agent you can be. However, lawyers exist alongside agents for good reason.

You will most likely have gauged throughout this book that an important aspect of being a successful agent is to be able to identify your own limitations and knowing when to seek professional support and advice. This is arguably no more important than when deciding to work with qualified and practising lawyers.

(Erkut) I am in the fortunate position that I studied law and legal systems for a decade in various universities across Europe. This has always helped me during my career as an agent as I have put in the hard work to have strong foundational knowledge on law that impacts football, from playing contracts, to tax obligations, to image rights agreements. However, despite this there have been many situations where, in order to protect the best interests of the player as much as possible, it was necessary to seek the help and professional advice of lawyers.

This chapter will explain the vital role that lawyers play in benefitting your performance as an agent for your client and the services and opportunities you are able to provide. It will also explain how these relationships are formed and materialise in practice.

When and Why?

Remember the integral underlying factor for being a good agent; everything you do must be for the sole purpose of benefiting your client as much as possible in each event. The biggest mistake you can make is to try and do something yourself when you do not have the necessary expertise and the consequences are detrimental to your client's career. This is often borne out of selfishness and may be financially motivated. For example, top lawyers charge high fees and you will have to pay them out of the money you make from commission. However, they charge these fees for good reason; they are the experts.

In almost every opportunity you identify for your client, there will be legal implications. When they sign for a new club or a contract extension, or in any endorsement deal as well as other off-pitch services you provide such as financial management, investments and social media, there will almost always be a contractual agreement and clauses that must be adhered to. Having a general understanding of contractual law, sports law or any legal knowledge will inevitably help you and we always recommend an agent to obtain some level of education in law. Nonetheless, recognising where and when you need expert opinions and guidance is vital. The need for this can be demonstrated more clearly through a practical example.

Let's say your client is looking to sign with a new club and they have sent through the contract they are offering. With your own knowledge, you can review the contract and make your own assessment that the contract is acceptable or not. However, as a responsible and successful agent, you call upon a lawyer who is a close contact of yours to give it a full proof read to ensure that it is legally sound. It is very common that the contract is returned with countless notes and pointers of clauses or elements that need to be reconsidered and addressed. If you had signed this contract without consulting the lawyer, you would have left your client in an unfavourable and undesired position. The worst case scenario in this is signing a contract that ties them in with a club and makes leaving very difficult even in circumstances when a move is vital for them to revive their career, or even failing to identify small print that renders your client far less financially strong than what you originally thought and had advised them.

For example, in a case involving a club and a manager (our client), the club included a suspicious clause within the contract. We sought the legal advice of a specialist lawyer as it was an old national law that only a qualified lawyer in that country would be able to interpret the implications of. The lawyer advised us that the clause implied that the club would be able to terminate the contract without just cause and without paying any further salary or compensation payments. Had it not been for our professionalism in consulting a lawyer, the clause may have been left in the contract and put the client into an incredibly vulnerable position.

If a situation like this does materialise, it is not only significantly negative for your client's career but also enormously damaging for your own. Remember that clients talk to their teammates and chatter amongst each other can often bring up the mistakes you may have made in their contracts. What begins as a simple saving of a small fee by avoiding paying a lawyer, suddenly culminates in a large loss of earnings as current clients and future clients lose faith in your commitment to sacrificing everything to achieve the best outcome for them. Bringing in a lawyer is always worth it if it protects the main goal of benefitting your client.

Finding the Right Lawyer

Sourcing and utilising the right lawyer brings us back to the overarching theme of building your network. As we have repeated throughout this book, the value of your network directly correlates to the value of service you are able to provide to your client. The previous section of this chapter should have demonstrated to you that collaborating with top quality lawyers is a necessity for a responsible and successful football agent. Hence, if you have built up strong and trusting relationships or connections with sports or contract law specialists over the years, you will be able to find the right help.

The best case scenario is that you are close friends with sports lawyers who you can text or chat with and they will offer their assistance to you throughout your time as an agent and beyond, particularly in contract negotiations and other legal issues. However, if you are not in the fortunate position of being closely connected to a lawyer, you must know how to seek and find a suitable standard of legal professional to help you.

Due diligence and research is imperative. Look at the sports law firms that are available to you and speak to other agents or sports industry personnel as they will be able to advise you on the best lawyers they may have come across. Once you have found an attractive candidate, be aware that when reaching out to them you are beginning a relationship that could last for a lengthy period of time if both parties come to trust one another and work productively alongside each other. Ensure that you present yourself in a professional and reputable manner and advertise yourself as someone they would want to work with. The impression you give of your trustworthiness and personal values will influence the likelihood of them working with you and of a long-lasting professional relationship.

Some Examples of Top Football Lawyers:

Country	Lawyers
UK	Daniel Geey
Spain	Jessie Engelhart
France	Christophe Bertrand
Germany	Dr Frank Rybak
Italy	Lorenzo Cantamessa
USA	Andrew Visnovsky
Belgium	Kristof De Saedeleer
Brazil	Marcos Motta

In-House Lawyers

A final brief point to note on this topic is that often when working with clubs or if you are a part of a large agency, they may have access to 'in-house' lawyers. Put simply, the organisation will have a partnership with or even directly employ specialist sports lawyers to help with legal issues. As an agent, you may be able to access the use of these experts if you go through the right channels and people. However, bear in mind that these lawyers are employed by the club or by the agency so they may not always have your client's best interests at heart.

Nevertheless, the strength of your network rears its head once more. If you have developed your personal network to include lawyers that are employed within clubs or agencies, you will be able to know who you can trust and who will be able to offer specialist advice that is, most importantly, impartial.

If you are acting on behalf of the club, in-house club lawyers will inevitably be involved in the process. It is important to collaborate and communicate well with them to ensure you reach a desirable outcome. Appeasing club lawyers can reflect well upon your reputation and help you to obtain the result you are looking for such as successfully acting on behalf of the buying club to sign a new player. The non-negotiable factor throughout any dealings with lawyers is that there must be an element of trust present and a mutual goal to satisfy the best interests of the party you are representing.

Expert's View: Jessie Engelhart

Women's football director at FC Barcelona &
Sports lawyer

"Sports attorneys and sports agents are often perceived as interchangeable professions with similar profiles and responsibilities. I believe this to be fundamentally untrue.

As a Sports lawyer, my role is complementary to that of an agent. Yes some sports agents have a legal background and some sports lawyers simultaneously work as agents, but by no means are these professions similar in nature or interchangeable by default.

Sports agents should collaborate with sports lawyers to complement their activities and ensure legal compliance, even when they may have a legal background themselves. Being aware of the latest amendments to regulations, the newest jurisprudence and the application and interpretation of certain legal rules in practice, are crucial for the proper execution of legal activities such as contract drafting and signings. When representing an athlete's career, meticulous legal scrutiny is required for all contract negotiations, image rights and brand endorsement deals, player transfers and contractual disputes between the player and the club.

Regardless, agents often choose to save costs by not initially hiring a lawyer but then, once a dispute does arise, will have no choice but to resort to a lawyer and they will then have to pay a far higher bill. Prevention is better (and cheaper!) than cure.

One of the most common issues that sports agents encounter when choosing to work independently without consulting a specialised lawyer, is the validity of their representation agreements with players. Standard representation contracts often lack enforceable jurisdiction and exclusivity clauses in case of a unilateral breach of the representation contract by the player.

Sports lawyers are able to help ensure agent practices, procedures and contracts are compliant with the legal regulations concerning such activities as well as affording as much protection as possible for both the agent and the player. Having a trusted and capable network of lawyers both locally and internationally will be a huge benefit to you as an agent."

Summary

- There is a lot of overlap between agents and lawyers and the skills of a lawyer are complimentary to your capabilities as an agent
- Recognising when and why you may require the services of a legal expertise professional is an essential attribute of a successful agent
- Knowing or finding the right lawyer to collaborate with to obtain the goal of protecting the best interests of your client stems from developing a strong network across a variety of sports industry personnel
- The most important thing is that if you think you need a lawyer, you do need a lawyer. Never try to take shortcuts for selfishly or financially motivated reasons. In the long run, spending money on a legal specialist will benefit the client and your reputation as an agent.

Further Reading

- The Sports Lawyer Masterclass - Jessie Engelhart
- Sports Agents versus Sports Lawyers: http://sportsagentblog.com/2013/10/30/sports-agent-vs-sports-lawyer/

Chapter 23: Endorsements, Boot Deals and Commercialisation

"It is the role of the agent to seek and negotiate the best deals whilst leaving the player to concentrate on their on-pitch performances"

Introduction

Alongside playing and employment contracts, agents will have to deal with several additional contracts that must be sufficiently understood in order to negotiate the best outcome for their player. With the rising popularity and 'celebrity' status of modern footballers, the players are being commercialised. In other words, they are now sought after to become brand ambassadors for companies from a variety of sectors such as clothing, cars, watches, headphones, airlines and more. There are also on pitch sponsorship opportunities such as boot deals which can be an extremely important contract for a player and the agent. This new era of player brand endorsement has given rise to image rights agreements and companies which we will also outline within this chapter.

Endorsements

The term 'endorsements' refers to the partnerships formed between players and brands for commercial and promotional purposes. This takes the form of a commercial sponsorship contract which an agent will have to negotiate. If you are looking after the most globally-recognised players in the world, there will be an array of prospective endorsement deals for the player and your job is to help guide them to what is best for their personality and image. However, for most clients, the top agents will work hard to try and seek extra sources of income through paid partnerships and deals that go beyond simply boots and apparel. In general, there are four key considerations before making any commercial agreement:

1. **Type of brand:** does this company fit your client's personality and values, and is it in conflict with a principal sponsor of their club? If the company doesn't reflect what your player feels is important or is interested in, then perhaps it isn't the right partner. Similarly, being endorsed by a business that goes against religious or cultural beliefs could obviously be detrimental. Remember, whatever the public's opinion of this brand may be, it is now inadvertently linked to your client – be that good or bad. It is your job as the agent to understand the market and only suggest or engage with companies and brands that are suitable for your client.

2. **Territory and Reach:** is the deal regional or global? Many large companies have region specific offshoots. Therefore, is the endorsement for the brand global, or simply confined to a certain country or continent? This is a very important differentiation – global partnerships will normally mean more money, but regional deals are normally less risky as they are less committal and *may* allow your client to enter into agreements with companies in (relatively) similar areas. This involves the concept of exclusivity, a vital area for agents to understand in the modern commercialised era of football. We will explore this further later in this chapter.

3. **Requirements and Obligations:** part of the negotiation process will be to agree on what is actually required from the player. Social media posts, photoshoots, live appearances, interviews can all be part of the contract between player and sponsor, so make sure that your client is comfortable with what they have to do. Agents must know their client well enough to understand their level of interest and confidence in appearing or participating in such activities and campaigns.

4. **Length and value of contract:** as with any agreement, how long it is and the remuneration are two of the most crucial aspects. Like with all deals, ensure that the length of commitment is adequately represented in what is being paid. This also involves considering the aforementioned requirements and obligations that your player is contracted to. If they are having to spend hours of their days off travelling around as an ambassador for the brand, the agent must make sure they are appropriately compensated or that they negotiate to reduce these commitments.

In general, just make sure you are cautious in your decision making and keep the player updated with key developments. Unless you represent an iconic superstar, the more endorsement deals you have results in each future one being worth less as the brand recognition decreases. This is sometimes why one-off social media posts or promotions (combined with some endorsements) can be a good alternative to having lots of long-term sponsorship deals. Moreover, the types of deals discussed so far are based on a purely monetary basis, and actually not all deals are solely financial. For example, an agreement with a car company or watch manufacturer may mainly be free gifts (and a small fee on the side) due to the worth of the item being so high. Again, this is where understanding your client is important as they may have a distinct interest in watches or cars and will happily engage with these sponsors for material compensation whilst others will prefer you to negotiate a cash sponsorship fee.

Sometimes as an agent it is important to be realistic with what you can advise a player on. It is absolutely essential to have a general understanding of all areas that a football career may become involved in. However, expertise in all of these areas is incredibly difficult. Part of the skill of a successful agent is knowing when to outsource work to experts and having a network which allows you to reach out to trusted experts in such areas. Hence, some footballers and agents collectively decide to sell the player's image rights to a media agency for a guaranteed fee plus a split of commission. Below is a list of some media and marketing agencies known for working directly with footballers:

Head office location	Agency
Los Angeles	Creative Artists Agency (CAA)
London	MediaCom
Munich	We Play Forward
London	CSM Sport & Entertainment
New York	Roc Nation
London	The Goat Agency

The role of these commercial agencies is to specifically focus upon finding the best commercial sponsorship opportunities for your player. We have worked with several fantastic commercial, marketing, endorsement and sponsorship specialists, particularly Erkut in his experiences with Mesut, and he has become very close friends with some. He can trust them to find the best deals for clients and they are able to offer an expert opinion and strategy to help achieve the greatest outcome for the player.

Image Rights

Image Rights Agreements are a relatively new addition to football contracts. They have risen as a result of the growing commercialisation and marketability of football players in the age of social media influencing, global recognition and lucrative sponsorships of clubs. These agreements are made in order to protect the players right to receive an income from the use of the personal attributes. Image Rights Agreements, therefore, provide a mechanism for which clubs can remunerate players for their off-pitch commercial activities with sponsors associated with the club which benefits the club itself commercially and financially.

The endorsement of products and the players' involvement in any kind of marketing affiliated with the club for which they play can vary greatly. Players often appear in television advertisements, on billboards and can be seen posing in or with a range of endorsed products. Image Rights Agreements also incorporate the use of the player and their image for activities such as photo shoots in the new season kit of the club or other official merchandise and team wear and the permissibility of distributing these images across the club's social media channels. It is important to note that the 'image' of a player refers to a broad scope. This includes; their face, haircut, voice, nickname, autograph, squad number and any other 'trademark' characteristics they might possess. Their following, publicity, reputation, personality, fame, status and personal fan-base then further influences the value of their image.

Players of particularly public status will often outsource their image rights to a company which the club will pay directly. The role of an agent here is firstly to negotiate the terms between the club and the image rights company to ensure that the client is properly remunerated for their off-pitch, commercial activities on behalf of the club. It is important to remember that this is of financial and commercial benefit to the club so the player must be valued as such.

Image Rights in Practice

For example, a company, in this case Emirates, that is an official airline partner of a major club such as Arsenal, is more prone to be interested in using the most recognisable faces of the club in their campaigns. Let's say, for the sake of this example, that Bukayo Saka was requested by Emirates to be a part of their latest advertisement, Arsenal would be able to call upon Saka for his services through their image rights agreement and a licence they will have obtained. This licence is obtained through demonstrating that the provision of Saka's image to the sponsor is commercially viable and generates additional income for the club.

On Saka's side, the young English star will most likely have set up his own Image Rights Company. This is commonplace for players of his stature. An agent will help the player sell their image rights to the company which will then be entitled to a fee directly from (in this case) Arsenal for the use of Saka's image. The benefits of this is that the money received directly from the club will only be taxed at a company rate of 19% rather than included in a player's 45% income tax if it were to be paid directly to Saka. Further tax may be paid at a future date once the player takes the money out of the company but it is most likely to be kept there and can be seen as security savings for once a player retires. Agents are also financial advisers so must help a client navigate this process and may even outsource this to tax experts to better inform their service to their client.

The agreement with the image rights company will have been set out when the player signs with the club in their employment contract. This avoids legal complications and sets out the parameters the clubs can use in exploiting the image of their star players. However, in some instances, disputes over image rights agreements can be a decisive factor in signing for a club. This was the case in 2019 when it seemed Paulo Dybala was set to transfer to Tottenham Hotspur in the English Premier League. Ultimately, the deal collapsed as a result of a failure to agree upon image rights clauses. Despite being irrelevant to the football on the pitch that a club is signing the player to play, in the modern era of commercialised football, it is interesting that image rights can take on a significant role in contract negotiations. Ultimately, these negotiations come down to the agent so image rights are something you must be aware of and consider in order to fulfil your duty to a player of obtaining the best possible contractual terms.

Boot Deals

Ultimately, football boots are the most essential piece of equipment for a player to carry out their job. A boot deal refers to a deal that is made between a player and a boot manufacturer in order to supply the player with boots. This also often includes shinpads and, in the case of goalkeepers, gloves. Of course, as with almost all contracts in football, it can become far more complicated than this.

First and foremost, it is important to understand that boot deals span far across the world of football. The majority of players at a professional level will have a boot deal unless they have deliberately chosen not to, all will at least have been offered or approached for one. Even several semi-professional footballers will have a boot deal of some kind. This may be what is known as a 'boot supply deal' where, for example, one or two pairs of boots are provided per season free of charge but with no additional monetary fee paid to the player.

In top level football, however, these deals can be enormously lucrative as well as providing a new pair of boots every few weeks if the player so desires. Furthermore, and arguably more importantly, for a player it is vital that their agent finds a deal with a boot manufacturer that they are comfortable with wearing and can perform to the best of their ability in.

The deals can be made via negotiation from the boot manufacturer with the player's agent. However, more common is for a player's agent to delegate this responsibility to a commercial team or lawyers that specialise in commercial contracts as mentioned in the first section of this chapter. The contracts themselves are complicated and can include an array of clauses such as performance-based add-ons on top of a fixed 'base' sponsorship compensation. This may include terms such as bonuses for televised appearances for the player's club or country; the percentage of minutes they play per game; the category of the club for which they play for and whether or not they are competing in international and continental competitions such as the UEFA Champions League.

Boot deals can be separated into three 'categories' which an agent must understand. These are summarised below:

1. **A supply contract:** a common form of boot deal for youth or lower league semi-professionals. If we consider that a youth player or their parents must source around £250 per pair of top quality boots, this is a significant expense each year. Brands or the agents themselves will usually assist with this by providing supply contracts to distribute boots to upcoming players. This could be a good opportunity for agents to show the player what they can provide and to build a relationship. The brand may also be willing to include other bits of sports apparel such as tracksuits.

2. **Boots + Budget:** the next step up also does not include a sponsorship fee for the player. Instead, players will be given complimentary boots as per a supply contract, as well as a non-cash budget for the brand. For exciting young players this may be between £2,000 and £10,000 to spend on the wider range that the brand sells from trainers to caps and other apparel. This type of contract may occur for a player who has signed their first professional contract or is playing in the middle divisions of national football.

3. **Full Sponsorship Boot Deal:** for the top players, this kind of deal involves a cash fee as remuneration on top of free boots and a higher budget to spend with the manufacturer. The value of this sponsorship deal depends on the categorisation of the club for which the player plays which are ranked as a, b, c, and d. The categorisation varies according to the exposure the club receives. For example, when Mesut Özil was at Real Madrid, they were competing in one of Europe's top leagues, on television every week and competing in the Champions League. They were an obvious category A club. This was the same when he moved to Arsenal although since Arsenal are now no longer in the Champions League they have become a category B club.

This can ultimately affect the transfer of players between clubs as it could cause a large financial loss to the player. For example, a category A club player may have a contract for £2million annually from their boot deal but if they move to a category B club, as per the terms stated in their contract, this may be halved or even quartered!

Agents should be aware of this when considering whether a transfer is the right option for their client.

Boot deals are an interesting concept for agents to monitor as we believe and predict that the future of boot deals differs from the modern situation we currently see. It makes sense to us that more and more players will move away from the contractual obligations that arise with boot deals. In the modern era, footballers have become celebrities and influencers and can develop their personal brands through social media and otherwise. The ability of players to grow, develop and promote their own personal brand is significantly restricted by signing a boot deal with a single brand.

The biggest names will instead create their own brand and enter into agreements with manufacturers. For example, Mesut Özil's M10 brand now has a contract with manufacturer, Concave, in order to design and sell his own range of boots. A consequence of this may be that brands offer larger sums for boot deals to convince players to stay but in the age of personal brands, it will most likely make more social and financial sense for the biggest players to go their own way through their personal brands. Rather than being contractually obliged to always wear a single brand in all of their apparel and accessories, they will be able to express themselves and their personal brand freely. Agents must be well-equipped in order to support such a commitment and decision.

Exclusivity

Exclusivity is a fairly straightforward term to comprehend. It refers to the idea that a player or a club that enters into an endorsement contract will likely have agreed to exclusivity to that product or brand. In other words, partnering with a certain brand or company will simultaneously prevent a similar agreement taking place between the same party and a rival company and therefore prevents the sponsored party from publicly promoting their products. The most prevalent example of this in football is between the two sports apparel giants, Nike and Adidas. Evidently, a player or club that is partnered with or sponsored by one is not permitted to advertise or even use the products of a rival company. This can raise issues when an Adidas sponsored player plays for a club that is sponsored by New Balance or a national team sponsored by Nike. Whilst this is permitted, it is something that players need to be careful with and it is your role as the agent to assist them in avoiding breaching their contractual obligations.

In more complex cases, exclusivity can also apply to things like using headphones, watches, leisurewear, cars and hats of a certain brand which sponsors the player. This can make things difficult and restricts what a player can and can't do; it is something they and their agent must be wary of when negotiating and signing an endorsement contract. It is the responsibility of the agent to ensure that no unreasonable exclusivity clauses are a part of the contract and that the player is made aware of the implications of exclusivity. Agents must note exclusivity when they are negotiating such deals to include in the agreement that if the player does have broader obligations of exclusivity to the brand that is providing them with a boot deal, for example, then they must be appropriately and sufficiently remunerated.

It is important to remember that the sole purpose of exclusivity is that your player must not be seen to be wearing or using and obviously promoting a rival brand, but it becomes more complicated once club partnerships are considered and agents need to consider this. This has impacted major stars such as Cristiano Ronaldo (Nike) at Real Madrid (Adidas) and even for managers such as Jose Mourinho (Jaguar) who experienced issues as manager of Manchester United who were affiliated with Chevrolet as their Official Vehicle Partner.

Agents need to be aware of the existence and possibility of 'matching clauses' in supplier contracts. These clauses are included to expressly state that suppliers are able to extend the contract of a player up until 180 days after its expiry date provided that they at least match any offer from a competitor. This binds the player to that brand unless they are unable to offer the same financial reward and additional benefits that another brand does. This often makes it difficult for a player to leave the brand and is a slight variation of an exclusivity rule. Be careful of clauses like this to prevent your client being locked down by one brand!

To give you a sense of the influence that these players can have and why the exclusivity clauses are so important to the sponsors; it is estimated that Cristiano Ronaldo generated approximated $216million in additional value for his sponsor's rivals Adidas simply by sporting it as part of his Real Madrid kit. Messi returned the favour himself and it is suggested that as he wore the Nike kit of Barcelona, he contributed around $110million in value to Adidas' rivals. So, despite the best efforts of the company to maximise exclusivity, the impact of such global stars still having to wear the rival's brand is strongly felt. Hence, brands will do all they can to ensure that the exclusivity clause is applicable in as many circumstances as is reasonably enforceable. This gives you as the agent another element of your client to consider and negotiate with when dealing with brands and possible sponsors. Avoid exclusivity as much as possible to keep your client's opportunities unrestricted and if it cannot be avoided, ensure they are compensated adequately.

Expert's View: Misha Sher

*Global Head of Sport, Entertainment &
Culture at MediaCom working with clients such
as Vinicius Jr, Adidas and Pele*

"Over the past 20 years, I've had the opportunity and the privilege to work with some of the biggest brands and players in developing high value commercial and strategic partnerships. There has never been a better time to be a player and create a personal brand that can be monetized and sustained many years after retirement. Unfortunately, in my experience, most players and their agents miss this opportunity and what I'd like to do is highlight how to avoid these pitfalls.

First and foremost, as you've already read in this chapter, it's absolutely imperative to work with experts. Every player knows that to perform and sustain a successful career on the pitch will require surrounding themselves with the very best people who can impact their performance. That means chefs, personal trainers, sports psychologists and so on. There isn't an agent on the planet that can claim to also be qualified to be the chef or nutritionist yet, most players trust their agents or friends to manage their commercial activities off the pitch. This is not how David Beckham, Lebron James, Lewis Hamilton or Roger Federer got to where they are in the world of business and brands. They surround themselves with the best and the best agents I've worked with understand this. Your job as an agent is to set your client up for success and that involves understanding your strengths and weaknesses. Working with trusted partners, as I have with Erkut for many years, is exactly what you should be striving to do.

Second, and I'll use the football analogy again, it's important to build a personal brand that can attract commercial opportunities. What exactly does this mean? As a footballer, the player has to put themselves in the best position possible to attract potential clubs. No matter how good or well-connected the agent may be, he or she will never be able to convince a top club to sign the player if they're not up to the standard. The same rule applies off the pitch. In today's world of celebrities, it's not near enough to be a good or well-known footballer. There are thousands of them. What you need to be is someone who transcends football and has relevance in popular culture. The reason being is that brands aren't just looking to high profile footballers to be their ambassadors. They don't care if the ambassador is a footballer, a gamer or a TikTok travel influencer. What they care about is the individual's influence and reach. I can name some amazing footballers, some of the best in the world, who have little to no value to brands because they don't have any influence off the pitch. Companies like Pepsi or Samsung, amongst others, want talent that gives them reach, relevance and connection with consumers that elevates anything they can do on their own. That's why Pepsi signs the likes of Pogba, Ronaldinho and Vini Jr. They're not just big names but players who have become universally known for their personality and charisma. They align with Pepsi's brand ethos and that's why they are the brand's global ambassadors. What this means is that players need to diligently craft a personal brand narrative and reinforce that narrative through social media, partnerships, appearances, philanthropy and so on. Players must become personalities that people are interested in beyond on-field performances.

Third, I have a little secret for everyone reading this chapter. Brands are not interested in whether your player needs a car, a watch or a personal care partner. If I had a dime for every agent that has told me that his player needs a car, I would be retired in Turks and Caicos. Brands are not interested in what you need, they are interested in what they need. So my advice to any agent who wants to increase his or her chances of developing long lasting, high value commercial partnerships, is to do their homework and understand why the player would be of interest to a particular brand. Erling Haaland recently signed a major deal with watch brand *Breitling* and when you read how it happened, it's no surprise. Haaland has always been into watches and had a particular preference for Breitling. All you need to do is look at his social media and his interest in watches is clear. As such, building a partnership with Breitling is a no-brainer as the story already exists in the eyes of the consumers. Breitling are not signing a random high-profile footballer. They are signing a player who is known to love watches and their brand in particular. Agents need to understand what their players are into and then help them build a narrative around those interests. Then, when it comes to approaching brand partners, give the brand a reason to care by focusing on their needs. Only when we've taken the time to understand what challenges brands are looking to solve, and where you players can be the answer, can we genuinely expect to engage in meaningful conversations.

To summarise, succeeding off the pitch and building significant commercial revenues requires a strategy, diligence and understanding that fame alone won't be enough. If you're in the business of 'doing deals', you risk always focusing on yourself and forgetting the deals are actually partnerships where 1+1=3. Like success on the pitch, it's impossible to achieve off-field success with shortcuts. Those who have the longest careers and those who have built significant off-field income have done so by working with the best and having a plan. Everyone else is missing a trick."

Summary

- To a large extent, football and its players have become commercialised.
- There are a variety of sponsorship opportunities available to players and it is the role of the agent to seek and negotiate the best deals whilst leaving the player to concentrate on their on-pitch performances
- There are companies who have specific expertise in commercial sponsorship deals and agents can collaborate with them in order to best serve their clients.
- Image rights agreements are important for agents to negotiate with clubs within contracts of top players.
- Image rights companies can be useful to a player in protecting their income from sponsorship deals and promotional activity.
- Boot deals are the most common and most important deal after the playing contract and should be treated as such by the agent.
- Exclusivity issues rear their heads in boot deals as well and contradiction between boot brands for players, clubs, and national teams will affect the player's income so should be considered.

Further Reading

- Football players as brand ambassadors: https://research.cbs.dk/en/studentProjects/football-players-as-brand-ambassadors-their-influence-on-consumer

- Football Player Boot Deals Explained | Daniel Geey: https://www.danielgeey.com/post/football-player-boot-deals-explained/

Chapter 24: Additional Off-Pitch Work of an Agent

"Service to others is the rent you pay for your room here on Earth." - Muhammad Ali

Introduction

So far, we have looked at the major areas away from the football field that agents have a responsibility in for their clients such as commercial sponsorships and post-retirement sustainability. However, there are also many other duties that have to be carried out with diligence in different sectors. Some of these tasks may seem relatively straightforward but they are things that can set you apart from other agents who do not devote enough attention to them. Remember, if you are competing with a number of agents who are equally as good as you at negotiating employment contracts, there has to be other little bits that you can offer your clients that distinguishes you above the rest. The top agents will do more than just negotiate a move from one club to another and will provide their client with a vast array of services, the final few of which we will outline in this chapter.

Charity

Although something like charity would never appear in a Representation Contract, or even cross most people's mind when thinking about the agency world, our opinion is that agents have a moral obligation to ensure their clients give back to those in a less fortunate position than themselves. For the most part, the charity work of a player is usually closely tied in with their club. Most teams have their own charitable foundation (or at least charities in which they are close to) that the players will have to help represent. Normally, charitable activities include team visits to hospitals or hosting training sessions for children and young adults at the stadium or training ground.

If you help your client understand the importance of philanthropic work, they will also build up a positive reputation. Consequently, they might even be asked to be part of a global campaign either on behalf of National Associations, large charitable organisations, FIFA or UEFA. These bodies sometimes use the top and most reputable players to help promote their charitable endeavours. Given the influence you have on the player, you must also try to make them aware that charity work shouldn't be confined to compulsory attendance days or visits with clubs or federations. There is a variety of independent initiatives that you and your client can undertake in order to help local and international communities:

1. **Your client creates their own foundation:** perhaps one of the more long-term initiatives when it comes to charitable contributions is to help your client to set up a foundation in their own name. Often, if a player has a foundation then themselves or a family member will be responsible for the running of it. The foundation can be targeted at anything that personally resonates with the player. This is important to consider as it helps create a meaningful charitable cause that a player can connect with on a more personal level and devote themselves to growing it. Throughout its development and existence, your role as an agent is one of guidance and assistance when and where it is appropriate.

2. **Tickets and memorabilia:** an easier way to give back on a regular basis is through matchday experiences or signed gifts. You as the agent can make this process more efficient by taking care of all the arrangements. This includes things such as sending out tickets and personal invites to charities or specific fans to attend a game and maybe even experience hospitality in the stadium. This becomes more feasible especially if you are looking after a top client that has a box or suite at the stadium. Alternatively, if you contact the club then they would more than likely assist in finding great seats. Similarly, giving away signed memorabilia (kits, boots, footballs, etc.) is such an easy yet powerful thing that you can push your client to do frequently. You can source the shirts or other items and arrange a time for your client to sit down and do some signing or write personal messages.

Case studies

-   Sadio Mané

- Donated £500,000 to build a hospital in his Senegalese home village of Bambali.
- Donated £41,000 and actively took a role in supporting the Senegalese government to help combat COVID-19 fatalities.
- Donated £250,000 to build a secondary school in Bambali.
- Regularly gifts shirts, memorabilia and other forms of donations to African children and partner charities.
- Mesut Özil
  - Mesut donated his 2010 World Cup earnings of £237,000 to fund surgeries for 23 children in Brazil.
  - He has been helping children receive vital operations every month ever since the 2014 Brazilian World Cup in any country where his support is needed.
  - He has also incited other big names to join forces and engage in similar charitable work as detailed below.
- **BigShoe:** Actively supported by Mesut Özil, Bukayo Saka, Antonio Rüdiger, Paul Pogba, Philipp Lahm
  - Providing funding and access to life changing services.
  - Including medical operations and specialist medical teams.
  - It has helped support over 1600 children with medical needs.
- Marcus Rashford
  - Has teamed up with FareShare to provide free school meals to impoverished children in Manchester and now in a nationwide campaign.
  - Provides 1.2m children with free school meal vouchers.
- Wayne Rooney
  - Created the Wayne Rooney Foundation.
  - Partners with NSPCC, Claire House Children's Hospice and other charities and fundraisers.

Property

One thing that an agent *may* have to advise on are living arrangements of the player. Whilst there is no formula for where and how players live, their on-pitch situation does normally dictate what happens. If you're representing a top player who has a stable position at their club, then it makes sense to secure a long-term rent or even purchase a property. Not only is the latter advantageous particularly if the player has (or is planning to start) a family, but also because property *can* be a good investment.

If your player has a growing portfolio of assets, then this can only be seen as positive so long as they maintain their worth in the market. Of course, like any investment, the buying of property is by no means a guaranteed profitable exercise, so do make sure you consult with some experts and lawyers beforehand.

Alternatively, most young players could possibly still live with their family, and not want to buy a property in case they are loaned out or transferred to another club. Similarly, if your client is on the fringes of the first-team and perhaps only on a short-term contract or looking likely to be transferred, it may be better to just rent somewhere until they are more secure and stable. Remember, whatever the footballing situation, it is partially your responsibility to ensure that the player is living comfortably, as this will only benefit on-pitch performances. In the modern era, clubs also have staff which are known as Player Care (or Welfare) Officers. It may be useful to network with and build relationships with them as their job description includes things like helping the players of a club with property and living queries.

Tax

Being an accountant and having an exhaustive knowledge of taxation is not a prerequisite skill to be a successful agent. If you are able to have some extent of an understanding of this then it will benefit the service you can provide but taxes may be one of the many instances where it is important to recognise that the best option for your client is to outsource to a professional financial adviser for their help.

If you are an agent who is (or aspires to be) doing everything for their player, then making sure they pay their taxes on time and legally is fundamentally important. Simply put, footballers are **not** above the law, and taxes and bills still have to be paid. There is no shortage of players in the news and media who have allegedly not paid tax or attempted to get around certain rules and regulations. Often, this comes about when certain people approach you, your client, or their family, detailing a great plan to save money and to reduce their tax bills. At the end of the day you represent the player's best interest, and ultimately making sure everything is done legally and properly is non-negotiable. Having a really trustworthy and reliable accountant in your network will make this a far simpler ambition. When starting out, speaking to other reliable agents or the players themselves about who they currently use is a good way to go about finding one to build a relationship with. A relationship with a tax adviser or accountant may last the duration of your career as an agent and help you serve many clients well.

Investments and Wealth Management

This topic is covered in greater detail in chapters 26, 27 and 28. To emphasise this point, whilst being an expert investor is also not an essential skill of an agent, it is important that you are able to help a client think about how best to utilise the financial security and wealth that they may accumulate during their career. From NFTs, to property, to stocks, there is a variety of options which you and your player might consider.

For investments it is once again important to outsource decisions and professional advice to those that do this as their job. Utilising your network will allow the player to access experts who can even invest their money for them. If done properly, this can provide financial sustainability even after the player has retired.

Case Studies

- Mathieu Flamini
    - Has now become the CEO of GF Biochemials.
    - Co-founded the biochemical company during his playing career and invested his earnings into its development.
    - The company is now estimated to be worth £21billion.
- Mesut Özil
    - Has invested in a 50% stake of a Mexican football club, club Necaxa alongside Hollywood Stars.
    - Alongside Aaron Ramsey and Petr Cech, Mesut has invested in the Essex-based, Lewin Sports Injury Clinic.
    - Mesut also owns a chain of coffee shops as well as his own streetwear clothing brand.
    - Has founded his own eSports team under the M10 brand.
- Cristiano Ronaldo

- o   Has built and invested into his own property empire including some of the most expensive properties in the UK, Portugal and Spain.
- o   Has built his own CR7 fashion brand which produces and distributes a variety of products including shoes, denim, underwear and fragrances.
- o   The CR7 brand is estimated to be worth around $63million
- o   Cristiano also owns a chain of 'lifestyle' hotels in New York City, Lisbon, Paris, Marrakesh, and Madrid, as well as a four-star hotel in Funchal Madeira, his birthplace.

eSports

One area that is somewhat linked with investments and post-career opportunities is that of eSports. Nowadays there exists eSports 'athletes', who play video games (such as FIFA) in a professional capacity. Although this modern concept may seem strange at first, eSports 'athletes', like real footballers, need professional representation too as many of them play for teams, which therefore requires contracts (and sometimes transfers!), in addition to marketing too. So, in this sense, you could also represent eSports players, alongside your other clients.

However, the way this links in with the ideas discussed in this chapter is that footballers and ex-footballers (as well as those from other sports) are engaging with this new phenomenon in many different ways. Some are investing into eSports companies and teams, whilst others are building their own professional squad that compete competitively. Although this market is somewhat still small, it is expected to see significant growth in the near future. Part of your education of becoming an agent might include expanding your breadth and depth of knowledge in the gaming sector as it may become more and more relevant as part of the job of being an agent.

Expert's View: We Play Forward

"PR and marketing is a vital component for any player in the modern era of football. Agents have had to adapt in recent times to understand and identify where possible opportunities may arise for their clients to boost their careers and fulfilment through alternative off-pitch work. This 'off-pitch activity' can take many forms, from charity work to a passion for investments but can add value in equal measure to a client's career and income.

Proactively seeking and thinking about off-pitch opportunities is the responsibility of the agent. A client will always recognise the extent of the value that an agent can add to their career in doing so which is only a benefit for your own career.

At We Play Forward, however, we have our own responsibilities in this process. The best agents will recognise their own shortfalls in terms of expertise in areas such as off-pitch work and will bring in the help of professional PR and marketing companies like ourselves. The result is usually that the player receives the best assistance possible in developing their presence away from the football pitch and to thrive in different sectors that are important to them.

For us, the relationship we have with certain agents is always something that helps us gauge the kind of projects we can work on and obtain the best outcomes. It isn't just down to the status and stance of the player but also involves the working relationship we can have with the agent and hence, their client."

Summary

- Always try to think one step ahead of everybody else – in planning projects and making key decisions, always think short-, medium-, and long-term when possible.
- Remember, do not try to do everything yourself. Serving your client's best interests is the priority for you. If this means outsourcing work or advice to experts and professionals in certain areas then do not refrain from doing so to reach the best outcome.
- You ought to be aware of (but not an expert in) all of the possible avenues away from the pitch that may be worth exploring for your client. Always educate yourself and keep up-to-date with how different industries are also evolving

and changing and be proactive in spotting the right opportunities for your client to involve themselves in.

Further Reading

- Why Has Nobody Told Me This Before - Dr Julie Smith

Chapter 25: Social Media and Client Marketing

Introduction

With the game of football no longer being confined to the pitch, as an agent you have to be constantly thinking about how to make the most of the platform that your client has. Remember, sports is one of the few industries in which its workers (i.e. the athletes) have a relatively short window of opportunity coupled with a brief time in the public spotlight. Given that the on-pitch career of a footballer is normally no longer than a 15-year period, you have to make sure that they build their foundations away from the pitch whilst still active and develop an engaged global fanbase. In the modern era, footballers have taken to social media as a platform for promoting themselves, their lifestyles and their personal image or 'brand'. This chapter explores the role that agents play in these sectors.

Social Media

A critical component of the commercialisation of footballers is social media, and it is vital that your client has a well-established social media presence on the key sites. Part of the reason why the players listed can attract the most valuable marketing deals is because their social media following is so large and can therefore reach the highest amount of potential customers for the brand. It is common for either the agent to control the social media of the player, or (for perhaps more famous clients) organise a digital agency to help with the accounts and posts. In both situations, it is important that the messages given to fans are positive (for example posting a picture of the player working hard at training or in the gym) and also conform to contractual agreements with the club and sponsors. For example, a company may sponsor the player to wear their sportswear, and the contract states that there is to be a minimum of five posts with that brand in a month.

You should also try to make your client have a presence in other countries' social media channels too. For example, Weibo (China) has twice as many users than Twitter - so this can be a very valuable tool to have. Whilst social media is great, it can also be very dangerous if not taken seriously or carefully. You have to make sure that your client avoids discussing injuries or tactics that can help an opponent, or post any 'sensitive' material that may cause serious offence. Overall, social media is almost a necessity when it comes to the marketing of football players. It allows the public to gain an almost unparalleled insight into the personality of their sporting heroes, therefore becoming a more attractive prospect for brands. It opens a more personal medium for players to directly interact and engage with their fan-base. If this is done in the right way it can become a significantly beneficial aspect of a player's career. Simply put, the more content and followers a player has on social media, the more of a brand they are able to build around themselves, which will only result in a greater number of commercial opportunities.

Below is a table of the most followed male and female players (current and retired) on the planet. Evidently, this is correlated with the number of advertisements and public promotions that you will see them appearing in as they are highly sought after by brands and companies:

Player	Instagram (M)	Facebook (M)	Twitter (M)	Overall (M)
Cristiano Ronaldo	538	153	103	794
Neymar Jr.	179	88	58	325
Lionel Messi	364	106	–	470
David Beckham	75	56	–	131
Kylian Mbappe	73	15	9	97
Mesut Özil	24	37	26	87
Robert Lewandowski	30	24	2.6	56.6
Alex Morgan	10	6	4	20
Megan Rapinoe	2	0.7	1	3.7

Sources: Instagram, Facebook, Twitter (correct as of September 2022)

What is interesting to see here is that a player's following can span across different social media platforms and each must be approached differently to attract and appeal to certain audiences and demographics. Furthermore, it is important to note that someone like David Beckham, who has been retired for a considerable number of years, can continue to generate post-career income through the brand and global popularity that they generated during their time as a footballer. Finally, Alex Morgan is a long way ahead of any other female player as she has seized the opportunity of the modern era of social media, coupled with the rise of women's football and has developed a hugely successful personal brand. She boasts the likes of Nike, Coca-Cola and Chapstick on her endorsement portfolio, which generates far more from off-field earnings than from her club wages.

Personal Brands

It has become a common trend in the modern football era, particularly with the top players, to work towards building a strong and popular personal brand that is attractive to potential sponsors. As we will see in the case study given in the following section, possessing a world-renowned personal brand opens up a unique variety of opportunities to companies and to players which comes hand-in-hand with lucrative remuneration and publicity.

Players may work directly with professional media agencies such as MediaCom and We Play Forward to develop personal brands and seek the best commercial opportunities. This process begins with the player establishing their own values, principles, behaviours and visions in order to inform those helping them as to what form of commercial partnership the player might best engage with. For example, religious and cultural beliefs may alter and restrict the companies that would be appropriate for a player to endorse, such as a personal objection to gambling or alcohol. This would mean the player is unlikely to enter an agreement with a betting or alcoholic beverage commercial partner! This was the case recently with Kylian Mbappe who took a stand and refused to be a part of a new gambling advert. However, a stance such as this may open up alternative opportunities such as partnering with a betting-rehabilitation charity or a responsible-drinking campaign. It is the responsibility of the player and their agent to find a sponsor that fits appropriately with the attributes, personality traits and interests of the individual player.

A player can build their own personal brand in a variety of ways. Through the manner of their interaction with their fanbase and the insight they provide them through their social media channels, the players begin to develop a specific public image. Their personality and interests shape the kind of commercial sponsorship deals they are likely to become involved in. Some players will become widely known for certain 'trademark' things or behaviours. The most typical example of this is Cristiano Ronaldo's 'Siiii' goal celebration. Other examples include Leroy Sané who includes #inSané on his social media posts, or the 'JLingz' hand sign seen being used by Jesse Lingard.

If developing a personal brand is successful enough, players may even venture beyond partnering with a large brand and take on the challenge of monetising their own brand through some platform. There are several examples of this such as the aforementioned JLingz brand which is now a line of clothing or the street apparel brand belonging to Mesut Özil, M10 Streetwear, named after his M10 trademark. Alternatively, players may enter collaborations with brands in a variety of ways that will name the product after them. There have been many examples of this such as the David Beckham Homme aftershave, the Chris Kamara Street Soccer video game or the CR7 Drive Sports Drink by Herbalife and Cristiano Ronaldo, one of many that Cristiano has developed as a result of his global brand.

Case Study: CR7

Predictably, in football at least, David Beckham, Neymar, Lionel Messi and Cristiano Ronaldo have accumulated the greatest earnings from commercial deals and other off-field ventures. Beckham continues to generate an annual income of approximately $40million, he laid the foundations of his personal brand early in his career and still works with major brands now such as H&M, Sainsbury's, Samsung, Adidas, Breitling and his own fashion brand, Kent & Curwen. For Neymar, his commercial income of over $20million is generated across a large variety of brands from Nike, clothing brand Relay Jenas, C&A underwear, GAGO MILANO watches with which he has three of his own branded pieces, Beats by Dre headphones, food and beverage giants McDonalds and Red Bull,

Gillette toiletries, Panini stickers and many other brands that have paid large sums to collaborate with the Brazilian. The full extent of his reach can be seen in the exhaustive list below:

To continue, Lionel Messi supposedly earns around $33million annually from endorsements with leading brands such as Adidas, Gatorade and Pepsi and a number of partnerships in different categories.. However, arguably the greatest personal brand in football and certainly the most lucrative is the *CR7* trademark, belonging to Portuguese superstar Cristiano Ronaldo.

In 2021, Cristiano was one of the world's highest paid athletes across any sport. He earned over $100million in that year alone. Notably for the purpose of this chapter, over half of that figure (approximately $55million) was earned through commercial sponsorship deals away from the football field. This placed him third in the world of sport for endorsement income, behind only Lebron James and now-retired Tennis star, Roger Federer. He has earned over $1billion across his illustrious career and his ability to balance his match performances with an extraordinary ability to globalise and monetise his personal brand has been a significant feature of his success.

Aside from the footballing ability, attention-capturing character, marketable appearance and catchy goal celebration, Cristiano's social media has played a vital role in catapulting both his fame and his fortunes away from the pitch. His Instagram following of over 500million users puts him way on top as the most followed person on the planet, streaks ahead of second-placed Kylie Jenner and third-placed sporting-rival, Lionel Messi. His Twitter following of over 100million also puts him near the top of the world, around 30million behind number-one ranked former US President, Barack Obama. To indicate this significance of Cristiano's influence, it is important to note that within the very first 24-hours following his departure to Italy, Real Madrid lost one million social media followers whilst Juventus gained over 6million. This was repeated recently as his new Saudi Arabian club, Al Nassr went from less than one million followers before Cristiano's unveiling to over 10million in a few days. The impact of his move to Juventus in 2018 and then subsequently rejoining Manchester United in 2020 is shown in the graphic below:

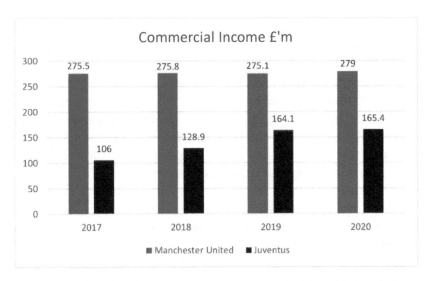

Commercial Income £'m

Source: The Conversation

These world-leading social media statistics have made what Cristiano has achieved commercially possible. His channels have provided him with an enormously powerful and influential platform to connect with his fans in a unique manner. Brands have identified this opportunity to have Cristiano promote and endorse their products to his engaged audience of millions and hence many have vied for his signature and commitment as an ambassador. This enthusiasm to sign one of the game's greatest states was reflected as he became only the third athlete in history, after Lebron James and Michael Jordan, and the very first footballer, to sign a lifetime deal with Nike worth over $1billion. Alongside the fundamental sportswear apparel and boots deal, the CR7 brand has been utilised widely. It is suggested that companies will pay around $1.5million per promotional Instagram post onto Cristiano's page.

Cristiano has taken on endorsements with an expansive variety of brands. These include nutrition brand Herbalife, through his own drink 'CR7 Drive'; streaming and media platform DAZN; Clear shampoo; and he is a global ambassador for the luxury watchmaker Tag Heuer, among many others during his career. He has been a part of an array of advertising campaigns and his face is seen across cities from bus stop posters to large LED Billboards. It is the perfect example of monetising one's position in the public spotlight.

Importantly, Cristiano has developed his own personal values and attributes that form his global brand known as CR7. The trademark has become synonymous with things like fitness, lifestyle, family-oriented and, of course, the 'Siii' celebration. This has enabled him to collaborate with companies and to set up his own ventures. CR7 has been used in naming his own fragrances; his own fashion brand of underwear, shoes and other apparel; a hair clinic; and even his own CR7 lifestyle hotels which can now be found in New York, Lisbon, Madrid, Paris and his home city of Madeira, which happens to be conjoined with the Cristiano Ronaldo museum.

His endorsements, partnerships and off-field work have not always been about attracting large and lucrative deals with major brands. It is almost imperative that a player of such calibre, and other footballers of any level that have the financial ability to do so, align their principles and their personal interests with charitable causes. In Cristiano's situation, he has often emphasised his family values through partnering and supporting charities such as UNICEF, Save The Children and the Red Cross. He is also a regular blood donor and even auctioned his 2013 Ballon d'Or trophy for $600,000 which was contributed to the Make-a-Wish foundation. Building a successful brand as a player is not just for the purpose of receiving pay packages; it is also about achieving a position and status in society that can be utilised to make a meaningful and positive difference to the world around the player.

As the agent, you play a pivotal role in all of this. From the development of your client's social media, to the subsequent exploitation of their enhanced following for off-pitch projects, be that endorsements or personal businesses. You must be knowledgeable in the field of social media and marketing to the extent that you are able to advise your client in a manner that helps them to establish and grow their own brand and become attractive to additional sources of income through endorsements.

Expert's View: We Play Forward

"Maybe even just over a decade ago, a full chapter on this topic would not have warranted a place in this book. However, as is typical of the ever-evolving and altering landscape of football, social media has had a substantial impact upon the sport, the clubs and, perhaps most profoundly, upon the players.

As a company that was established as recently as 2015, we have always operated within a world where social media is a priority for football players that are in the public spotlight. Working alongside the agents is vital for this to be a success as they are often the direct line of communication with the player when developing and discussing ideas. It is important for the agent to have a good understanding of their client so that when we begin to explore possible projects and areas of social media to utilise, the agent knows which ones will resonate most with their client, avoiding the need to hassle the client when they are more concerned with playing football.

Another thing to note is that each individual player will engage differently and to different extents with social media. Some players are incredibly private and are unlikely to want to exploit their public image through a very open social media platform. The agent needs to understand this and communicate with specialist marketing companies such as ourselves as to whether or not the player would be willing to commit to certain things.

The pertinence of social media in modern society and modern football is demonstrated by the lucrativeness of brand deals and sponsorships that are agreed and activated through social media promotion by a player. Thousands can be paid for a single post, tweet or story and hence, needless to say it can be a substantial source of income for the top well-known clients.

As this chapter has discussed, the financial opportunity is not solely restricted to brand deals and commercial endorsements. Additionally, social media can be the perfect platform for a player, the agent and a specialist company to implement, establish, promote and grow the client's personal brand. This can be incredibly powerful and social media, if used correctly, is the tool that can facilitate this. The role of the agent is to be creative and to envisage the kind of personal brand their client could develop. Then throughout the process the agent needs to work with professional partners to ensure that this vision comes to life in a manner that appropriately reflects their client."

Summary

- The age of social media provides an exciting platform for your player to express themselves and interact with their fan-base.
- Your role as an agent is to help them grow their presence on a regional and global scale and to align their endorsement deals and other business ventures with their personality and reputation.
- Clients of the highest calibre are able to monetise their personal brand. An agent must identify if this is the right option and assist the player in its development.

Further Reading

- Break the Internet - Olivia Yallop
- The Power of You - Hannah Power

Chapter 26: The Second Career of a Football Player

"The agent who represents the best players is the agent who does the best business" - Jörg Neubauer

[Written in conjunction with **Stéphane Ehrhart**. After a playing and coaching career, Stéphane is now working with UEFA and specialises in the transition of footballers from playing to post-career opportunities. With over 12 years of experience, Stéphane has worked on high-profile projects and is himself an author.]

Introduction

The average duration of a European professional footballer career is only five years. Worryingly, within the first five years following retirement, 40% of players declare bankruptcy. The top footballers who receive the extraordinary salaries throughout their career only represent a tiny proportion of the reality. For 80% of players, their career ends prematurely because of injury or the inability to find another contract. They are forced away from professional football and will need to find a new career path to bring in an income.

Whilst something should be done in the industry as a whole to better support these players after their career, agents can play a significant role here too. Planning for the 'second career' of your client is pivotal. Having projects and ventures already in motion before their retirement is something that the top agents may prioritise to an extent during their time with a player. Your responsibility with a client should be one of duty of care and this extends beyond their footballing career to ensure they are set up suitably for life after football.

Facing the Reality of Retirement

Retirement is inevitable for footballers, even the likes of the relentless Lionel Messi or the goalkeepers who play until their forties. In other words, no matter how talented, famous, or successful the player is, there will be a day where their footballing career will cease...

and it will hurt. As such, agents should be aware that players will normally come across three major changes and challenges in their lives that agents can help with:

1. **Physical change:** players are no longer required to train every day, and as such their bodies will burn less calories and it will face a serious lack of dopamine and adrenaline which came from the competition and playing. Suddenly, the meals provided by the club at training no longer exist, and their diet will suddenly differ. Agents need to be a point of encouragement to ensure that they do not lose a healthy lifestyle altogether and instead find new ways of living and eating well. For footballers, other activities like Golf and running are often popular.

2. **Physiological change:** usually, players will miss their team-mates, the 'banter' and comradery that came with being with the same similarly-minded people day in, day out. Moreover, feeling as though they are less relevant can be psychologically damaging. They are talked about less in the press and may not be recognised as much in public. Agents need to help players understand that this is not what is important in life and help them see the benefits. This includes being able to prioritise family time away from the public spotlight. They may have seen their teammates as 'family' but it is part of the transition to move away from this whilst keeping friends-for-life made through football.

   The same goes for their close ones. Their entourage, spouse, children, friends might all be subject to similar psychological changes, sometimes resulting in periods of depression, feeling burn-out, sadness or divorce. An agent needs to be human in these times, relatable and trusted and to understand when it is appropriate to offer assistance and guidance.

3. **Logistical change:** most of the times, when a football career comes to an end, the player and his family will relocate to a new city, or a new house. This means that the whole family environment and routine will completely change. Of course, it's inevitable that the level of income will also decrease, which might force the family to change their spending habits, thereby creating new pressures and tensions. Agents play many different roles here whether it be finding new properties and the best areas to relocate or whether it is

financial guidance in readjusting to life after a football salary. However, if a 'second career' has already been planned ahead, money struggles may not be an issue.

Combined, these factors clearly demonstrate the vast change that retirement brings to a football player. It also shows that a player (and therefore their agent) has to start thinking about what comes next far before retirement comes. There is no right or wrong answer as to when is the right age to start exploring opportunities for a player's second career. If we were forced to attach a number to it, it would be between the ages of 25-29 depending upon how far into their thirties they feel physically and mentally capable of playing. 5 or 6 years is ample time to prepare for a secondary career and is late enough into their twenties that they are likely to be established and settled in their playing career so it will not be a distraction. Beginning to think about second careers in their early twenties can sometimes be too distracting and is not necessary.

Going About a Player's Second Career

Each player, agent and family member will have their own ideas about how to go about post-career opportunities. Whilst all situations do differ, there is a simple method that can be followed to help build a successful post-career for your client. Depending on what exactly you do with your client, it is still always a good idea to work hand in hand with specialists or professionals in order to prepare players properly and offer them the best possible advice, support and training. Work through the options methodically and stick to the general rules below and you should be set to provide your client with a sustainable 'second career':

1. **Avoiding mistakes & protecting funds:** part of preparing your client for post-career involves giving advice and guidance in terms of managing (or at least safeguarding) their wealth. Put simply, if your client has spent a large part of their income on material items, then it leaves very little to pursue business opportunities once they have retired. Financial advisers, investors and you yourself may be able to direct the player towards better options and sensible investments in order to protect and grow the purse they have leftover from football.

2. **Who to involve:** the specifics of each player and agent can obviously differ vastly, but as already mentioned, having somebody else working closely alongside the agent for such ventures can be beneficial. As such, there could be someone you (or your client) already had in mind. This is another demonstration as to why networking and having a good reach of contacts is vital, as you'll incidentally meet experts and professionals in these areas during your career who can help your player succeed after their football retirement. The earlier you find the right partners the better, as it will give the player time to see that the people involved are trustworthy, knowledgeable and reliable. Organisations such as Afterfoot are prominent in this field, as well as UEFA and some other national associations providing this type of support.

3. **Timing:** often, because of the stark changes to their lives, players will waste a lot of time between the end of their football career and the start of their 'second career'. Consequently, they can get frustrated if things aren't moving quickly enough and will lose patience and confidence in a project. This is why it is always advantageous if these ventures that serve a purpose for post-career are actually put into motion whilst the player is still playing. Remember, having an active player means that their audience and fanbase are still engaged and gives post-career projects a bigger launchpad and platform and a chance for greater success after their career ends. An agent needs to emphasise the importance of this to their clients whilst they are playing without distracting them from their current career.

Football-Related Opportunities

Whilst what has been discussed thus far relates to ventures away from the pitch, there are still plenty of ways to get your client paid footballing opportunities even after retirement. This may be the ideal outcome for your player. However, an agent must understand that footballers have a variety of desires once their career has ended. Some remain obsessed with, and adoring of, the sport and would love to seek a football-related opportunity. Whereas others may want to move away from the football industry altogether. Having served their time as a professional, an agent must know if they would rather pursue a second career totally unrelated to the sport.

As the table below indicates, many well-known players have become managers, pundits, or work with clubs in various capacities:

Player	Current role
Frank Lampard	Managed Derby County, Chelsea and now Everton
Steven Gerrard	Managed Rangers and Aston Villa
Mikel Arteta	Assistant manager at Manchester City, now manager of Arsenal
Phil Neville	Managed England Women's and now Inter Miami
Xavi	Manager of FC Barcelona
Zinedine Zidane	Managed Real Madrid
Xabi Alonso	Manager of Bayer 04 Leverkusen
Wayne Rooney	Managed Derby County and now D.C. United
Gary Lineker	Pundit
Jamie Carragher	Pundit
Michael Owen	Pundit
Jamie Redknapp	Pundit
Paul Scholes	Pundit
Gary Neville	Pundit
David Beckham	Co-owner – Inter Miami FC, Salford City (Still has commercial deals with global brands)
Edwin van der Sar	CEO – AFC Ajax
Thomas Hal Robson-Kanu	Pundit & Entrepreneur - his company now sponsors many football teams

If, for example, you represented a footballer who wanted to work as a pundit or analyst for a TV channel, the agent's role is to help them with this goal. Much like with a player moving from one club to another, these things require discussions and negotiations to take place before a deal is agreed. Similarly, before one can become a manager, you have to gain coaching experience and obtain badges and certificates. In most cases, players will begin by using their contacts from the clubs they played for in their career to secure a role as the coach of one of their youth academy age-group teams. Essentially, for the agent, you would be the one to enquire on your client's behalf to obtain precise details and information about the next steps if and when your client wanted to pursue them.

Commercial Opportunities

Although one would be correct in assuming that a player's endorsement and sponsorship value reduces post-retirement, this doesn't mean that these types of deals cannot be done. In fact, they are far easier given the lack of contractual obligations and restrictions that comes with an Playing Employment Contract, and obviously a client will have more free time to devote to commercial activities.

Remember, the foundations for this are laid during their career when they are most in the public spotlight. If you are able to successfully build a personal brand for your client and an engaged fanbase, commercial opportunities after retirement are possible, especially if your client goes on to remain in the football industry in some capacity that may still be in the public eye such as a TV pundit. In extreme cases, players such as David Beckham have earned far more post-career through sponsorships and endorsements than he did during his career. It is something for agents to bear in mind but may not always be possible depending upon the status of your player.

Expert's View: Jorg Neubauer

Agent of Leon Goretzka and Kevin Trapp

This expert's view was also featured in the second edition of this book. Jörg provides a fantastic insight and assessment that adds a vital element to his chapter. Since the second edition, it is with great sadness that Jörg has passed away. We wanted to take this opportunity to thank him for his services to football as an agent and particularly to the German market.

"I started working in the field of football agency in 1990, at a time where the profession was simply limited to helping broker deals. However, during that time I began to understand that a player needs more than just someone who could negotiate a contract. As a result, I started to learn about areas such as tax and insurance, legal advice, public relations and press activities – many of which seem like relative necessities for the agency business. For me, this was the step towards the professionalisation of player consulting. In addition, it was clear that there was a huge transformation occurring – something which I describe as the 'transparency of footballers'. Through the internet, social media and data collection, there is absolutely no room for secrets anymore. Nowadays, everything is public and easy to access – this represents the most fundamental shift and transition of the business over the last twenty-five years.

The football market has always been interesting and the game of football itself has had its own individual development ongoing. Nevertheless, the greatest steps taken have not been towards sporting success, but rather regarding monetary terms. The huge increase in commercialisation within football, especially through the increased income outside of the stadium (such as broadcasting rights and sponsorships) means there is more money available. Consequently, this has led to the aforementioned change in the nature of football agency. Whereas during the 1990s an agent was an individual, today agencies are in the majority, and this has somewhat led to the disappearance of the individual within the industry. As a pioneer in this field I started to establish a scouting network for young players at the end of the 1990s, and with a scout I was able to find the best talents. This area also shows rapid development. Similar to football clubs, the agencies started to build their own national as well as international scouting systems. The result was that the growth of a player started much younger.

Summing up, this business has gone through an enormous transition since I started. Despite this, one thing has remained a constant in all these years – the agent who represents the best players is the agent who does the best business."

Summary

- If you wanted continued success in this profession, then working with players once they have retired is a great opportunity to do so. The best agents maintain their duty of care and ensure their clients are set up for life after football.
- Understand and pursue post-career options that your player will enjoy and be suitable for. Communicate with them and collaboratively find the best options.
- Working with the right partner and associate who can elevate the success of ventures in your client's 'second career' is important, and you should be looking for people with shared values of trust and loyalty.
- Like with any part of the profession, making sure the player is aware of your plans and what you're doing is key – being open and honest is the only way to ensure your client's trust. Ultimately, it is them who decides what they want to do with their life after they retire, your role is one of guidance and not authority.

Further Reading

- Preparing players for life after football should begin before the final whistle: https://www.theguardian.com/football/blog/2019/nov/16/preparing-footballers-for-life-after-final-game

Chapter 27: NFT's and Cryptocurrency

"Nobody ever changed the world by doing what everyone else was doing" - Mark Cuban

Introduction

The chances are you may have heard or seen the acronym 'NFT' in some capacity and almost certainly it has been impossible to avoid the term 'Cryptocurrency'. For many, these can be daunting and futuristic sectors whilst for others, they have created a new obsession and fascination and have become a part of their lives. One area that these concepts have integrated into is the World of Football and soccer.

The theme is mirrored within football too; some players have so far avoided becoming involved in such an area as they view it as a riskful, unknown entity. For others, especially those in the fortunate position of financial comfort, these sectors present an exciting modern opportunity away from the football pitch. For agents, this may be a daunting prospect if they are required to advise players on such a volatile market as part of their role. However, these concepts are becoming more integral to modern football and this chapter is now more important than ever in helping you become a well-rounded agent and face any challenge that may arise during your career.

In this chapter, we will explain what NFTs and Cryptocurrency involves, their applicability to and place within football and the role of the agent. We will include a case study of how a footballer can benefit from these areas as well as considering the risks involved, as is the case to some extent with any investment.

What are NFTs?

The acronym 'NFT' stands for Non-Fungible Tokens. To break this down, the term 'Non-Fungible' simply means an object, item or 'thing' that is irreplaceable with another identical item. In other words, it cannot be replicated and is therefore 'one-of-a-kind'. A Non-Fungible Token is a digital collectible item that can be bought, sold and tracked on a digital blockchain. It can take the form of videos, GIFs, images and animated characters or 'avatars' as we will explore later. In football, NFT's appear through match highlights, iconic moments, digitalised trophies, football music and fan chants and other football-specific collectible items. It is a rapidly expanding area that is rising in popularity, interest and value.

To simplify the idea, imagine buying a piece of art. However, this art happens to only be available digitally. On a purpose-built network you are able to purchase and sell the 'data' that makes up this piece of art. There is only one very specific data coding that creates this officially authenticated version of the art. Therefore, you will be the sole owner of this piece of art and any copies that are made of it will not be the 'official' version. This can be an investment as this piece of digital art may rise in value and can be sold on for profit to interested buyers. Another way to think about this concept is to imagine they are similar to football trading cards that you may have collected before, with the caveat that only one person can have each card in the world and that the card is digital.

What About Cryptocurrency?

Cryptocurrency is a slightly older concept than NFTs. You have most likely heard people, news platforms or social media discussing the likes of Bitcoin, the infamous Dogecoin, and Ethereum, amongst others, since the beginning of the last decade. Crypto, as it is often referred to, comes under many titles or 'coins' as digital currency which can be bought and sold. Just like any currency around the world, the different crypto 'coins' can rise and fall in value. The medium of exchange for cryptocurrency is only through a digital network where all transactions pass through rather than via a bank or other institution.

NFTs and Crypto in Football

We have decided to cover both of these concepts within this chapter as they are both interlinked. Often, NFTs are purchased using Cryptocurrency such as Ethereum. Footballers, particularly those at the top, are in a position financially and socially to get ahead in these markets. These sectors present a new and exciting opportunity for investing their money into. This is where agents must also have a level of knowledge and understanding in order to inform their clients of the safest and most appropriate ways of making significant returns on NFTs and Crypto.

For NFTs, players can leverage their public following and fanbase, assisted by their agent, to increase the value of their digital art and produce a successful investment, made financially possible from their high salaries at the top level. NFTs can certainly be a significant financial opportunity as some can be worth enormous amounts. Players may pay hundreds-of-thousands of pounds, dollars or euros to secure a piece of digital art, in the hope that it will rise in value.

The most common area of NTFs that players engage with is known as 'Bored Ape Yacht Club' and you may have seen this in the form of well-known players changing their social media icons to a cartoon ape. These include current and retired footballers such as Bobby Zamora, Tammy Abraham, Reece James, Ashley Cole, Trent Alexander-Arnold and John Terry. The BAYC, as it is abbreviated to, uses Ethereum and charges a minimum of £163,000 for one of its specific 'bored ape' icons.

The record sale for a football player is Erkut's client, Mesut Özil, who sold a single piece for £75,000. Elsewhere, an Mbappe GIF is believed to have sold for £47,000. Paul Pogba has purchased 'NFT eggs' and has partnered with the Cryptodragons Project as an official ambassador. This is a rising theme in football as the likes of Antoine Griezmann, Gerard Pique and Rio Ferdinand have also invested into various platforms that deal with NFTs or Cryptocurrency. It presents another off-field opportunity during and post-career to partner and collaborate with a modern and unique commercial endorsement.

It isn't just players either; clubs are also engaging with these sectors. Seventeen Premier League clubs currently have commercial deals with a Cryptocurrency company and so do Paris Saint Germain and UEFA - a true sign that this digital phenomenon is firmly embedded into football. Even clubs like Southampton and Championship team Watford, sport Cryptocurrency platforms as their front-of-shirt sponsor. Another argument in favour of these concepts is that they are a new space to engage with fans around the world through a new and exciting medium. For agents, it may be possible to take on the role as a broker in such deals between the clubs and the Cryptocurrency platforms. Your task would be to act on behalf of the club and negotiate a lucrative sponsorship deal with the Cryptocurrency company.

The table below shows just how valuable some of these deals can be for football associations and clubs in 2022:

Team	Sponsor	Total Value ($USD million)	Length
Premier League	Consensys	589	4
Atletico Madrid	Whale Fin	210	5
Inter Milan	Zytara Labs	100	3
AS Roma	Zytara Labs	42	3
Manchester City	OKX	20	1
Manchester United	Tezos	27	Per year
Inter Milan	Socios	23	1
Chelsea	Whale Fin	24	Per year

Source: Mondaq

The Risks Involved

This section differs little from any that may be written about investments of any kind. Particularly in Cryptocurrency and NFTs, the market is highly volatile. These are modern concepts that are still unknown entities to an extent. Furthermore, the regulations and laws governing the markets are not fully formed nor comprehensive. This means that there are many aspects of these sectors that create risks for those investing within it. Players may be in the fortunate position of financial stability and can afford to take such a risk but they must be aware of this before investing. The agent must ensure they bring this awareness to the client. Remember, you are an adviser and your client has entrusted you to guide them to make the best decisions for their career. Ensure that you are able to do this, or outsource it to other experts, if your client enquires about a possible NFT, Crypto, or any other investment for that matter.

Another part of this risk that players and their agents ought to be aware of is rogue coin-creators who pitch an idea to a player and try to take advantage of their popularity in the public eye. These creators will make some quick money from the players building hype as ambassadors before exiting with their own profit, leaving the player behind. This is sometimes referred to as the "pump and dump" concept, using false and misleading information and using a players face to inflate the value of their coin and creating what is known as a 'buying frenzy' before selling their own shares. These scams must be avoided if possible and due diligence and research is imperative in order to mitigate against the risk of entering such deals, this again, is part of your role as the agent.

The Cryptocurrency market alone has experienced a 500% growth during the years of COVID-19 and this is likely to continue to rise. Whilst this presents a significant financial opportunity and the possibility of dramatic investment returns, it also raises the level of risk of the loss of money. After all, this is a modern form of speculative trading and profit is never guaranteed. The graph below shows the extraordinary rise and also the possibility of loss of cryptocurrency since 2015:

Market Capitalization of Cryptocurrencies, 2015-22 (USD Billions)

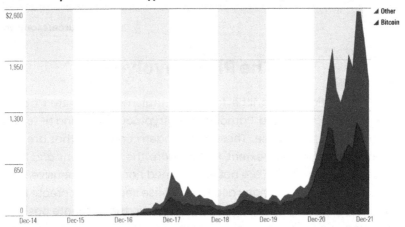

Source: CoinGecko

Expert's View: Dr Erkut Sogut & Mesut Özil

"My client, Mesut Özil, has been a successful pioneer in these sectors for football. As well as holding the record sale for a player of £75,000, he was also the very first individual across any sport to create NFT 'genies', an idea that was only otherwise previously emulated by Justin Bieber and Cardi B. We had explored and considered the ideal for a while before taking the step as we believed it was an avenue that could produce great results. It was my role as his agent to do due-diligence around the topic and research into this specific area so that I could advise him adequately.

These genies or 'avatars' were similar to the concept of 'bitmojis' and had its own digital custom clothing range. This generated enormous interest and goes to show the influence and impact that top-level football players collaborating with digital platforms such as NFTs and Cryptocurrency can have globally. The range sold out in 6.7 minutes and generated over $500,000, demonstrating Özil's global reach and fanbase. To acknowledge this extraordinary achievement he wore the number 67 after his move to Fenerbahce.

Özil and I are also shareholders in Mexican football club, *Club Necaxa*. The club's board formulated the idea of selling 1% of his ownership stake to the public and the fans through digital NFTs. An exciting opportunity for fan engagement which was unfortunately blocked by the Mexican Football Federation although it is possible that this may be an indication as to the direction in which football is going alongside NFTs and Cryptocurrency. Agents must look out for such patterns and trends and establish whether they are worth involving their client in. I truly believe we suggested this concept ahead of its time and that this kind of NFT ownership sale is part of the future.

This case study demonstrates how powerful the spheres of Cryptocurrency, NFTs and the Metaverse can be for players as a new avenue for them to invest their finances well. Although there is significant risk that must be considered and experts must be consulted, as agents we should not hesitate in supporting our clients in such exciting ventures as long as they are embarked upon and conducted in the right manner."

Summary

- In this modern era of football, Cryptocurrency and NFTs are certainly something one should be aware of, and not just in the football sector.
- As an agent you must understand the concept to some extent in order to best serve your client.
- They may be slightly alien concepts still but their continuing rise in society is unavoidable. Players and clubs will engage more and more with these sectors.
- The extent to which they will become an integral part of the world of football is still unpredictable.
- Your role as an agent could be to advise your players on investing into these sectors or in brokering a deal with a Crypto sponsor for a club.
- Your clients must be aware of the risks involved in investing in a volatile sector.
- Think outside the box. Develop a concept utilising NFTs and Cryptocurrency before anyone else does and it can be a great opportunity for your player to make a substantial sum.

Further Reading

- The Crypto Book - Siam Kidd
- The Age of Cryptocurrency - Paul Vigna
- The Meta-Verse - Matthew Ball
- NFTs for Dummies - Tiana Laurence

Chapter 28: 'Show me the Money'

"Use the opportunities wisely, then the money will come to you" - Pere Guardiola

Introduction

Like any profession, money is always a crucial factor when deciding whether to pursue it or not. Especially in the current financial climate of some countries across the world, income is an influential consideration in people's lives and their careers. For some, the risk of a career that may be based purely on widely fluctuating commission rather than a stable salary is enough to put them off. For others, they are drawn to football agency by the possibility of truly life-changing money.

The positive news is that there is certainly no shortage of money in football! With the ever-expanding commercialisation of the football industry, the value of contracts and transfer continues to grow alongside. The football industry is expansive and this chapter will identify the major sources of income that may be possible to you as an agent within the industry.

The graphic below is an initial summary of the main sources of commission in a football transfer:

DEAL BROKERING: WHO CAN HIRE YOU?

PLAYERS

The player hires the agent and pays them commission on their salary.

Selling Club

The club wants to sell a player and will compensate the agent for brokering the transfer.

Buying Club

The club instructs the agent to contact a player or the agent of a player that is a target for them and to convince them to join the club.

The regularity of each possible party is exemplified below for 2022 for all international transfers:

Who uses intermediaries?

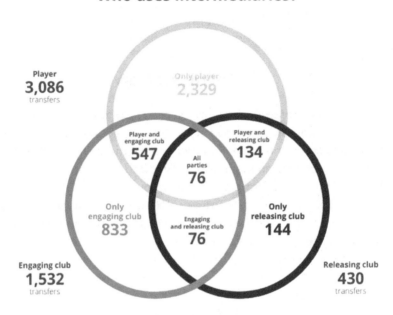

Player
3,086
transfers

Only player
2,329

Player and
engaging club
547

Player and
releasing club
134

All
parties
76

Only
engaging club
833

Engaging
and releasing club
76

Only
releasing club
144

Engaging club
1,532
transfers

Releasing club
430
transfers

Source: FIFA Intermediary Report 2022

Wages

Your constant source of income comes from the Representation and Employment Contracts that you have agreed with your client. These entitle you to your agreed commission and agents fee, and is normally paid to you by the club itself. It is common practice for clubs to pay on behalf of your client for a variety of reasons.

Your salary relying upon a small percentage (often between 5-10%) of someone else's wages may seem unattractive on the surface but remember that football wages are astronomical, particularly at the top level. It is estimated that the total European wage bill for footballers is around £9.5 billion per year and thus there is certainly room for you to take a slice of this substantial and continually-growing market. Bear in mind that if you negotiate well and seek the best deal for your clients, you will inevitably come away with more money for yourself - without this getting in the way of prioritising the best interests of your client.

It is important to note that in most cases and in most countries, the percentage of commission you earn will be taken from the player's gross salary and therefore means you will earn more than if it was taken as a net salary. However, in some countries such as Turkey or those in the Middle-East region, the agent's commission is based upon the player's net (post-tax) salary and this needs to be considered as the agent may end up making far less than they expected if it is not accounted for.

Transfers

In the majority of situations, you as the agent will receive money from the player's employment contract. In other words, your commission comes from the percentage of their salary that your client owes to you. The general public perception is that the norm is for an agent to receive 10% of any transfer fee. For example, they believe a €100million transfer results in €10million being given to the agent. The reality is actually that this is very rare ever since the FIFA ban on third-party ownership and only occurs in some very infrequent circumstances.

For the most part, agents will not have any level of participation or financial gain in the transfer fee. One example where this may arise though is if there is a release clause which may not be public knowledge. If this release clause exists, the agent may be entitled to additional commission for any money the club receives for the transfer fee that is above the release clause. For example, if the agent is in the knowledge that the release clause for a player is €3million but does not disclose this to other clubs and finds an agreement for €5million for the player, the selling club may compensate the agent around 50% (€1million) of the additional transfer income. Note that sometimes there still may be clauses put into employment contracts that entitles agents to compensation on a future transfer fee but this is something that you must be very careful with and consult a lawyer as if it is not done correctly, it will be seen as third-party ownership.

Despite the infrequency of this as you may have previously thought, transfers can occasionally provide an alternative bonus source of income for you as an agent, with wages offering you a more steady flow of money. Whether you have a mandate for a player's transfer, or you are their registered agent, there is the potential to make an immediate large sum of money as a one-time payment when your client moves to a club if you are able to be entitled to any of the fee.

If you are working on behalf of a club directly then the transfer agreement may include a set fee for the agent as a commission for brokering the deal. It is down to you to negotiate this once you have finalised all the terms within the contract that are relevant to your client. You should not let your commission influence your decision or discourage you from making a deal if it is the right one for your client. More and more clubs are willing to pay agents due to increased pressure for success, and they know how important agents are in getting a deal over the line.

Agency fees at almost all levels of professional football are proportionately significant. They are paid as a result of services to the player, the club or perhaps even the coach. Under the current rules you may even be remunerated for representing all three although this will be changing as soon as the new regulations come into force. Nevertheless, at the very top level there are enormous sums of money exchanged between clubs and agents. Such a notion is evidenced by the fact that Premier League clubs spent just over £200m on agents' fees in 2021 which was over 10% of the overall spending in the 2022 summer transfer window:

Club	Estimated spending 2022 Summer Window	Estimated agents spending 2021
AFC Bournemouth	£24.21m	£3,505,603
Arsenal	£118.86m	£18,652,818
Aston Villa	£63.0m	£9,557,057
Brentford	£45.45m	£3,499,285
Brighton & Hove Albion	£43.02m	£6,244,039
Chelsea	£253.79m	£28,227,858
Crystal Palace	£31.14m	£8,865,484
Everton	£78.48m	£11,494,820
Fulham	£55.26m	£10,160,399
Leeds United	£99.13m	£11,396, 947
Leicester City	£15.3m	£12,046,495
Liverpool	£81.27m	£22,136,224

Manchester City	£125.55m	£35,046,646
Manchester United	£214.22m	£29,036,141
Newcastle United	£122.40m	£7,717,687
Nottingham Forest	£145.76m	£2,388,090
Southampton	£59.76m	£4,941,761
Tottenham Hotspur	£152.91m	£13,938,231
West Ham United	£163.80m	£10, 532, 927
Wolves	£122.94m	£11,958,945

Total	£2.016bn	£227,458,638

Source: The Sporting News, 90MIN, ESPN

Note: these figures are still slightly tainted due to the financial impact of COVID-19 upon football clubs. This is shown in the graphic used in chapter 13 from the FIFA Intermediary Report 2022.

This is, of course, not just the case in the Premier League, although the statistics and agent expenditure is the highest there. No matter the value of the transfer fee nor the national association(s) it takes place between, the agent will be entitled to a service fee if they are acting on behalf of the club, the topic that is covered in chapter 13. The graph below shows the number of club agents in international transfers by the size of the transfer fee and hence, the service fees as a percentage of the transfer fee:

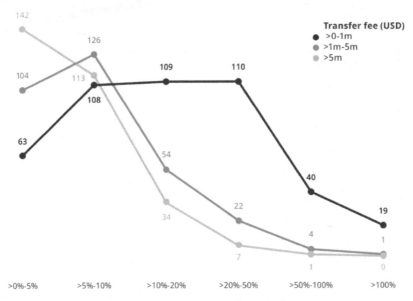

Source: FIFA Intermediary Report 2022

How the Agent is Paid

When a transfer deal is made, the agent could be paid their fee by the club through a variety of methods. For the following example we will outline how the agent's commission might be received:

CASE: A client signs a 5-year contract with a club where they will earn a £2,000,000 gross annual salary, the agent's commission is £200,000 a year if they have agreed a 10% remuneration fee. Hence totalling £1,000,000 across the five years.

1. **Non-guaranteed instalments:** this often occurs as two annual payments (one every six months) of £100,000. However, as they are not guaranteed, if the player leaves the club then they will cease from paying these instalments.

2. **Guaranteed instalments:** the same as the above but in this case, perhaps as an additional incentive to the agent, the club guarantees full payment of the commission owed, even if the player leaves the club before the end of their contract.

3. In some cases, the full fee of £1,000,000 will be paid to the agent up front if agreed upon between the club and the agent.
4. Most commonly, half of the fee will be paid upfront, in this case £500,000, whilst the other half will be paid in instalments that the club and the agent will agree upon and detail their structure.
5. The club may also offer the agent an incentive by paying 5% commission upfront rather than the original 10%. Then from thereafter they will pay 5% on top of the upfront payment. Inevitably this means slightly less money overall for the agent but an immediate payment upon completion of the deal may be desirable in some cases.

Other Projects

Another way in which an agent can make money is through other projects, which are inherently linked with their existing clients. Due to the power and attraction that football players have, they can easily open doors for agents to pursue further business ventures. The types of projects are crucial to your income as well, as the agent will often get some shares in the business, which will give you (as well as the player) a source of income post-retirement. This should be further encouragement to be proactive in areas away from football to acquire a new source of income. For example, Erkut has been fortunate enough to work as business partners with clients Mesut Özil and Mathieu Flamini on ventures such as Unitee and has shares alongside both of them.

Note that the commission percentage that agents are entitled to is often higher and less legally restricted in commercial deals; often around 20%.

More details on other projects can be found in chapters 23-27.

Ownership and M&A (Mergers & Acquisitions)

Another area in which agents can get involved in is that of the more business-related side by acting on behalf of the clubs themselves. If you're an agent who is determined to expand their network as far and wide as possible, you may cross paths with extremely wealthy business people wanting to get into the world of football. Years of reputation and admirable work may one day land you with the role of acting as the agent in brokering a deal for a takeover of a club. When partnering with an affluent businessperson, they may use you in order to help put together the deal, and may even give you shares in the team as a result as a part of your commission.

If this rare opportunity did arise, it is a clear sign of your success and something you would have to contemplate. As exciting as such an offer may be, it is important to note the regulations around this for agents, and it is certainly a grey area. In some countries, agents are permitted to own up to 5% of a football club. This is the maximum cap so as not to create any conflict of interest that may arise.

There is less of a clear-cut ruling on an agent brokering the takeover of a club, without receiving any shares. As just mentioned, this is an ill-defined area of football, and could well be subject to more rigorous regulations in the future. Perhaps if you reach such a stage you may consider moving on from your successes in agency and could explore a new venture of part-owning a club and everything that comes with it. However, if you are in the position already then it is unlikely you need to read this book. For most of you, the focus for now will be starting out as an agent and beginning to achieve success in the industry. However, it is important to mention now to give you extra incentive to flourish in and dedicate yourself to the industry with all the additional and unexpected opportunities and sources of income it could produce further down the line.

Expert's View: Pere Guardiola

*Agent, Sports Entertainment Group, brother
of Pep Guardiola*

"I am fortunate enough to have had the opportunity of working in the sports business for many years now. One of the most important things that you should know is that football is such a big industry and the possibilities of making money are endless. So if you don't have contacts to get you an internship at a large agency, or a friend who is playing professionally, it doesn't matter.

There are many ways to make a successful living in the football industry. Of course, there are the better- known methods as already mentioned in this book such as transfers (where you can work on either the club or player side – or in some cases both) as well as commercial deals for your client. Additionally, there are further opportunities relating to football itself such as M&A (mergers and acquisitions), where you can use the network you have to put together a club looking to sell and an investor looking to buy, taking a percentage of the total sale as your commission or introductory fee.

Moreover, away from the pitch, you can advise your client(s) on investments in a range of industries, including, for example, restaurants and coffee shops. subsequently, you would be entitled to take a share in the business as your commission. The same can also be said for property and other tangible investments.

Remember, the opportunities that present themselves to you in this business are extremely valuable. Take them and use them wisely, then the money will come to you!"

Summary

- Whilst it shouldn't be the main motivating factor, the money available for you to make by being an agent may be enticing. It is realistic that someone who thrives in the industry will make a significantly life-changing sum of money.
- The commission that you receive from representing a client can be your only source of income, but not capitalising on the business opportunities that stem from the player's popularity is a missed opportunity. The very best agents are

able to proactively seek and utilise this sector away from the football pitch and find further opportunities for themselves and for their clients.

- Never forget, there is a strong distinction to be made between good business and simply taking advantage of your player's fame and wealth – you ought to be open, honest and transparent, as well as always incorporating your client within any relevant and appropriate business, if you decide to pursue off-the-pitch work on their behalf.
- The interests of the client should never be undermined by your own greed!

Further Reading

- The Price of Football - Kieran Maguire

Chapter 29: Around the World of Agency

Global View: Australia

Paddy Dominguez (Owner, Republic Sports Management)

"Modern day football management is very much an international business. Although, as with any business there are varying levels through which an agent progresses. Generally, a football agent will commence working in their local domestic market and grow to gain experience and knowledge of other international territories over time, and with an ever-expanding list of clients who will transfer between leagues. Purely from a business perspective, a football agent is effectively, and needs to be, heavily involved in the import/export trade. The global nature of the football industry means that most agents will encounter transfers between different leagues worldwide at some point in their careers.

With this in mind, it is important for football agents to be up to date on FIFA regulations as they relate to international transfers. The vast majority of agents over time will build a network, and work in partnership with other agents who have local knowledge. Some of the benefits of utilising local agents and their knowledge in this kind of relationship are that:

- Local agents will know the pay structures of the clubs in their territory
- Local agents will have existing relationships with clubs in their respective territories
- Local agents will know of any anomalies to FIFA rules in their territory*
- Local agents will have existing relationships with local media
- Local agents will be able to advise on lifestyle choices for the player
- Local agents can provide day-to-day assistance for the player on the ground

*There can be some additional regulations in certain territories such as Australia, USA, etc… although all of the fundamental FIFA rules and regulations are adopted by Member Associations.

There are only two salary capped leagues in world football currently, being the A-League (Australia) and the MLS (North America). This creates a unique working environment for agents working in these territories as the limits on finances creates a market where player's salaries fall into certain categories of earning, which is a natural default position based on the number of players in each squad and the limit of the salary cap. Clubs in these countries will have an unofficial range of salary for players in each position. For example, defenders can earn in the range of $250k-$400k maximum, midfielders $300k-$450k, etc… These leagues will generally provide a set number of exemptions for Marquee players who will be considered outside the cap. The rationale behind these players receiving an exemption is based on their value in driving marketing, publicity, attendances and general interest in their respective league.

The Australian A-League is predominantly a feeder league in the global sense of where it stands. One of the youngest leagues in the world (commenced in 2005), it continues to mature season by season and almost all of the best players in this league have the aim of transferring to other clubs in Europe or Asia. Consistently there is debate around whether the salary cap promotes the export of players from this league as footballers can earn a lot more in leagues where players are not paid within a salary cap structure.

Australian players qualify as Asian qualified players and as such they are very attractive to clubs in the Asian market. The diverse heritage of most Australian families also permits many Australian players access to European passports, and therefore they qualify as European and this in turn, is the other main destination for players from Australia.

In such a vast country with cities spread far apart from each other it is critical for any agent to build a strong scouting network to identify talent. It is simply impossible for any football agent to scout everywhere, although there are only 10 teams in the A-League and this makes it far easier to track players in the top professional league in the country.

Australia has a proud tradition in exporting quality players to Europe, mainly to England, Scotland, Holland and Italy. The general pathway, historically, for most Australian players has been through the National team. As Australia has appeared at every World Cup since 2006, and the stature of the National team has continued to grow, it has naturally provided a platform for the best players from Australia to get noticed and impress overseas clubs. As the A-League continues to improve this will allow players from this territory another pathway to seek overseas opportunities."

Global View: South America

*Matthieu Rios-Grossin (Owner of Alinea
Sports Management, Agent of David Ospina)*

"As in all different businesses, it is very important to know who is the party you will negotiate with. It is also vital to understand what their interests and objectives are so you can be in control of the negotiation. It may sound easy and straightforward, but its importance can't be underestimated, as a deal can become extremely complicated if you don't identify the aims of the club/the entity you're negotiating with.

You can see the significance of the above advice when put into a practical example:

- As an agent, you are asked by a club to check on a South American player and construct a deal, or, as an agent, you want to get a mandate from a player and his agent/club to move them to a European club.
- You can ask the player who their agent is and usually they will give you an answer with a name or saying that he has no agent.
- Despite this, you will sometimes see that the player has signed mandates to different people, and in the middle of a negotiation someone who you have never heard of will work their way into the conversation staking their claim in the deal.
- If this is the case, it is important that you immediately get all the documents authorising your action before you move forward in order to validate yourself to all the parties involved.

When compared to Europe, the industry in South America operates totally differently. In Europe, people are used to a player having a contract with a club and a full-time agent, so it is easy to know who to contact and negotiate with. However, it is far from this straightforward in South America. Often, the club where the player is contracted to will share 'economic rights' (sometimes referred to as ownership) with former clubs, agents, and companies who have helped pay relevant bills.

Of course, this is neither legal or official as it goes against all the third-party ownership rules and regulations. People cover it up by referring to them as 'private contracts' (frequently with political motivations) that are not disclosed to the football associations. Therefore, you will have to battle against vested interests, personal conflicts, egos, etc. when trying to get a deal done.

If you manage to get through all of this, it probably means you have gained the trust of the buying club by simplifying this unfavourable situation and can now look to proceed with the deal! Now, just make sure everything is legally sound, all the numbers and percentages add up, and double-check all the paperwork."

National View: Colombia

Paolo Cucalon (Former Professional Tennis Player turned Colombian Soccer Agent)

- "The most popular sport in Colombia is football/soccer, this is because Colombia has become a football powerhouse worldwide.
- Colombia is the third country in South America that produces the greatest volume of professional players after Argentina and Brazil.
- Colombia is a big country with a population of over 50million people, it is culturally diverse and well geographically connected.

Professional League

The professional football in Colombia is ruled by the Major Division of Colombian Football, DIMAYOR. It is the entity in charge of organising, managing, and regulating theColombian Professional Football Championships. It has two divisions named Categoría A, which means A category, and Categoría B, meaning B category. Categoría A is the top division. Currently, the DIMAYOR organises 5 professional tournaments as follows:

- **Liga BetPlay Dimayor:** a contest in which the 20 teams of Categoría A compete and two champions are crowned per year. Each of them obtains the respective title and additionally a place in the Copa Libertadores the following year.
- **Torneo BetPlay Dimayor:** in which 16 teams of Categoría B face each other. At the end of the year, two clubs are promoted to the higher category, A, and enter to compete in the BetPlay DIMAYOR League for the following season.
- **Liga Femenina BetPlay:** a competition in which the 17 women's clubs of the Professional Colombian Football, FPC, participate in an annual championship. The champion and runner-up team have the right to participate in the 2022 Women's Copa Libertadores as representatives for Colombia.
- **Superliga BetPlay Dimayor:** the two champions of the year from the BetPlay League face each other. In the event that the same team wins both events, the Super League is played

by that club, against the best team in the reclassification table.

- **Copa BetPlay Dimayor:** is the championship that brings together the 35 clubs of categoría A and B. The champion, in addition to the title, gets a place in the next Copa Libertadores.

It is important to mention that the league's format is going to be restructured. It seems that the Liga BetPlay DIMAYOR will go back as it used to be prior to 2001, which was one tournament per year, thus there would be only one champion instead of two.

As an agent:

From my experience as a Colombian, is important to have good and trustworthy

relationships in the country before making any decisions. The best way to access the market would be via joint venture or with a local partner that has real knowledge on how the football business is structured in the country and contacts to be able to make it happen in a legal and secure way. The acquisition of a professional football club in Colombia from a foreign investor is a complement because it adds value to the professional league."

Global View: Africa

Yussif Alhassan Chibsah (CEO & Founder,
Club Consult Africa)

"I have been surrounded by football nearly my whole life! Being an ex-professional footballer, I was fortunate enough to have played for all the various national teams of Ghana from the youth to senior level. I captained the Ghanaian Olympic football team (Black Meteors) at the Athens Olympic Games in 2004, and I was also a member of the Black Stars squad in the lead up to the 2006 World Cup in Germany.

At club level, I played professional football in Italy, Finland, Germany, Israel, Sweden and Turkey. Among all these countries, Sweden was where I played the longest, with 10 years of professional football there in total.

Whilst playing, I started to mentor young African players in Sweden and other Scandinavia countries (Denmark, Finland & Norway), acting as a role model and giving any advice or help I could.

My educational background was in banking and finance, and it had been my intention to practise this after my footballing career had come to an end. However, some of the young African players I was mentoring suggested that I become an agent and representative.

Football agency in Africa is certainly behind the European industry. I therefore felt the worry and pain of these young players, and when I thought about how different I felt playing in Africa compared to Europe, I decided it was better to work on improving the agency business in my home continent.

I decided to use all that I have learnt in Europe as a professional footballer and the experience I have gathered from all agents I encountered to help those back home in Africa.

The Industry in Africa

Before the introduction of the intermediary system, there were very few licensed FIFA agents in Ghana and across Africa, and even those that were licensed tended to be based in Europe.

Back then there was an exam, and this deterred a lot of people, but at the same time gave the profession perhaps a higher standard of intermediary due to the restrictive nature of the system.

Either way, the agency world in Africa has huge potential. There is an abundance of footballing talent across the continent that could really benefit from high-level representation.

How the industry operated

Because there were few licensed agents around, the industry operated through local people who called themselves the 'managers' of players. These people were not licensed, but essentially played the role of agents and did everything for the player, whether it be acting as their guardian, or providing sponsorship. This could be in the form of giving them football boots, training kits, or a monthly allowance.

In exchange for these services, they would become the decision maker for the players. Domestic clubs would have to contact them if they need the services of the players. They get paid either by the buying club or the player, and even though these 'managers' have no licence to operate, the system accepted them. Essentially therefore, they operated as agents for a very long time.

Players with a bad character and attitude will keep changing their 'managers' anytime they want to, by jumping from one rich person to another. The one with the highest bid always wins, as there is no proper structure or regulation in the system. Some 'managers' did very well for themselves with good returns on their investments, whilst others lost out heavily.

But at the end of the day, there is no loyalty in this system. Players will tend to just ignore their 'manager' when a European agent comes along with interest from a European club.

Similarly, there is no professionalism. In Africa, some players do not even know the duration of their contracts, nor how much they earn per month.

Scouting

There are also some differences when it comes to scouting in Africa. The negative part is that there lacks structure and regulation. One can visit any game, identify a talent and straight away become the representative of the player, especially in cases where the 'manager' involved is rich. Due to the fact that most domestic clubs do not have the finances to operate a youth side, they rely on these 'managers' to provide them with young talent because they don't have to invest in them.

Often, small tournaments are organised which have some of the top players from the best clubs. These events are organised by both local and European agents, as well as clubs, foreign club representatives, and 'managers'. Subsequently, these players are offered to European teams.

Introduction of the intermediary system

The introduction of the various FIFA regulations has brought about a little bit of structure, but still more work needs to be done!

In my own opinion, the system of allowing individual federations to have the power and control is an issue in Africa, because the associations are more interested about the intermediary fee they collect rather than the standard of the industry. Almost every football fan became an intermediary because all they needed to do is to register. Family members and friends of footballers all became intermediaries without any technical knowledge of the game, and many talents are misled because of a lack of knowledge. All they are interested in is the money.

That is why education is so key!

Personally, I think we need greater education and regulation to improve the agency business in Africa. Right now we have many fraudsters who registered as intermediaries and all they do is go onto the internet and pull pictures of famous managers and agents, create photoshops, and deceive players by claiming they are partners with these big names. The promise of a 'big contract' means many fall for their tricks. Players who are so desperate to play in Europe are victims of these plans, and as such lose money and opportunities.

At the end of the day, the system is currently failing the players. It is them that are losing out, as innocent talent is being deceived. There needs to be change, and as I said before, education and regulation are two key components of what the future should be like!"

Global View: North America

Dr Erkut Sogut

"The North American 'soccer' market is incredibly exciting at the moment. I recently moved from London to Los Angeles in recognition of the potential this region, and particularly the MLS, has. I strongly believe that by 2026, following the World Cup in the USA, Major League Soccer will be one of the top leagues in the world after the Premier League and another European League such as La Liga. The US is an enormous country with a staggering population of over 300million; it is a global powerhouse in almost every aspect and soccer is likely to come next.

The sheer scale of the progress that the MLS is making is extraordinary. There are new stadiums being built to hold between 40,000 and 60,000 fans around the country, new fan groups are emerging and even new teams. Following the new St Louis franchise's introduction in the 2023 season, there will be 30 teams in the MLS. There is also set to be a new cup competition played between clubs in the US and in Mexico. The unique and world-beating marketing strategies of American sports federations is exemplary and will only benefit the MLS to become one of the best in global soccer. The spectacle of American Football, Baseball, Basketball and Ice Hockey is an extraordinary experience for anyone, even those that are not particularly fans of the sport. This is being replicated in the MLS and is responsible for the continuing rapid rise and expansion of soccer in the US.

Part of this is the pioneering approach to women's football that has been long standing. For the national team, both the men and women are paid the same for representing their country and many of the women are household names, commercially valuable and are helping to promote the sport amongst the female population across the US. The players, both male and female, are given a spotlight and unique status in North America. Hence, it is arguably more important in the US than in other countries to capitalise on the potential of clients as commercial entities. There are endless opportunities to find sponsors and endorsement deals for your clients and makes the MLS an attractive option.

The MLS has been known in the past as a 'retirement home' for some of Europe's top talents in the twilight of their careers. The likes of Wayne Rooney, David Beckham, David Villa, Gareth Bale, Bastian

Schweinsteiger and Frank Lampard have all chosen the MLS as the final destination of their illustrious careers. However, this is changing and the MLS is transitioning into a league that attracts players at the peak of their careers and a strong career option in its own right. It is also becoming more and more common for players to move in the direction of Europe having developed in the MLS and the American youth system rather than players transferring from Europe to the US.

A significant factor for this is the extensive investment into the grassroots system in North America. With a greater focus on development and sufficient funding that correlates with its importance, the youth academy setup in the US has established itself as a very good system. Consequently, the US is producing greater talents such as Chrisitan Pulisic. This not only makes the MLS and the national team stronger and more competitive but it also makes the soccer market more enticing for European clubs to scout in and for players to play in. Historically, the greatest talents in South America have been scouted and poached by the top European clubs but as this transition continues it is frequently the case that these young talents will move to the US instead, as it is more convenient and is able to offer the same opportunity and facilitates for development in the same way that Europe would. For the youth that are involved in the grassroots system but do not become professional players, they are still exposed more than ever to the sport and many will choose to be lifelong devoted fans of soccer alongside the other sporting attractions in North America.

Coupled with the American approach to promotion and marketing, this creates an entity of irresistible growth and expansion. The 2026 World Cup will be another boost in shining a light upon the stature of North American soccer as it reaches its goal of being a top global league. It is a league for the future and of that I am certain. For agents, it is integral that you understand and monitor the North American market, establish your network here and consider the value it can have for your clients."

National View: Italy

Nicola Giuliani (Agent of Roberto Mancini and Marco Rossi)

- "You still must get a licence through the FIFA examination.
- Only then can you be registered as *agente sportivo stabilito*. You either need to work with another registered agent at this point unless you meet specific criteria outlined by the Italian Football Federation (FIGC) which allows you to work independently.
- This process is national law and both agent and agency must be registered first with the FIGC and then once they have obtained their full certificate, they must also register with CONI, the national sports governing body here in Italy.
- There are a couple of other key points that must be noted for agents based in Italy:
- A club can not pay or give you an official mandate without officially documented registration.
- Professional insurance is mandatory otherwise you will be sanctioned.
- Italy is the same as France in that when the new FIFA agent regulations come into force, we will continue to implement our additional national laws."

National View: Japan

Lucas Arbelo (Football Agent at FujiProject)

"The Japanese football market is growing day by day and the potential of players and the production of talent is continually proving. There is an emphasis upon good technical footballers and a dedicated work ethic. Currently, many of the players in the national team are playing in Europe. Germany is a major export market for Japanese footballers.

Some obstacles remain prevalent. Japan is now a very developed country but it has some catching up to do in football to compete with European leagues for example. It needs to raise its level further in order to attract more lucrative investors and thus be able to grow as a world-renowned league. The best players on the production line are tempted to go to Europe too early and the league loses its prized assets before they have a chance to boost the image of the Japanese league.

From my point of view, as an agent in the market, the academy system needs greater investment and improvement. Today many young people end up starting their football career at 22 years old after finishing university. It's something that has to change if Japanese football is to develop, I'm not saying that it's not good to go to university, but rather that they need to have the necessary tools to be able to continue growing as footballers and the level of the university is not so good yet. Hopefully, in the near future, the academy system will take on a similar structure to those seen elsewhere in the football world and will facilitate the top talents flourishing alongside Japanese football as a whole.

In order to register in Japan as an agent, you currently do not need to pass any type of exam, there are minimal requirements, a registration fee (outlined below) and then monthly payments. Perhaps the most significant element is an interview that is conducted for prospective agents although this is a very straightforward formality. As a result, there are a large number of registered agents in Japan.

What do you need to do to register as an Agent under the Japanese Football Association?

- First-time registration: 100,000 yen per fiscal year (plus tax)

- Subsequent registration in the following fiscal year or after: 30,000 yen per fiscal year (plus tax)
- Interview

Below I have outlined some interesting details regarding playing contracts in Japan:

Three Options for Contracts

1. Contract A | Conditions
   a. Player needs to earn ¥ 4.600.000 per year or more
   b. Minutes played
      i. J 1 (First Division) = 460 minutes or more
      ii. J 2 (Second Division) = 900 minutes or more
      iii. J 3 (Third Division) or JFL (Fourth Division) = 1350 or more
2. Contract B | Conditions
   a. Player needs to earn less than ¥ 4.600.000 per year
   b. Minutes played
      i. J 1 (First Division) = 460 minutes or more
      ii. J 2 (Second Division) = 900 minutes or more
      iii. J 3 (Third Division) or JFL (Fourth Division) = 1350 or more
3. Contract C | Conditions
   a. Player needs to earn less than ¥ 4.600.000 per year
   b. Minimum salary is not defined.
   c. The minutes played required are not defined
   d. When the players exceed a certain number minutes in the league, it is obligatory to alter the contract to fit the details of contract A or B
      i. J 1 (First Division) = 460 minutes or more
      ii. J 2 (Second Division) = 900 minutes or more
      iii. J 3 (Third Division) or JFL (Fourth Division) = 1350 or more"

National View: India

Ali Sharaballi (Agent at Triton eSporte, India)

The registration process

"In 2017, the All India Football Federation (AIFF), introduced its own Regulations on Working with Intermediaries, 2017, pursuant to and based on the FIFA Regulations on Working with Intermediaries (FIFA Intermediary Regulations 2015), which came into effect on April 01, 2015. The regulations were put into place with the aim to promote and safeguard high ethical standards in the relations between clubs, players and intermediaries, and to protect players & clubs from being involved in any unethical/illegal practices as well as avoiding situations leading to a conflict of interest.

In order to become an AIFF Registered Intermediary, an intermediary has the option to either register prior to representing a player or club by submitting an Intermediary Declaration Form as either a natural or legal person, in accordance with the FIFA Intermediary Regulations 2015, and must disclose personal information, business information (if a legal person/entity), criminal history information, and any potential conflicts of interest, in compliance with Article 8 of the FIFA Intermediary Regulations 2015. Another option is to register during or at the conclusion of a transaction/transfer agreement, wherein a player and/or club must submit to the AIFF an Intermediary Declaration form duly executed by said Intermediary, which has to be submitted at the same time as the Representation Contract. In both cases, applicants are also required to pay a registration fee of INR 50,000 + taxes to the AIFF for a one year registration period, which will need to be renewed on an annual basis in order to continue Intermediary activity. However, in the instance of a lawyer being engaged by a club or player to provide legal services in relation to a transfer agreement, he/she is not required to submit an Intermediary Declaration form, only a written acknowledgement from the club or player to the AIFF mentioning said Lawyer is the Intermediary would suffice.

At the end of every financial year in the month of March, the AIFF publicly publishes the names of all Intermediaries registered in the AIFF Centralised Registration System (CRS) as well as a list of every transaction in which an Intermediary was involved.

Representation contract

According to the AIFF Regulations on Working with Intermediaries 2017, if an Intermediary is engaged by a player or club in respect of a transaction, then the parties must enter into a duly executed Representation Contract. Besides, an Intermediary is allowed to simultaneously represent both a player and club, provided both parties provide written consent prior to the start of relevant negotiations, avoiding any conflict of interest. Also, the player and club must confirm in writing which party (player and/or club) will remunerate the Intermediary and such documentation must be lodged with the AIFF at the same time as the Representation Contract.

Difficulties for an agent in the Indian football landscape

The AIFF's implementation of just the minimum standards and requirements to its intermediary registration system brings to the fore certain advantages as well as disadvantages to its agents and football landscape. The advantage being that the industry is open to a wider audience, irrespective of what background or sector one may belong to. As for the disadvantages, though an agent is required to possess an impeccable reputation, the AIFF does not require its registered agents to possess any particular qualification, certification or tangible expertise to handle a player's contract or transfer agreement. The efficient handling of a player's contract with a club as well as negotiating a transfer agreement involves complex legal & contractual issues, employment issues, intellectual property issues etc., thus requiring a highly developed and diverse skillset. With no dedicated football agent education program, it's safe to say the industry lacks structure.

Furthermore, in a still developing market such as India, there are also concerns regarding the practicality of the proposed commission caps by FIFA, as there are no transfer fees involved in a majority of the deals taking place within the country, except in very rare instances. Hence, being a football agent in such a market is not as lucrative for all as one might be led to believe.

The future holds promise

Despite the obvious hurdles and difficulties there's still steady progress being made, partly thanks to the advent of The Indian Super League (ISL) which has led to more business opportunities for local intermediaries, and also the AIFF, through its constant endeavours to promote professionalism and transparency. With the newly launched strategic roadmap - 'Vision 2047', the AIFF aims to redefine, rebrand and restructure Indian football right from the bottom up, promising much cause for optimism.

However, there is a need now more than ever, for football agents to come together and align in demanding and achieving higher standards of professionalism, organisation and industry specific education to further encourage transparency as well as legal and ethical practice in doing business."

National View: South Korea

*Dee Hong (Head of International Affairs,
Footballade, Agent of Min-jae Kim)*

"The life of an agent in Korea may not differ much from that of my counterparts in Europe or elsewhere in the world. I start my day with a cup of coffee and check on my phone to navigate through emails, news, Instagram, and other social media channels to see what the football world has to offer. On a weekly basis I attend matches, speak with my players and chat with some club authorities whenever it is possible.

The movie 'Jerry Maguire' inspired me the most and attracted me to get a foothold into the football industry. However, in this profession nothing comes easy. It takes a long time for any agent to establish themselves, and I was no different! I was very lucky with my background, as I worked with the Korean FA, sponsors and clubs, enabling me to get valuable experiences. The only missing piece to complete the puzzle was working with the players directly, and I'm proud to finally be able to have this opportunity now. Even though I am still a newbie, my previous experiences have really helped me since I'm now acquainted with many important and interesting people in the industry whilst also gaining crucial interactive skills. I am certainly not the first (and definitely not the last) to state how vital it is to establish this network of contacts in the football world.

In recent years the Korean football industry has had to compete with its financially superior neighbours in Japan and China. Since the Korean game is played at a very high level within the region, the infrastructure and surrounding environments will hopefully keep improving and match the strong sportive performance.

In doing so, this opportunity may serve to boost the business surrounding football. In order to make the most out of this increase in funding and infrastructure, more transfers to different countries or continents have to be executed. Although language barriers may delay the process, the more we try the better we will become. The region still remains a learning curve for the whole industry, but eventually it will benefit the market in general.

We have had some fantastic players over the years, including Son, Ki, Park and Lee in our national team lineup. I hope that in the near future Korea could also introduce a Sogut who can represent high calibre players. My utmost goal as a football agent is to fulfil my clients' dreams while also keeping the fans entertained."

Chapter 30: The Future of Football Agency

"You must be able to demonstrate your value and importance to clients and to the footballing world continually"

Introduction

Perhaps one of the most important questions for prospective agents and those with years ahead in their careers, is where the football agency occupation is heading next. The answer is not objective and calls for calculated speculation. It is not possible to research factual information on what future awaits the profession. However, it is an intriguing proposition that presents several undisputed predictions. It can be guaranteed that, inevitably, the role of an agent will continue to expand and adapt in alignment with the evolving nature of football. The overall outlook and positioning of agents inside the sphere of football will change.

In an episode of Erkut's blog that can be found on his website (www.erkutsogut.com/blog) we attempted to make some other, more debatable, key predictions for the future of our profession. Some of these predictions might still seem to imply drastic changes to the industry whilst others were simply suggesting a continuation of the pattern of change that has already been seen in recent years and since the emergence of agents in football and wider sport. Some were more speculative than others but all of them were alterations to the role of agents that we believed warranted genuine consideration as possible outcomes which may be reached from the direction in which football agency was going and importantly at the time of writing, is still going. We will re-outline the predictions that we made as we hope it provides enough information and insight to help motivate and guide your careers following on from the knowledge, skills and lifestyle that you have learned and developed from this book.

From Player Representatives to Sports Agents and Club Agents

There has been a gradual move in this direction already over the last few years. Player agents at the top end of the industry have begun to act on behalf of clubs, coaches, TV presenters and even sporting directors. We believe it is just the beginning of a limitless diversification in the clientele that current football agents will face in the future.

First and foremost, we predict that 'club agents' will likely become set as a norm within the agency profession. With FIFA's new regulations, there is a higher rate of commission remuneration obtainable through representing the selling club or the exclusively permitted dual-representation of the player and buying club, and we expect agents to become the representatives of clubs more frequently than of players. This will see a shift in the primary roles and responsibilities of an agent as the job is no longer caring for an individual human being but instead, the task is representing and attaining the best interests and outcomes of an entity, in the form of a football club.

For similar reasons, we also believe that agents will also be more prone to representing clients commercially rather than concerning themselves with employment contracts at football clubs. Those agents that continue to represent players are once again restricted on the percentage of commission they can take from the contracts that they negotiate with clubs. A far higher commission of up to 20% from commercial endorsements and player sponsorships is likely to be far more attractive to agents.

The commercialisation of football shows no sign of diminishing. More and more commercial opportunities are becoming available to players as the age of technology, social media and the extraordinary fame and public spotlight that accompanies being a professional footballer, comes with the perks of attracting interest from major sponsors. The marketability of player clients is continually improving as they develop their own personal brand through the most modern and popular forms of promotion such as Tik Tok, Twitch and Instagram. Hence, the chapters within this book that concern the commercial side of how to be an agent are vital beacons of information that we would strongly advise you ingest and act upon.

The increasing number of platforms on which players can have a presence and influence on wider society correlates with a rise in commercial interest and the value of endorsement contracts as brands vie for the best talent to push their products into the public sphere. The modern world of football and wider sport encapsulates a significant commercial aspect and agents will continue to broaden their roles to fulfil these demands. Importantly, this is likely to also be a growing aspect of representing female clients. The rapid growth and expansion in the financial backing and popularity of the women's game will be reflected in a rise in the number of agents that represent female players and invest vast amounts of time in seeking commercial endorsements for their clients.

There are other unpredictable elements that may play a significant role in the future of football and, consequently, for agents. Cryptocurrency, NFT's and e-Sports are examples of relatively new phenomena that are gradually becoming intertwined within football and other sports as I explained in the chapter specifically dedicated to these. Once more, one would imagine that these will have a part to play in the future and agents will have to add yet another skillset to be able to fulfil their role in acting in the best interests of their client. Whilst already playing a role in financial guidance for clients, agents may, to some extent, engage with ventures such as crypto or NFT-asset management or perhaps securing a source of income for their clients in futuristic technological areas such as e-Sports and Twitch.

Evidently, agents will no longer be just 'football agents'. We believe the more appropriate term in future will be 'sports agents'. This incorporates more of what the work of an agent will likely entail across all of the sports world. From representing clubs to advising their clients on developing as a brand and commercial entity, agents must understand how best to serve their client in the future world of sport and hopefully this book has encapsulated a clear direction as to how to comprehend this and carry it out.

This future world incorporates the commercial side of sport and we also believe will lessen the narrowed approach of agents to a singular sport. As the more prominent responsibilities of an agent become dealing with off-field activities and interests of their clients, the sport they play is less important. Instead, we predict that agents will broaden their client base across many sports, from athletics to basketball to golf. We think that agents operating in a singular sport will become less common and less focussed upon the sport being played but rather the off-field opportunities of their clients.

Importantly, a good agent will not endeavour to carry out all of these responsibilities in all of these sports and areas alone. Whilst I'd advocate for possessing a basic overview or understanding of every venture the client goes for and every aspect covered within this book, the skill in the task sometimes lies in the ability to delegate to experts. It is also the agent's role to manage all of these outsourced and external team members and ensure that everyone is working in conjunction; aiming to achieve the best possible outcomes that are in the interests of the client. It would be ludicrous to think that one individual could be an expert in every facet or every sport we have mentioned but they must be an expert in directing and leading a team with the same mutual goal on behalf of the same client.

The Issues in the Lower Leagues

From what we have predicted so far, a lot of the extra responsibilities that we suggest will become an integral part of an agent's career rely on the client having a considerable amount of public popularity and global status in order to build up off-field opportunities such as personal brands and monetising social media channels. However, the future of lower leagues in football has a collateral impact on the agency world too. Many agents operate solely within these leagues during their careers and this is an area that could suffer in the future.

With the new commission cap regulations implementing a hard cap on agent remuneration, it may prove difficult to make a living from clients in lower divisions of football. The consequences of this may be a fall in the number of agents, particularly those working within lower leagues, as they are unable to achieve financial sustainability through the profession. Alternatively, this could have an additional negative effect as agents in that region could seek to find different ways of sourcing more income or unethical practices. Perhaps they will simply have to take on large volumes of clients which inevitably is of detriment to the holistic and personally-targeted service that they would be able to provide to each individual client.

This may further encourage agents to adapt into different areas of the industry such as representing clubs or other more lucrative clients rather than players at the lower end of professional football.

However, it is my hope that this concern and genuine fear might be realised and acknowledged by the policy makers within football. A revision of the regulations to include factors such as tiered commission cap restrictions in order to maintain the survivability of agents operating in lower divisions may occur at some point. This would avoid these negative outcomes and the decline of agents that are vitally willing to work with players that are not in such a category that opens up a vast array of off-field opportunities.

However, as agents you must be prepared that the going is never easy and in the future there may be even more pressure to take on more than one can effectively handle. We cannot make it clear enough that our primary duty as agents is to serve the interests of our clients and hence we should never sacrifice this. Part of taking on the role of an agent is to face and overcome these challenges and adversities that our industry may face in the future without compromising on our core principles and responsibilities.

Political Advisors

Another significant trend that has emerged as a component of the growing fame and attention that players receive is an increasing readiness to openly express their opinions of the world. Well-known players are utilising their position to share their thoughts about topics far away from the world of football such as politics, economics, inequality, religion, world hunger, animal cruelty and other global points of public discussion.

In the future, we believe this pattern will continue. The power, status and influence that players possess will become extortionate. This will open up an array of opportunities that can reflect positively upon the player or can jeopardise their careers. It will become a part of the remit of an agent to have an acute awareness of the personal beliefs and opinions that their clients hold.

We predict that agents will come to have distinct responsibility in ensuring that their players feel empowered to use their position to have a positive impact on a matter that they feel passionately about and that is important to the world beyond football. However, they are also responsible for assessing the consequences of being outspoken on sensitive topics and suggesting the best manner in which a player can deliver their opinions to the world. In this situation, the agent will have to offer informed guidance to try and achieve the outcome that their client desires such as meaningful change or positive political action.

The future magnitude of 'player-power' offers dangers and rewards aplenty. The future agent will likely be obliged to carry out the thankless task of monitoring how their client conducts themselves and uses, without abusing, this power. Ultimately, the agent's main role, as we continue to reiterate, is to care for the client. In the future, the extent of this care across elements of their client's lifestyle outside of football or the sport that they play, will broaden, and the agent must keep up with such changes and be able to fulfil their overriding duty.

Incorporating Data and Analytics

One of the major driving factors behind the future of agency is technology. The advancement of all things tech-related underpins the growth in social media platforms and the ability to market clients. However, another area that technology is increasingly having a presence within is in contract negotiations for employment contracts and transfer deals. There have already been examples of how data and analytics that are collated by technological computer programs and analyst teams can be used in contract negotiations. Most notably in recent times and as discussed in chapter 19, Kevin De Bruyne of Manchester City, one of the finest midfielders in the game, negotiated a contract worth an estimated £83million after bringing in data scientists as part of his team which saw him become one of the highest paid players in the league.

A drastic, sceptical suggestion to this example could be that there is no future for agents as data analytics and experts can be used instead to demonstrate to the club the on-field and off-field value that a player holds. However, there are two significant factors in this proposition which we argue make this an unlikely eventuality.

The four-year deal that 'data' obtained for KDB was not solely thanks to the analysts who presented the statistics. He still entered the contract negotiation with a team around him; his father, his lawyer and importantly, his two agents from Rockstar Sports. This is a telling indicator that players still seek the advice and knowledge of agents.

Whilst data played a vital role in helping the agents, alongside De Bruyne, to demonstrate to the club that he was worth forking out £83million (an extra 30% on what he was earning previously) for over four years, it was still the agents who played the pivotal role of getting the deal over the line. The bottom line is that footballers do not want the burden of responsibility for this aspect of the industry to lie with them. Their job is to focus upon performing on the pitch and even if they can call upon data to help with finalising contracts, there will always be a desire for agents to take on the responsibility of ensuring they are getting the best deal possible for their client.

Secondly to note on such a deal is that the level of data and off-field value that the data scientists were able to present to Man City were only possible because of the calibre and status of a player such as Kevin De Bruyne. It is far-fetched to think that, in the future, players that are in a lower division or even those not in the top bracket of top divisions will also call upon data and statistics. This would most likely not be the most realistic and cost efficient way of finalising a new contract and would fail to produce any significant advantage over what an agent could have done. Hence, we conclude that the future of data statistics and agency is, instead, one of harmony and mutual benefit. Agents can utilise data as a useful tool as and when it is appropriate and advantageous in reaching a more preferable and lucrative agreement for their client.

The main takeout from this is that we as agents need to continue to operate in a way that is considered vital to a player or the client that we are representing. If we are able to demonstrate our value and importance to clients and to the footballing world continually, then our place in football is not threatened. We are a necessity, as long as we act and work in the right way by adopting the skills and professionalism that you have learned within this book.

Further Reading

- The Football Code - James Tippett
- More Than a Game - Mark Gregory

Chapter 31: Important Contracts

The following pages contain updated copies of contracts from different areas of football that are important for an agent to familiarise themselves with.

England (FA – Football Association) Representation Contract

<u>STANDARD REPRESENTATION CONTRACT between INTERMEDIARY and PLAYER</u>

THIS STANDARD REPRESENTATION CONTRACT ("THE CONTRACT") is made BETWEEN

NAME OF INTERMEDIARY:
(the 'Intermediary') of

COMPANY NAME (where applicable):
ADDRESS:
NAME OF PLAYER (the 'Player'):
ADDRESS:
DATE OF BIRTH:

IT IS HEREBY AGREED as follows:

APPOINTMENT

1.   The Intermediary is appointed by the Player to provide services on the following terms:

....

DURATION

2.   The Contract shall take effect on .... and will terminate on (maximum two years) without notice.

EXCLUSIVITY

3.   The Player is contracted to the Intermediary on: *an exclusive basis*   ☐

a non-exclusive basis   ☐

REMUNERATION

4.   The Player shall pay to the Intermediary a commission amounting to .... % of the Player's Basic Gross Income as a result of any employment contract negotiated or renegotiated by the Intermediary, payable as follows:

- *a lump sum payment at the start of the employment contract*   ☐
- *annual payments at the end of each contractual year*   ☐

- *other (specify):*

(No remuneration will be due to the Intermediary while the Player remains a Minor).

TERMINATION

5.   The Contract shall be automatically terminated with immediate effect if the Intermediary's Registration expires during the term of the Contract and the Intermediary does not renew his Registration within 14 days of being requested to do so in writing by the Player.

SUPPLEMENTAL TERMS AND CONDITIONS

6.   Any other arrangements between the parties in any way connected to the provision of the services set out in clause 1 that are supplemental to the Contract shall be in accordance with the requirements of The FA Regulations on Working with Intermediaries and the FIFA Regulations on Working with Intermediaries, and must be attached to the Contract and lodged with The FA together with the Contract.

DISPUTES

7.   Any dispute between the parties arising out of or in connection with the Contract, including but not limited to any question regarding its existence, validity or termination, shall be referred to and finally resolved by arbitration under Rule K of the Rules of The FA (as amended from time to time).

GOVERNING LAW

8.   The Contract and any non-contractual obligation arising out of or in connection to it is governed by and shall be construed in accordance with the laws of England and Wales and subject to Clause 6 above, the parties hereby submit to the exclusive jurisdiction of the courts of England and Wales.

SIGNATURES

A copy of the Contract has been provided to the Player and lodged with The FA.

Signed by the Player: _____   **Date:**

Signed by the Guardian: _____   **Date:**

(if the Player is a Minor)

Print Name: _____

Signed by/on behalf of the Intermediary: _____ **Date:**

Print Name: _____

Mandate for Transfer

(Mandate for transfer: in this case, the agent has a mandate to conduct a transfer of the player to the English Premier League and Championship, the Turkish Süperlig, and America's Major League Soccer. Furthermore, it is between the agent seeking to make a deal, and the full-time agent of the player. As discussed in Chapter -, mandates can either be an agent-player *or* agent-agent agreement and depends on what is stated on the initial Representation Contract. The following example is relatively concise, and mandates can be longer than this, but do not have to be.)

INTERMEDIATION CONTRACT

This contract is between

(Company of the intermediary)
(Person Name) [Intermediary Number]
(Address)

Onwards **"the Intermediary"**

Company of the agent
Name of the agent [Intermediary Number]
Address

Onwards **"the Agent"**.

It is hereby agreed as follows:

1.1 Preamble

1.1 The agent represents exclusively the interests of the professional football _____, who currently plays for _____**(Club)** (the **"Player"**), with regards to the negotiation or renegotiation of a contract to a football club (the **"Transfer"**).

2. Authorization

2.1 The Agent authorizes the Intermediary to represent the Player for the following football clubs (the "**Clubs**"):
- All Clubs in the **English Premier League** and **Championship**. (First and second division)
- All Clubs in the **Süperlig of Turkey** (First Division)
- All Clubs in the **Major League Soccer** of the United States of America

2.2 The intermediary is authorised to initiate and direct discussions with the Clubs and to negotiate a Transfer for the Player to one of the Clubs. The intermediary must inform the agent of every discussion and negotiation.
2.3 The intermediary has the right to make a final decision, only with the previous consent of the agent, with regards to an agreement for a Transfer of the Player to a Club.

2.4 Every proposal, agreement and contracts issued by the Player, the Club or the Intermediary must be presented to the Agent. For the Transfer to be valid, the approval of the Player and the Agent is required.

2.5 The Contract shall take effect on _____ and will terminate on _____ without notice.

3. Remuneration

The Intermediary and the Agent agree to split the negotiated commission for the transfer of the player as follows:

- 50% for the Intermediary.
- 50% for the Agent.

4. Termination

The Contract shall be automatically terminated with immediate effect if the Intermediary's Registration expires during the term of the Contract and the Intermediary does not renew his Registration within 14 days of being requested to do so in writing by the Player.

5. Disputes

Any dispute arising from or related to the present contract will be submitted exclusively to the Court of Arbitration for Sport in Lausanne, Switzerland, and resolved definitively in accordance with the Code of sports-related arbitration.

6. Governing Law

The Contract and any non-contractual obligation arising out of or in connection to it is governed by and shall be construed in accordance with the laws of England and Wales and subject to Clause 5 above, the parties hereby submit to the exclusive jurisdiction of the courts of England and Wales.

7. Final Notes

7.1 In case any of the articles in the Contract are ineffective or inapplicable, the remaining articles will not be affected. The contracting parties agree to solve the issues that arise in the best way possible and in good faith to provide a valid article that is as similar as possible to the ineffective article.

7.2 This contract will be signed in two copies. Copies will be as follows:

1. Agent.

2. Intermediary.

Date: _____

Intermediary: Print Name   **Agent:** Print Name

_____   _____

_____(Signature)   _____(Signature)

Premier League Employment Contract

(Employment Contract: this is an example of 'Schedule 2' of a Premier League Employment Contract. This part of the agreement is where aspects like length of deal and salary are to be found. This is where bonuses and performance-based clauses would also be stated.)

Schedule 2 – *Insert Player's Name* ....

Supplemental Provisions and Employment Rights Act 1996

The following provisions shall apply to supplement the provisions of this contract and the information as set out herein in order to comply with the requirements of Part 1 of the Employment Rights Act 1996.

1. The Player's employment with the Club began on ....

2. The date of termination of this contract is **30 June 20**...........

3. No employment with a previous employer shall count as part of the Player's continuous period of employment hereunder.

4. The Player's hours of work are such as the Club may from time to time reasonably require of him to carry out his duties and the Player shall not be entitled to any additional remuneration for work done outside normal working hours.

5. The place of employment shall be at the Club's ground and training ground but the Club shall be entitled to require the Player to play and to undertake his duties hereunder at any other place throughout the world.

6. No contracting out certificate pursuant to the Pensions Scheme Act 1993 is in force in respect of the Player's employment under this contract.

7. **The Professional Footballers' Pension Scheme**

   7.1 Immediately on signing this contract, the Player shall:

   7.1.1 be automatically enrolled as; or

   7.1.2 or continue to be;

   a member of the 2011 Section of the Professional Footballers' Pension Scheme (the **"Scheme"**) and shall remain so during the continuance of his employment hereunder unless he:

7.1.3 notifies the Scheme Administrator in writing that he wishes to opt out of the Scheme;

7.1.4 has previously registered with HM Revenue & Customs for Fixed or Enhanced Protection; or

7.1.5 is otherwise ineligible for membership of the Scheme in accordance with the terms of the Scheme's definitive trust deed and rules as amended from time to time.

7.2 For as long as the Player remains a member of the 2011 Section, an annual contribution (funded by the levy on transfer fees) will be paid into the Scheme for the benefit of the Player. The annual contribution shall be £5,208 or such other amount as determined by the Trustees of the Scheme from time to time.

7.3 The Player shall not be required to contribute to the 2011 Section but may elect to contribute such amount as he notifies to the Scheme Administrator in writing. When a Player decides to contribute to the 2011 Section he can agree with his Club and the Scheme Administrator for the contribution to be made through a salary sacrifice arrangement.

7.4 Where, by virtue of previous membership of the Scheme, the Player has built up benefits under its Cash Section and/or Income Section, those benefits are frozen and will be revalued until his retirement from the Scheme. The Player shall be entitled to such benefits (including death benefits) from each section of the Scheme in which he has participated on such conditions as are set out in the Scheme's definitive trust deed and rules as amended from time to time.

7.5 The Player further agrees that the Club may disclose his name, address, gender, date of birth, National Insurance number, salary information and dates of commencement and termination of employment to the League and the administrators of the Scheme for the purposes of facilitating the administration of the Scheme.

8. **Remuneration**

The Player's remuneration shall be:

8.1 Basic Wage:

£ **per week/per annum** payable by monthly instalments in arrear from
.... to ....

£ **per week/per annum** payable by monthly instalments in arrear from
.... to ....

£ **per week/per annum** payable by monthly instalments in arrear from
.... to ....

£ **per week/per annum** payable by monthly instalments in arrear from
.... to ....

£ **per week/per annum** payable by monthly instalments in arrear from
.... to ....

8.2 Such of the bonuses and incentives as the Player shall be entitled to receive under the terms of the Club's bonus and incentive scheme as are set out below/a copy of which is annexed hereto.

....
....

8.3 Any other payments as follows:

....
....

9. Insurances (if any) maintained for the benefit of the Player subject to the terms and conditions thereof during currency of this contract the premiums of which are paid by the Club.

Nature of Policy   Amount

....
....

10. Benefits (if any) to be provided to the Player during the currency of this contract
....
....
....
....

11. The Player's normal retirement age is 35 years.

12. The terms and conditions of this contract form part of a number of collective agreements between the Club (through the League) and the Player (through the PFA) affecting the Player's employment and full details thereof are set out in the Code of Practice.

13. (If applicable) The following provisions which are additional or supplemental to those set out in clause 4 have been agreed between the Club and the Player as referred to in clause 4.11.

....
....
....
....

14. Any other provisions:

....
....
....
....

SIGNED by the Player ....
in the presence of: ....
(Witness signature) ....
(Address) ....
Occupation ....

SIGNED by the Player's parent or guardian (if the player is under 18)
....
in the presence of: ....
(Witness signature) ....
(Address) ....
Occupation ....
SIGNED by (name) ....
for and on behalf of the Club in the presence of:
....
(Witness signature) ....
(Address) ....
Occupation ....

Did Player use the services of an Intermediary   yes/no
If yes, name of Intermediary ....
Signature of Intermediary ....

Did the Club use the services of an Intermediary   yes/no
If yes, name of Intermediary ....
Signature of Intermediary ....

Marketing Deal

(Marketing deal: the following contract covers the most important parts discussed in Chapter 23. Although these contracts will likely include more legal definitions and technical jargon from the company, the basics are covered. This particular example is that of a headphones company.)

Talent: _____

Lender: _____

Effective Date: _____

Company: _____

Licensed IP:
The name, likeness, image, or digitised image, video or film portrayal, photograph, biography, voice and endorsement of Talent, including any autograph, initials, facsimile signature, nickname, symbol or other means of endorsement or identification.

Products:
Headphones, earphones, speakers and other audio products and accessories (as are agreed between the parties from time to time) that are branded as _____

Term:
A period of two (2) years beginning on the date of full execution of this Talent Agreement by all parties; provided that any Content captured from a Shoot may be used until the later of the end of the Term or six months from date of first use (provided such Content is initially used during the Term); provided, further that any results of Talent's services hereunder (including the Content) may be used in perpetuity for internal and/or archival purposes, editorial purposes and other non-advertising purposes (such as, without limitation, in advertising awards competitions, film festivals, retrospectives and archival and/or historical sections of Company websites and social media pages). Each consecutive twelve (12) month period commencing on the date of mutual execution of this Talent Agreement during the Term is referred to herein as a "Contract Year".

Payment/Payment Terms:
As full and complete compensation for any and all personal services rendered and the grant of rights herein, Company will pay Lender an annual fee for each Contract Year equal to _____ (the "Annual Compensation"), in quarterly payments during the Contract Year, to be invoiced in arrears. All payments of the Annual Compensation will be made within 45 days of receipt by Company of Lender's proper invoice therefore in accordance with Company's instructions.

Performance Bonuses:
In the event that Talent achieves any of the following, Company shall pay to Lender a Bonus Payment (a "Bonus") in the amount described below in respect of each such achievement, such Bonus payable no more than once per Contract Year. Lender shall invoice Company for such Bonus within thirty (30) days of the closing of achievement and Company will pay such Bonus within forty five (45) days of receipt of Lender's proper invoice therefore, in accordance with Company's instructions.

Achievement Bonus:
- Premier League Winner £_____
- Champions League Winner (on pitch) £_____
- Premier League Player of The Year £_____
- Ballon d'Or £_____
- UEFA Euro 2020 Winner £_____
- UEFA Euro 2020 Player of Tournament £_____

Territory: _____

Marketing Obligations:
Lender will cause Talent to endorse the Products and provide other marketing support for the benefit of the Company pursuant to a plan developed by the parties, including promotional appearances, photographic/film/voice shoots and similar activities, which plan shall include at a minimum, the following marketing support services

- Talent shall participate in two (2) full photograph/film/voice shoot days (6 hours each) per Contract Year, on such dates and locations as otherwise mutually agreed by the Parties (collectively, the "Shoots").

- Wear, when appropriate, the Products (to be provided by Company).

- Coordinated social messaging through Talent's Social Media channels as mutually agreed upon between the parties hereto across all of Talent's social media platforms (i.e., Facebook, Instagram, Twitter) with Product (approximately 1 post per month across all channels); tagging of official channels will be coordinated on request of Company. During campaigns, social media post frequency will increase to 2 posts per month across all channels. Company social media accounts may re-tweet and/or re-post Talent's social media messages and may promote and/or whitelist Talent's social media messages on all social media platforms including Facebook and Twitter.

- One (1) promotional appearance per Contract Year of at least four (4) hours. Each promotional appearance may include private and public events or clinics with Company's customers or consumers. At any such promotional appearance, Talent will pose for a reasonable number of photographs and privately sign a reasonable amount of autographs. Company will determine the dates, times and locations for any personal appearances subject to consultation with and the prior approval of Lender based upon Talent's prior personal professionally and commercial commitments, and provided that Talent will treat Company no less favourably than his other commercial commitments in terms of availability.

If Talent is required to travel for the purpose of attending a Shoot or an appearance, Company shall pay for actual and reasonable business class travel and premium lodging expenses in accordance with Company's Travel Policy for Suppliers. All Talent's services and the results and proceeds of the services rendered and/or created hereunder (including, without limitation, any commercials, photographs, marketing or promotional materials, films, recordings and any Shoot assets) shall be referred to herein as "Content".

Company Obligations:
After the beginning of the Term, Company shall provide a reasonable amount of a selection of its newest and/or custom Products, as designed by Company, to Talent for his own use, or (at Talent's discretion) for certain individuals such as Talent's coaches and other athletes (the retail value of such Products to be approximately $5,000 each Contract Year during the Term).

Exclusivity Restrictions:
Lender agrees that, during the Term, neither Lender nor Talent will use or grant any license or rights to any other party in the Licensed IP or any portion thereof in any way, manner or form in connection with the manufacture, distribution, marketing, promotion and/or sale of headphones, earphones, speakers and other audio products and accessories. Further, Lender agrees that Talent shall not wear or display any other brand of headphones or earphones in public during the Term

Termination: A party may immediately terminate this Talent Agreement if the other party is in material breach of this Talent Agreement and that party fails to cure that breach within thirty (30) days after receiving written notice of breach from the non-breaching party. Further, Company may, in its opinion, deem Lender to be in material breach of this Talent Agreement and immediately suspend its performance, including, but not limited to, payment of any compensation, or terminate this Talent Agreement immediately if (i) Talent engages in Negative Behaviour or is charged with a felony during the Term or (ii) Talent (a) fails to remain on the active roster (excluding the injured list) of _____ or other UEFA team and the _____ National team for any continuous ninety (90) day period during the Term or (b) incurs an injury, suffers an illness or develops a medical condition (other than resulting from illegal or illicit drug use) that prevents Talent from playing professional soccer for a continuous period of more than ninety (90) days. "Negative Behaviour" means any action or statement by Talent that brings Talent into public disrepute, contempt, scandal or ridicule, or that shocks or offends the community or any group or class thereof, or that reflects unfavourably on Company, including making any or authorising any statements in derogation of Company or its brand or its products which become or are made known to the public.

Signed by _____
Duly authorised for and on behalf of _____
Dated _____

Signed by _____
Duly authorised for and on behalf of _____
Dated _____

Conclusion

This book was written in the latter stages of 2022 and early 2023, as FIFA's new regulations came into force. If you are reading this a couple of years later, the chances are that rules and regulations may have changed further. Whilst throughout this book we have endeavoured to comprehensively deliver our collective knowledge of each aspect, sector, task, challenge, role, regulation, responsibility, opportunity, dilemma and success that an agent might encounter, the reality of the agency world is too complex to put into writing. As we can see from the history of the profession, the fluctuation between strict and relaxed regulation and the inklings we have for the future of football agents, this is a tough, volatile and unpredictable industry.

Having said this, it is one of boundless excitement and opportunity. It is impossible to hide from the fact that it takes a serious graft and element of dedication to learn and ply the craft effectively. An understanding of all the different elements involved; from the laws governing agents; to working with youth players; sourcing commercial deals; working with lawyers; collaborating with journalists; and differing practices in each corner of the footballing world, will help you set out on your journey of becoming a successful agent.

Furthermore, there are a handful of key non-negotiables that we hope you have gathered from this book and taken away as golden nuggets that will become practices and habits that you live by each day whether you end up in the agency profession or otherwise. These 'takeaways' may be something along the lines of 'protecting your process', reading and understanding your industry, becoming an expert, your network is your net-worth. Or perhaps more classic cliches have been reinforced in your mind such as 'hard work is the key to success'. These have all never been more relevant than to the world of agency.

Agency is a diverse and unique profession but we hope that reading this book may have progressed you somewhere along the line of your journey. Whether we have helped you formulate your opinions on agency, put you on the first rung of the ladder and fueled your ambitions of becoming an agent, helped you improve and develop your current behaviours and understanding in your already-established career, or whether we have put you off altogether; we hope that you have enjoyed this book and found the contents of it useful, insightful and comprehensive.

We would like to wish you all the best of luck in your future as a football agent or otherwise and thank you for reading!

Keep updated on social media

Get in touch for more information and advice on becoming a football agent! Furthermore, keep up-to-date with our teaching and seminar events worldwide. These include masterclasses, webinars, courses, a *youtube* channel, summits and more.

Education

Website: www.erkutsogut.com
LinkedIn: Erkut Sogut Academy
Instagram: @erkutsogutacademy
Facebook: Erkut Sogut Academy
Twitter: @ESogutAcademy
Youtube: @DrErkutSogut
Course: How to Become a Football Agent, 3 month taught course
Masterclass: 6-weeks online, self-taught course

Agency

Website: www.grow-talents.com
LinkedIn: GROW Talents
Instagram: @grow.talents

Made in the USA
Coppell, TX
06 April 2024

30874839R20184